HowExpert Antiques & Collectibles

The Ultimate Handbook for Identifying, Valuing, and Preserving Antiques and Collectibles

HowExpert

For more tips related to this topic, visit HowExpert.com/antiquescollectibles.

Recommended Resources

- HowExpert.com – How To Guides on All Topics from A to Z by Everyday Experts.
- HowExpert.com/free – Free HowExpert Email Newsletter.
- HowExpert.com/books – HowExpert Books
- HowExpert.com/courses – HowExpert Courses
- HowExpert.com/clothing – HowExpert Clothing
- HowExpert.com/membership – HowExpert Membership Site
- HowExpert.com/affiliates – HowExpert Affiliate Program
- HowExpert.com/jobs – HowExpert Jobs
- HowExpert.com/writers – Write About Your #1 Passion/Knowledge/Expertise & Become a HowExpert Author.
- HowExpert.com/resources – Additional HowExpert Recommended Resources
- YouTube.com/HowExpert – Subscribe to HowExpert YouTube.
- Instagram.com/HowExpert – Follow HowExpert on Instagram.
- Facebook.com/HowExpert – Follow HowExpert on Facebook.
- TikTok.com/@HowExpert – Follow HowExpert on TikTok.

Publisher's Foreword

Dear HowExpert Reader,

HowExpert publishes quick 'how to' guides on all topics from A to Z by everyday experts.

At HowExpert, our mission is to discover, empower, and maximize everyday people's talents to ultimately make a positive impact in the world for all topics from A to Z...one everyday expert at a time!

HowExpert guides are written by everyday people just like you and me, who have a passion, knowledge, and expertise for a specific topic.

We take great pride in selecting everyday experts who have a passion, real-life experience in a topic, and excellent writing skills to teach you about the topic you are also passionate about and eager to learn.

We hope you get a lot of value from our HowExpert guides, and it can make a positive impact on your life in some way. All of our readers, including you, help us continue living our mission of positively impacting the world for all spheres of influences from A to Z.

If you enjoyed one of our HowExpert guides, then please take a moment to send us your feedback from wherever you got this book.

Thank you, and I wish you all the best in all aspects of life.

To your success,

Byungjoon "BJ" Min   민병준
Founder & Publisher of HowExpert
HowExpert.com

PS...If you are also interested in becoming a HowExpert author, then please visit our website at HowExpert.com/writers. Thank you & again, all the best! John 3:16

Table of Contents

Book Overview

HowExpert Guide to Antiques and Collectibles: The Ultimate Handbook for Identifying, Valuing, and Preserving Antiques and Collectibles

Unlock the secrets to the fascinating world of antiques and collectibles with the HowExpert Guide to Antiques and Collectibles: The Ultimate Handbook for Identifying, Valuing, and Preserving Antiques and Collectibles. This comprehensive guide is your ultimate resource for everything you need to know about collecting, from identifying and valuing precious items to preserving and caring for them.

What You'll Discover Inside:

- Chapter 1: Introduction - Welcome to the world of antiques and collectibles, where you'll explore the significance and appeal of collecting and how to make the most out of this guide.

- Chapter 2: Understanding Antiques and Collectibles - Learn the key definitions and distinctions, delve into the historical significance and cultural value of collectibles, and explore various categories and types.

- Chapter 3: Identifying Antiques and Collectibles - Master the art of recognizing authentic items with insights into common marks and signatures, distinguishing features by category, essential tools and techniques for identification, and avoiding common pitfalls.

- Chapter 4: Valuing Your Collection - Discover the factors affecting value, various appraisal methods, valuable resources for valuation, understanding market trends, and tips for maximizing value.

- Chapter 5: Preserving and Caring for Antiques - Protect your treasures with proper storage techniques, effective cleaning and maintenance tips, strategies to prevent damage and deterioration, the difference between restoration and preservation, and safe handling practices.

- Chapter 6: Buying Antiques and Collectibles - Navigate the market with confidence by learning where to find antiques, tips for successful negotiation, the ins and outs of auction houses, markets, and online platforms, evaluating sellers and sources, and understanding auction etiquette.

- Chapter 7: Selling Antiques and Collectibles - Prepare items for sale, set the right price, discover the best selling venues and platforms, learn how to market your collection, and master the art of negotiating sales.

- Chapter 8: Historical Context and Case Studies - Be inspired by famous antiques and their stories, lessons from notable collectors, unique case studies, the impact of historical events on collecting, and how to research your antiques.

- Chapter 9: Legal and Ethical Considerations - Understand provenance, navigate the legal aspects of buying and selling, adhere to ethical collecting practices, deal with fakes and forgeries, and comply with import and export regulations.

- Chapter 10: Building and Managing Your Collection - Start and expand your collection with tips on organizing and cataloging, diversifying your collection, securing insurance, ensuring the security of your collection, and planning for the future of your collection.

- Chapter 11: Connecting with the Collecting Community - Join collectors' clubs and associations, attend conventions and fairs, engage in online forums and social media, network with other collectors, and find mentors and experts.

- Chapter 12: Resources and Further Reading - Access recommended books and guides, online resources and databases, museums and exhibitions, educational courses and workshops, and find reliable information to further your knowledge.

- Chapter 13: Conclusion - Reflect on your collecting journey, receive encouragement for continued exploration, gain final tips and advice, and look ahead to the future of antiques and collectibles.

- Chapter 14: Appendices - Utilize a glossary of terms, checklists for collectors, contact information for appraisers and experts, sample valuation forms, and quick reference guides.

With its in-depth content and practical advice, this guide is designed for both novice and experienced collectors. Whether you're just starting your journey or looking to enhance your existing knowledge, the HowExpert Guide to Antiques and Collectibles provides everything you need to become a confident and successful collector. Dive into the enchanting world of antiques and collectibles and discover the treasures that await you.

HowExpert publishes how to guides on all topics from A to Z. Visit HowExpert.com to learn more.

Chapter 1: Introduction

Chapter 1 of *HowExpert Guide to Antiques and Collectibles: The Ultimate Handbook for Identifying, Valuing, and Preserving Antiques and Collectibles* introduces you to the captivating world of antiques and collectibles, setting the stage for your journey into the art of collecting. This chapter emphasizes the significance of antiques as connections to history and culture, highlighting the unique stories that each piece carries. It explores the importance and appeal of collecting, from the joy of discovery to the preservation of cultural heritage and potential financial benefits. Whether you're new to collecting or an experienced enthusiast, this chapter provides a welcoming introduction, guiding you through the foundational concepts that will enrich your collecting experience.

1.1 Welcome to the World of Antiques and Collectibles

Welcome to *HowExpert Guide to Antiques and Collectibles: The Ultimate Handbook for Identifying, Valuing, and Preserving Antiques and Collectibles*. Whether you're a novice collector or a seasoned enthusiast, this guide opens the door to a fascinating world where history, art, and culture converge. Antiques and collectibles are not just relics of the past; they are tangible connections to bygone eras, each piece carrying its own story, significance, and value.

As you embark on this journey, you will discover the joy of uncovering hidden treasures and the satisfaction of preserving history. The world of antiques is vast and varied, encompassing everything from exquisite furniture and fine art to vintage toys, rare books, and precious jewelry. Each item you encounter is a window into the past, offering insights into the lives, tastes, and technologies of those who came before us.

This section welcomes you into the community of collectors—individuals driven by a passion for preserving history and a curiosity about the stories behind the objects they acquire. Here, you'll begin to understand the allure of collecting, which blends the thrill of discovery with the intellectual challenge of research and the practical skills of preservation. Whether your interest lies in specific categories or you enjoy the broad spectrum of collectibles, this guide will equip you with the knowledge and tools to navigate the world of antiques confidently.

Through this journey, you will not only learn how to identify and value antiques but also how to care for them, ensuring they remain cherished possessions for generations to come. Welcome to the world of antiques and collectibles—where every object has a story waiting to be discovered.

1.2 Importance and Appeal of Collecting

Collecting antiques and collectibles is much more than a pastime; it's a meaningful pursuit that connects us to history, culture, and artistry in a uniquely personal way. The importance of collecting lies in its ability to preserve tangible pieces of our heritage, ensuring that future generations can experience and appreciate the craftsmanship, design, and stories that these objects embody. As a collector, you become a steward of history, safeguarding artifacts that might otherwise be lost or forgotten.

The appeal of collecting is multifaceted. For many, it begins with a love of history or an admiration for the beauty and craftsmanship of certain items. The thrill of discovering a rare or valuable piece can be incredibly rewarding, offering a sense of accomplishment that comes from knowing you've uncovered something special. Collecting also provides intellectual stimulation; researching the origins, makers, and historical context of your items can be as engaging as the act of collecting itself.

Beyond the personal satisfaction, collecting can also be a social activity. The world of antiques and collectibles is a community filled with passionate individuals who share their knowledge, experiences, and discoveries. Whether through clubs, conventions, or online forums, collectors often find camaraderie and mutual support among like-minded enthusiasts.

Additionally, collecting can be a savvy financial investment. Over time, well-curated collections can appreciate in value, turning a hobby into a valuable asset. Understanding market trends, learning how to properly care for items, and knowing when to buy or sell are all part of the collector's skill set that can lead to significant financial returns.

In *HowExpert Guide to Antiques and Collectibles: The Ultimate Handbook for Identifying, Valuing, and Preserving Antiques and Collectibles*, you'll learn how to navigate the many aspects of collecting, from the historical and cultural significance of items to the practicalities of valuation and preservation. The world of collecting offers endless possibilities for enrichment—intellectually, socially, and financially—and this guide will help you make the most of your collecting journey.

1.3 How to Use This Guide

HowExpert Guide to Antiques and Collectibles: The Ultimate Handbook for Identifying, Valuing, and Preserving Antiques and Collectibles is designed to be both an educational resource and a practical tool that you can refer to throughout your collecting journey. This guide is structured to provide comprehensive information on every aspect of antiques and collectibles, from understanding their historical significance to mastering the skills needed to identify, value, and preserve them.

Here's how to make the most of this guide:

1. Start with the Basics

- If you're new to collecting, begin with the early chapters that introduce you to the world of antiques and collectibles. Chapters 1 and 2 lay the groundwork by exploring the importance of collecting, key definitions, and the historical and cultural value of antiques. These sections will provide you with a strong foundation in the essential concepts and terminology used in the field.

2. Deep Dive into Specific Topics

- As you progress, delve into the chapters that cover more specialized topics such as identification techniques, valuation methods, and preservation practices. Each chapter is designed to stand on its own, so you can jump directly to the sections that are most relevant to your current interests or needs. For example, if you're focused on identifying items in your collection, Chapter 3 offers detailed guidance on recognizing authentic antiques and distinguishing features by category.

3. Use the Tools and Resources Provided

- Throughout the guide, you'll find practical tools, checklists, and examples that you can apply directly to your collecting activities. Whether you're preparing for an appraisal, organizing your collection, or researching a particular item, these resources are designed to be user-friendly and actionable.

4. Refer to the Appendices for Quick Access

- The appendices at the end of the guide include a glossary of terms, checklists, and sample forms that you can use for quick reference. These sections are particularly useful when you need to clarify terminology, ensure you've covered all the necessary steps in a process, or access additional resources for further reading and research.

A. Navigating the Guide

- The guide is structured to be easy to navigate, with clear headings and subheadings that allow you to quickly find the information you need. Whether you're reading it cover to cover or using it as a reference for specific questions, the logical flow of topics will help you stay on track and make the most of the content.

B. Applying What You Learn

- As you move through the guide, consider how the information applies to your own collecting goals. Each chapter includes practical advice and examples that you can adapt to your situation, whether you're building a new collection or refining an existing one. Take notes, highlight key points, and think about how you can integrate the insights you gain into your collecting strategy.

C. Engaging with the Collecting Community

- Finally, remember that collecting is not just a solitary activity. Use this guide to connect with the broader collecting community, whether through the recommended resources, by joining clubs and associations, or by participating in online forums. Sharing your experiences and learning from others will enrich your collecting journey and open up new opportunities for discovery.

By following these steps and making full use of the resources in *HowExpert Guide to Antiques and Collectibles*, you'll be well-equipped to navigate the world of antiques with confidence and expertise. This guide is your companion in the exciting and rewarding pursuit of collecting, helping you to unlock the full potential of your passion for antiques and collectibles.

Chapter 1 Review: Introduction to Antiques and Collectibles

Chapter 1 provides a foundational overview that introduces readers to the world of antiques and collectibles, highlighting the appeal of collecting and offering guidance on how to make the most of this guide. Here's a breakdown of the key sections:

1.1 Welcome to the World of Antiques and Collectibles

- Invitation to Explore: The chapter begins by inviting readers to explore the diverse and fascinating world of antiques and collectibles, emphasizing the wide range of items that can be collected.

- Universal Appeal: It highlights how collecting can be enjoyed by people of all ages and backgrounds, offering a personal connection to history, art, and culture.

- Introduction to Collecting: Readers are introduced to the idea that collecting is not just about owning objects, but about preserving history, understanding craftsmanship, and appreciating beauty.

1.2 Importance and Appeal of Collecting

- Cultural and Historical Value: This section emphasizes the significance of collecting as a way to preserve and celebrate cultural and historical heritage.

- Personal Fulfillment: Collecting is presented as a deeply rewarding activity that brings personal satisfaction, whether through the thrill of the hunt, the joy of discovery, or the pride in building a curated collection.

- Investment Potential: The chapter also touches on the potential financial benefits of collecting, noting that certain items can appreciate in value, making collecting both a passion and a smart investment.

1.3 How to Use This Guide

- Navigating the Book: Readers are provided with practical advice on how to use the guide, whether they prefer to read it sequentially or focus on specific sections relevant to their interests.

- Comprehensive Resource: The book is described as a comprehensive resource, covering everything from identifying and valuing items to preserving and selling them, making it a valuable tool for both novice and experienced collectors.

- Reference Tool: The guide is designed to be a reference that readers can return to as they progress in their collecting journey, offering insights and tips tailored to various aspects of the hobby.

Chapter 1 effectively sets the stage for the rest of the book by introducing the reader to the world of antiques and collectibles. It highlights the broad appeal and importance of collecting, both as a cultural and personal pursuit, and provides clear guidance on how to use the guide as a comprehensive resource throughout the collecting journey.

Chapter 2: Understanding Antiques and Collectibles

Chapter 2 of *HowExpert Guide to Antiques and Collectibles: The Ultimate Handbook for Identifying, Valuing, and Preserving Antiques and Collectibles* is designed to build a foundational understanding of what constitutes an antique or collectible and why these items hold such significant historical and cultural value. This chapter will equip you with the knowledge to distinguish between various types of antiques and collectibles and appreciate their importance in the broader context of history and society.

2.1 Definitions and Distinctions

Understanding the difference between an "antique" and a "collectible" is fundamental for any collector. These terms are often used interchangeably, but they have distinct meanings that can influence how items are valued, preserved, and appreciated. In this section, we'll define these key terms and explore the distinctions between them.

1. Antiques

A. Definition

- Age and Significance: Traditionally, an antique is defined as an item that is at least 100 years old. These items are valued not just for their age but also for their craftsmanship, rarity, and historical significance.

B. Examples

- Classic Items: Common examples of antiques include Georgian furniture, early American silverware, and ancient artifacts. These items typically embody the artistic styles, materials, and techniques of their respective periods.

2. Collectibles

A. Definition

- Modern Rarities: Collectibles are items that are less than 100 years old but are sought after by collectors due to their rarity, uniqueness, or cultural significance. These can include anything from comic books to mid-century modern furniture.

B. Examples

- Popular Collectibles: Examples of collectibles include vintage toys, limited edition art prints, and memorabilia from the 20th century. Unlike antiques, the value of collectibles often depends on current trends and the demand within specific collector communities.

3. Key Distinctions

A. Age vs. Rarity

- Fundamental Difference: The primary distinction between antiques and collectibles lies in age. Antiques are valued primarily for their historical significance, while collectibles are often prized for their rarity or unique qualities, even if they are relatively modern.

B. Historical vs. Cultural Value

- Different Values: Antiques typically carry historical value, representing a particular period in history. In contrast, collectibles may have more cultural or nostalgic value, often reflecting trends or popular culture of their time.

4. The Grey Area

- Blurred Lines: As items approach the 100-year mark, they often straddle the line between being considered antiques or collectibles. Some items may be classified as both, depending on their context and the market trends. For example, a piece of furniture from the 1920s might be considered an antique by some and a collectible by others, particularly if it reflects a significant design trend from that era.

5. Factors Influencing Classification

A. Market Trends

- Demand-Driven Classification: The classification of an item can be influenced by market demand. An item that is highly sought after due to its rarity might be considered a collectible, even if it is on the verge of being an antique.

B. Cultural Impact

- Cultural Significance: Items that have had a significant cultural impact, such as movie memorabilia or items associated with iconic historical events, may also blur the lines between collectibles and antiques.

Understanding these definitions and distinctions will help you approach your collection with greater clarity and insight. By recognizing the unique characteristics of antiques and collectibles, you can better appreciate their value and significance, and make informed decisions about how to identify, purchase, and preserve these items.

2.2 Historical Significance and Cultural Value

Antiques and collectibles are more than just objects; they are tangible connections to the past, serving as windows into the lives, cultures, and societies of previous generations. This section delves into the historical significance and cultural value that these items hold, helping collectors understand why preserving and appreciating these pieces is so important.

1. Historical Significance

A. Preserving History

- Tangible Links to the Past: Antiques are tangible pieces of history that offer insights into the technologies, artistic expressions, and daily lives of past generations. By collecting and preserving these items, we maintain a direct connection to our heritage, allowing us to study and appreciate the advancements and traditions that have shaped the modern world.

- Continuity of Traditions: These objects serve as a bridge between the past and the present, helping us to maintain and continue cultural traditions and historical practices.

B. Educational Value

- Lessons in History and Art: Studying antiques can provide valuable lessons in history, art, and sociology. Each piece tells a story about the time and place it was created, offering a unique perspective on historical events and everyday life. For example, a simple household item like a Victorian-era tea set can reveal much about social customs, manufacturing techniques, and trade routes of that period.

- In-depth Understanding: Through antiques, collectors and historians can gain a deeper understanding of societal norms, technological advancements, and the economic conditions of different eras.

2. Cultural Value

A. Reflection of Society

- Capturing Cultural Trends: Collectibles often reflect the culture of the time in which they were produced, capturing the trends, interests, and values of a particular era. For instance, pop culture memorabilia from the 1960s, such as Beatles merchandise or posters from Woodstock, encapsulates the spirit and cultural movements of that decade in a way that written records alone cannot.

- Snapshot of an Era: These items serve as cultural snapshots, preserving the essence of a specific time and place, and offering a more relatable and personal connection to history.

B. Cultural Identity

- Connection to Heritage: Collecting can also be a way to connect with one's cultural identity or heritage. For example, collecting items from your ancestors' country of origin can be a meaningful way to maintain a connection to your roots. These items not only serve as a link to the past but also help preserve the cultural heritage of a community or family.

- Cultural Preservation: By collecting and preserving items of cultural significance, collectors contribute to the preservation of cultural heritage, ensuring that future generations can learn about and appreciate their ancestry.

3. The Role of Antiques in Modern Culture

A. Influence on Contemporary Design

- Inspiration for Modern Trends: Many antiques continue to influence modern design, fashion, and art, demonstrating their lasting impact on culture and aesthetics. For example, the clean lines and functional forms of mid-century modern furniture have seen a resurgence in popularity, influencing contemporary furniture design and home decor trends.

- Timeless Appeal: The enduring appeal of certain antique styles highlights the cyclical nature of design trends and the timeless qualities of well-crafted objects.

B. Symbol of Status and Taste

- Reflection of Personal Values: Antiques and collectibles often serve as symbols of status and taste, reflecting the collector's appreciation for history, craftsmanship, and uniqueness. Owning and displaying such items can convey a deep understanding of cultural history and an appreciation for the finer things in life.

- Cultural Capital: Possessing and curating a collection of antiques can elevate one's cultural capital, showcasing not only wealth but also a refined sense of history and aesthetics.

Understanding the historical significance and cultural value of antiques and collectibles enhances their appeal and importance, making them not just valuable possessions but vital pieces of our shared heritage. As you build your collection, recognizing the stories and cultural contexts behind each item will deepen your appreciation and enrich your collecting experience.

2.3 Key Categories and Types of Collectibles

The world of antiques and collectibles is vast, encompassing a wide range of items that appeal to different interests and passions. In this section, we'll explore some of the most popular categories and types of collectibles, providing insights into what makes each category unique and valuable to collectors.

1. Furniture

A. Antique Furniture

- Historical Significance: Antique furniture includes pieces from various historical periods, such as Georgian, Victorian, and Art Deco. These items are known for their craftsmanship, quality materials, and unique design elements that reflect the aesthetics of their respective eras.

- Examples: Georgian mahogany chests, Victorian dining tables, and Art Deco cabinets.

B. Collectible Furniture

- Modern Appeal: Collectible furniture often refers to more modern pieces, such as mid-century modern designs, which have gained popularity due to their sleek, functional design and iconic status in 20th-century decor.

- Examples: Eames lounge chairs, Scandinavian teak sideboards, and Knoll dining sets.

2. Art and Sculptures

A. Fine Art

- Timeless Masterpieces: Fine art includes original paintings, drawings, and sculptures created by renowned artists. These pieces are often highly valued for their aesthetic qualities, historical significance, and the reputation of the artist.

- Examples: Paintings by Rembrandt, sculptures by Rodin, and drawings by Michelangelo.

B. Collectible Art

- Contemporary Significance: Collectible art includes limited edition prints, contemporary art, and works by emerging artists. While these pieces may not have the centuries-old history of fine art, they are often sought after for their unique perspectives and the potential for appreciation in value.

- Examples: Limited edition prints by Andy Warhol, contemporary sculptures by Jeff Koons, and photography by Ansel Adams.

3. Jewelry and Watches

A. Antique Jewelry

- Historical Craftsmanship: Antique jewelry showcases the styles and techniques of different historical periods, such as Edwardian, Victorian, or Art Nouveau. These pieces are often handcrafted, using precious metals and gemstones, and are valued for their beauty and historical significance.

- Examples: Edwardian diamond brooches, Victorian lockets, and Art Nouveau enamel necklaces.

B. Collectible Watches

- Prestige and Craftsmanship: Collectible watches include vintage timepieces from iconic brands that are prized for their craftsmanship, design, and the prestige associated with the brand. These watches are often seen as both functional items and status symbols.

- Examples: Rolex Submariner, Patek Philippe Calatrava, and Omega Speedmaster.

4. Toys and Games

A. Vintage Toys

- Nostalgia and Rarity: Vintage toys are often sought after for their nostalgia and rarity. These items can range from early tin wind-up toys to the first editions of popular action figures and dolls.

- Examples: Tin wind-up robots, original G.I. Joe action figures, and 1950s Barbie dolls.

B. Modern Collectibles

- Pop Culture Appeal: Modern collectibles include limited edition toys and games, often associated with popular culture. These items can gain significant value over time, especially if they are kept in mint condition or have unique features.

- Examples: Limited edition LEGO sets, Funko Pop! figures, and rare video game cartridges.

5. Books and Manuscripts

A. Rare Books

- Literary Treasures: Rare books are highly valued for their age, rarity, and historical importance. This category includes first editions, signed copies, and books that have played a significant role in history or literature.

- Examples: First edition of Charles Dickens' "A Christmas Carol," signed copies of Ernest Hemingway's works, and illuminated medieval manuscripts.

B. Collectible Manuscripts

- Historical Documentation: Collectible manuscripts include historical documents, letters, and autographs that provide insights into significant events or figures in history. These items are often treasured for their direct connection to the past.

- Examples: Letters from Abraham Lincoln, handwritten manuscripts by Shakespeare, and autographed speeches by Winston Churchill.

Understanding the various categories and types of collectibles allows you to focus your collecting efforts on areas that resonate with your interests and passions. Whether you are drawn to the timeless elegance of antique furniture, the artistry of fine jewelry, or the nostalgia of vintage toys, there is a world of possibilities awaiting your exploration.

Chapter 2 Review: Understanding Antiques and Collectibles

Chapter 2 of *HowExpert Guide to Antiques and Collectibles* delves into the essential concepts that every collector needs to grasp. It provides clear definitions, explores the historical and cultural significance of antiques and collectibles, and introduces the key categories that define this diverse field.

2.1 Definitions and Distinctions

- Understanding Antiques: Antiques are defined as items typically over 100 years old, valued for their craftsmanship, rarity, and historical importance. These pieces often serve as tangible links to the past, offering insight into the lifestyles, artistry, and materials of earlier times.

- Defining Collectibles: Collectibles, on the other hand, are more modern items that are prized for their rarity, uniqueness, or cultural significance. These can range from limited-edition toys to contemporary art, reflecting the trends and values of their time.

- Overlap and Grey Areas: The chapter also addresses the overlap between antiques and collectibles, noting that certain items may straddle both categories depending on their context, age, and market trends. For example, an early 20th-century object might be considered both an antique and a collectible.

2.2 Historical Significance and Cultural Value

- Preserving History: Antiques and collectibles are more than just objects; they are custodians of history. Collecting these items allows individuals to preserve pieces of the past, offering educational insights and a connection to previous generations.

- Cultural Reflection: Collectibles, in particular, reflect the cultural values, trends, and societal norms of the periods in which they were produced. They often serve as symbols of cultural identity and heritage, capturing the essence of a specific era.

- Influence on Modern Culture: The chapter also explores how antiques and collectibles continue to influence modern design, aesthetics, and even cultural trends, highlighting their enduring relevance in contemporary society.

2.3 Key Categories and Types of Collectibles

- Popular Collecting Categories: The chapter introduces a variety of popular collecting categories, including:

  - Furniture: Antique furniture pieces, often prized for their craftsmanship and materials, are key highlights.

  - Art and Sculptures: Both antique and modern art are discussed, with a focus on their cultural and aesthetic value.

- Jewelry and Watches: Collecting jewelry and watches combines an appreciation for design with an interest in precious materials.

- Toys and Games: From vintage toys to modern collectibles, this category appeals to nostalgia and the preservation of childhood memories.

- Books and Manuscripts: Rare books and historical documents offer a unique glimpse into the literary and intellectual history.

- Identifying Interests: Each category is broken down into examples of both antiques and modern collectibles, helping collectors identify which types resonate most with their personal interests and passions.

Chapter 2 equips collectors with a thorough understanding of the foundational concepts in the world of antiques and collectibles. By defining what constitutes an antique versus a collectible, exploring their historical and cultural significance, and breaking down key categories, this chapter lays the groundwork for informed and thoughtful collecting. Whether you're drawn to the historical depth of an antique or the cultural resonance of a modern collectible, this chapter provides the knowledge needed to navigate the collecting world with confidence.

Chapter 3: Identifying Antiques and Collectibles

Identifying antiques and collectibles accurately is one of the most crucial skills for any collector. Being able to recognize authentic items, understand common marks and signatures, and distinguish features by category can significantly impact the value and significance of your collection. In this chapter, we will explore the tools and techniques necessary for accurate identification, as well as how to avoid common pitfalls in the process.

3.1 Recognizing Authentic Items

Accurately recognizing authentic antiques and collectibles is a critical skill for any collector. The value and historical significance of an item are directly tied to its authenticity, and being able to distinguish genuine pieces from reproductions or forgeries can significantly impact your collection. This section outlines the key factors and strategies to help you identify authentic items with confidence.

1. Research and Knowledge

A. Understanding Historical Context

- Familiarization with the Era: Familiarize yourself with the historical period or style of the item in question. Knowing the typical materials, construction methods, and design trends of the era can provide important clues about the item's authenticity.

- Study Comparable Items: Study similar items in museums, auctions, or reference books to build a solid foundation of knowledge. This comparative research helps in recognizing patterns and anomalies that might indicate a fake.

B. Identifying Characteristics of Authentic Items

- Signs of Authentic Aging: Authentic items often show signs of age that are difficult to replicate, such as patina, wear, and small imperfections. These characteristics add to the item's charm and historical value.

- Beware of Artificial Aging: Reproductions may lack these natural signs or may exhibit artificially induced wear that does not match the item's supposed age. Look for inconsistencies that suggest the item has been deliberately aged.

2. Physical Examination

A. Inspecting for Age and Wear

- Natural Wear Indicators: Look for natural wear in areas where the item would have been frequently handled or used. For example, antique furniture might show wear on armrests, while vintage jewelry may have slight scratches from regular use.

- Lighting Techniques: Examine the item under different lighting conditions to spot inconsistencies in color, texture, or material that could indicate a reproduction or repair.

B. Analyzing Construction Techniques

- Handcrafted Techniques: Authentic antiques were typically made using handcrafting techniques that are not commonly used today. For example, dovetail joints in furniture, hand-blown glass, or hand-stitched textiles are indicators of authenticity.

- Comparison with Period Examples: Compare the construction methods used in the item with known examples from the period to verify its age and origin. This can include examining the type of wood, stitching methods, or metalwork.

3. Provenance and Documentation

A. The Importance of Provenance

- Documented History: Provenance refers to the documented history of an item, including previous ownership, sales records, and any related documentation. An item with a well-documented provenance is more likely to be authentic and can be more valuable.

- Supporting Evidence: Provenance can include receipts, letters, or photographs that confirm the item's history and authenticity, providing a continuous chain of ownership that enhances credibility.

B. Verifying Documentation

- Scrutiny of Documents: Always verify the authenticity of any documents associated with the item. Look for inconsistencies, such as incorrect dates, mismatched names, or signs of tampering.

- Expert Verification: If possible, consult with experts or appraisers who can help confirm the validity of the provenance. This is especially important for high-value items where provenance can significantly impact value.

4. Consulting Experts

A. Seeking Professional Opinions

- Expert Insight: When in doubt, consult with experts who specialize in the type of item you are evaluating. Professional appraisers, museum curators, or experienced collectors can provide valuable insights and help you determine the authenticity of an item.

- Importance for High-Value Items: Expert opinions are particularly important when dealing with high-value items, where the risk of forgery or misrepresentation is higher.

B. Utilizing Authentication Services

- Specialized Services: Consider using authentication services that specialize in verifying the authenticity of specific types of collectibles, such as art, coins, or vintage watches. These services often provide certificates of authenticity that can enhance the value and credibility of your collection.

- Added Security: Authentication services offer an added layer of security, ensuring that your investment is protected by professional verification processes.

Recognizing authentic items requires a combination of research, physical examination, and expert consultation. By developing these skills, you can confidently identify and acquire genuine antiques and collectibles, ensuring that your collection is both valuable and historically significant.

3.2 Common Marks and Signatures

Identifying the common marks and signatures on antiques and collectibles is a crucial aspect of determining their authenticity, origin, and value. Many items, especially those made by renowned manufacturers or artists, bear specific marks or signatures that serve as important clues to their history and authenticity. This section will guide you through understanding and identifying these marks and signatures.

1. Maker's Marks

A. Identifying Maker's Marks

- Location and Appearance: Maker's marks are often found on the underside or back of an item and typically include the manufacturer's name, logo, or initials. These marks help to identify the creator of the item, providing insight into its origin and, in many cases, its quality.

- Common Placement: Common places to find maker's marks include the bottom of ceramics, the back of silverware, or hidden areas of furniture.

B. Importance of Maker's Marks

- Verification and Value: Items with identifiable maker's marks are generally more valuable because the mark verifies the origin and authenticity of the piece. It also allows collectors to trace the item's history and connect it to a specific maker or period.

- Example of Significance: For example, a piece of furniture marked with "Chippendale" is instantly recognized as valuable due to the association with the famous 18th-century cabinetmaker.

2. Hallmarks and Date Marks

A. Recognizing Hallmarks

- Definition and Purpose: Hallmarks are official stamps found on precious metals such as silver, gold, and platinum, indicating the metal's purity, origin, and sometimes the date of manufacture. These marks are typically small and may require a magnifying glass to see clearly.

- Usage in Identification: Hallmarks are particularly important in identifying silverware and jewelry. For instance, a sterling silver hallmark with a lion passant indicates British origin and a high level of purity.

B. Interpreting Date Marks

- Date Indicators: Date marks are used to indicate the year of manufacture, often seen alongside hallmarks. These marks can be symbols, letters, or numbers that correspond to specific years according to a standardized chart.

- Understanding the System: Understanding these marks requires familiarity with the symbols used by different countries and periods. For example, British silver often uses a letter to represent the year, with each letter corresponding to a specific date range.

3. Artist Signatures

A. Importance of Artist Signatures

- Impact on Value: In the case of art, pottery, and other handcrafted items, an artist's signature can significantly impact the value and authenticity of the piece. A recognized artist's signature confirms the creator and often enhances the item's desirability.

- Location of Signatures: Signatures may appear on the front, back, or base of an item, depending on the medium. In paintings, they are often found in the lower corners, while on pottery, they are typically on the bottom.

B. Verifying Authenticity of Signatures

- Avoiding Forgeries: Not all signatures are genuine; some may be forged to increase the value of an item. It is essential to compare the signature with verified examples from the artist, checking for consistency in style, placement, and medium.

- Consulting Experts: Consulting reference books, databases, or experts specializing in the artist or period can help confirm the authenticity of a signature.

4. Factory and Production Marks

A. Recognizing Factory Marks

- Identification of Origin: Many collectibles, especially ceramics, porcelain, and glass, carry factory marks that indicate the place of manufacture. These marks can include symbols, initials, or numbers that identify the specific factory and sometimes the production line.

- Notable Examples: For example, the Meissen porcelain factory is known for its crossed swords mark, which has been used since the 18th century to signify authenticity.

B. Understanding Production Marks

- Significance of Production Numbers: Production marks may also include information about the production run or series number, which can indicate rarity. Limited edition items often have numbered marks, such as "1/500," indicating they are part of a limited run.

- Impact on Value: These marks can greatly affect the item's value, especially if the production run was small or the item is particularly sought after.

5. Regional and Cultural Marks

A. Identifying Regional Marks

- Cultural Signifiers: Some marks are specific to certain regions or cultures, reflecting the local styles and traditions of craftsmanship. For example, Chinese porcelain often features marks that include the dynasty name, reign period, and sometimes the emperor's name.

- Importance of Knowledge: Recognizing these regional marks requires knowledge of the history and cultural significance of the area where the item was produced.

B. Cultural Significance of Marks

- Beyond Identification: Regional and cultural marks often carry additional significance, indicating not just the maker or place of origin but also the item's role within that culture. For instance, Japanese ceramics may have marks related to specific kilns or schools of pottery, which are highly respected in the art world.

Understanding and identifying common marks and signatures is essential for any collector looking to accurately appraise and authenticate their items. These marks provide valuable information about the item's origin, maker, and sometimes even its history. By learning to recognize and interpret these marks, you can make more informed decisions about the items in your collection and ensure that they hold both historical and monetary value.

3.3 Distinguishing Features by Category

Antiques and collectibles come in a wide variety of forms, each with unique characteristics that help to determine their authenticity, origin, and value. Understanding the distinguishing features within specific categories is essential for accurately identifying and appraising items in your collection. This section will guide you through the key features to look for in different categories of antiques and collectibles.

1. Furniture

A. Construction Techniques

- Traditional Joinery: Look for traditional construction methods, such as dovetail joints in drawers, mortise-and-tenon joints in frames, and hand-carved details. These techniques indicate quality craftsmanship typical of genuine antique furniture.

- Material Authenticity: The use of solid wood, rather than veneers or composite materials, is another indicator of an authentic piece, especially in older furniture. Examine the underside or back of the furniture for signs of solid wood construction.

B. Wood Type and Aging

- Historical Wood Usage: The type of wood used can help date the piece and determine its origin. For example, oak was commonly used in English furniture, while mahogany was popular in American and British pieces during the 18th century.

- Signs of Natural Aging: Natural aging signs, such as a darkened patina, shrinkage, or slight warping, are common in genuine antique furniture. These features can distinguish authentic items from reproductions, which may lack these characteristics.

2. Ceramics and Porcelain

A. Glaze and Finish

- Handcrafted Glazing: The quality and type of glaze can be a telltale sign of an item's age and origin. Older ceramics often have a thicker, more uneven glaze due to the hand-dipping process, while modern reproductions may have a more uniform finish.

- Crazing Patterns: Crazing, or the network of fine cracks in the glaze, is common in older ceramics and can indicate authenticity, although it can also be artificially induced to mimic age.

B. Hand-Painted vs. Transferware

- Hand-Painted Designs: Hand-painted designs, especially those with slight variations or imperfections, are typically more valuable and indicative of older pieces. Transferware, where patterns are applied via a transfer process, became popular in the 19th century and can be identified by its more uniform and consistent patterns.

- Magnification Checks: Examine the edges of patterns and designs under magnification to distinguish between hand-painted and transfer-applied decoration. Hand-painted items often show brushstrokes and irregularities that transferware lacks.

3. Jewelry and Watches

A. Hallmarks and Maker's Marks

- Purity and Origin Indicators: Jewelry often features hallmarks that indicate the metal's purity, as well as maker's marks that identify the creator. These marks are usually found on the inner band of rings, the back of pendants, or the clasp of bracelets and necklaces.

- Assay and Date Marks: The presence of multiple marks, including those for assay offices and date letters, can add to the authenticity and value of the piece. These marks can also help trace the item's history and origin.

B. Gemstone Setting Techniques

- Hand-Set Stones: The way gemstones are set into the jewelry can indicate its age. Older pieces often feature hand-set stones with more intricate settings, while modern pieces may use more uniform, machine-made settings.

- Wear Patterns: Look for signs of wear around the setting, as genuine antique pieces will show some natural wear from years of use. The wear should be consistent with the age and type of the piece.

4. Art and Sculptures

A. Signature and Style Consistency

- Artist's Signature: In artwork, the artist's signature is a crucial factor in determining authenticity. Consistency in the signature, placement, and style compared to other known works by the artist can confirm authenticity.

- Period-Consistent Techniques: The style and techniques used should be consistent with the period in which the artist worked. For instance, Impressionist works should show the characteristic brushstrokes and color usage of that movement.

B. Materials and Medium

- Authentic Materials: The materials used in sculptures, such as bronze, marble, or wood, can help identify the period and authenticity. Genuine pieces often have a patina that has developed over time, while reproductions may lack this natural aging process.

- Quality of Medium: The quality of the materials, such as the type of canvas or pigments in a painting, can also be indicators of authenticity and value. For example, older paintings may show signs of craquelure (fine cracks) in the paint, indicating age.

5. Textiles and Rugs

A. Weaving Techniques

- Handwoven Indicators: The weaving technique is a key factor in identifying the age and origin of textiles and rugs. Handwoven items, especially those with intricate patterns and slight irregularities, are typically more valuable and authentic than machine-made pieces.

- Knotting Variations: Look for signs of hand-knotting in rugs, where the knots may be uneven and show slight variations, indicating a hand-crafted item. This irregularity is a hallmark of genuine, traditional craftsmanship.

B. Natural vs. Synthetic Dyes

- Dye Sources: Older textiles and rugs often use natural dyes derived from plants and minerals, which can fade naturally over time. Synthetic dyes, which became common in the late 19th century, tend to have brighter, more uniform colors.

- Dye Testing: Testing for natural dyes can involve examining the color under natural light or using a dye testing kit to see if the colors bleed or fade in a manner consistent with natural dyes.

6. Books and Manuscripts

A. Binding and Paper Quality

- Historical Binding Techniques: The quality of the binding and paper can help date a book or manuscript. Older books often have leather bindings and handmade paper, which may show signs of aging, such as foxing (brown spots) or a slight brittleness.

- Watermark Identification: Look for watermarks in the paper, which can indicate the paper mill and sometimes the date of production. Watermarks are often visible when the paper is held up to the light.

B. Edition and Printing Techniques

- First Editions and Rarity: First editions, particularly of important works, are highly valued. Identifying a first edition often requires knowledge of the publisher's practices and the specific markings that denote a first edition.

- Printing Techniques: Examine the printing techniques, such as letterpress for older books versus modern offset printing, to help date the book and assess its authenticity. Letterpress printing leaves a slight indentation on the paper, which can be felt and seen.

Understanding the distinguishing features within each category of antiques and collectibles is essential for accurate identification and valuation. By focusing on these specific characteristics, you can better assess the authenticity and value of items in your collection, making informed decisions that enhance your collecting experience.

3.4 Tools and Techniques for Identification

Successfully identifying antiques and collectibles requires not only knowledge but also the right tools and techniques. These tools can help you examine items more closely, reveal hidden details, and verify authenticity. In this section, we'll explore some of the most useful tools and techniques for identifying antiques and collectibles with accuracy and confidence.

1. Magnification Tools

A. Loupes and Magnifying Glasses

- Essential for Detail Work: A loupe or magnifying glass is essential for examining small details such as maker's marks, hallmarks, or fine cracks in the glaze of ceramics. These tools allow you to see minute details that are invisible to the naked eye, helping to verify the authenticity of an item.

- Recommended Magnification: Choose a loupe with at least 10x magnification for detailed work. Higher magnification may be necessary for intricate items like jewelry or coins.

B. Microscopes

- For In-Depth Analysis: For more detailed analysis, especially of very small items like stamps or gemstones, a microscope can be invaluable. Microscopes allow you to examine surface textures, engraving details, and even the structure of materials at a microscopic level.

- Digital Options: Digital microscopes, which can display images on a screen, are particularly useful for sharing your findings with others or capturing images for documentation.

2. Ultraviolet (UV) Light

A. Detecting Repairs and Alterations

- Revealing Hidden Repairs: UV light is an effective tool for revealing repairs or alterations that are not visible under normal lighting. For example, it can help you detect glue repairs on ceramics or touch-ups in paintings.

- Material Fluorescence: When shined on an object, UV light can cause certain materials to fluoresce differently, indicating the presence of newer materials or repairs.

B. Verifying Signatures and Inscriptions

- Authenticating Inscriptions: UV light can also be used to verify signatures and inscriptions on artwork and documents. It can reveal whether a signature was added later or if different inks were used, which can be a red flag for forgeries.

3. Weighing and Measuring Tools

A. Scales

- Weight as an Authenticity Check: Accurate scales are important for weighing items such as coins, jewelry, and silverware. The weight can provide clues about the item's authenticity, as genuine pieces will have specific weights depending on their materials and design.

- Precision Measurement: Precision scales that measure in grams or even finer units are recommended for small and valuable items.

B. Calipers and Measuring Tapes

- Exact Measurements: Calipers and measuring tapes are useful for taking precise measurements of items. For example, the dimensions of a piece of furniture can help verify its period and style, while the thickness of a coin can indicate whether it has been altered or is a reproduction.

- Digital Accuracy: Digital calipers can provide highly accurate measurements and are easy to use for items of varying sizes.

4. Chemical Testing Kits

A. Metal Testing Kits

- Verifying Metal Purity: Metal testing kits are used to verify the composition of metals, such as gold, silver, and platinum. These kits often include acids that react differently with various metals, allowing you to determine the metal's purity.

- Safety Precautions: Always follow safety precautions when using chemical testing kits, as the acids can be harmful if mishandled.

B. Dye Testing Kits

- Identifying Natural Dyes: Dye testing kits can help you identify whether the dyes in textiles and rugs are natural or synthetic. These kits often involve applying a small amount of a testing solution to the fabric to see how the dye reacts, helping to date the item and verify its authenticity.

5. Reference Guides and Databases

A. Printed Reference Books

- Invaluable Resources: Having a collection of reference books is invaluable for any serious collector. These books often include images, descriptions, and historical information that can help you identify and verify items in your collection.

- Category-Specific Information: Popular reference books cover specific categories like furniture, ceramics, or coins, providing detailed information on marks, styles, and periods.

B. Online Databases and Resources

- Searchable Archives: Online databases offer searchable archives of maker's marks, hallmarks, and artist signatures. These resources can be especially useful for quick identification and verification.

- Museum and Auction House Resources: Many museums and auction houses provide online access to their collections and past sales, allowing you to compare items and see how similar pieces have been valued.

6. Digital Tools and Apps

A. Digital Magnifiers and Cameras

- High-Resolution Imaging: Digital magnifiers and cameras can capture high-resolution images of items, making it easier to share your findings with experts or document the condition of an item over time.

- Built-In Features: Some digital magnifiers come with built-in lighting and adjustable magnification, providing clear and detailed images.

B. Identification Apps

- Image Recognition Technology: Several apps are designed to help collectors identify and value antiques and collectibles. These apps often use image recognition technology to match your item with a database of known pieces, offering instant identification and valuation.

- Complementary Tool: While these apps are a helpful starting point, they should be used in conjunction with more traditional methods and expert consultation for the most accurate results.

Utilizing the right tools and techniques is crucial for accurately identifying antiques and collectibles. Whether you're inspecting the fine details with a loupe, verifying materials with chemical tests, or cross-referencing with a trusted guide, these resources empower you to make informed decisions about the items in your collection. By combining these tools with your growing knowledge, you can enhance your ability to distinguish genuine pieces from imitations and confidently build a valuable collection.

3.5 Common Pitfalls and How to Avoid Them

When collecting antiques and collectibles, even seasoned collectors can fall into certain traps that can lead to acquiring inauthentic items, overpaying, or missing out on valuable pieces. Being aware of these common pitfalls and knowing how to avoid them is essential for building a successful collection. This section will highlight some of the most common mistakes collectors make and provide strategies to help you avoid them.

1. Over-Reliance on Marks and Signatures

A. Misleading Marks

- Deceptive Replicas: While maker's marks, hallmarks, and signatures are important indicators of authenticity, they can sometimes be misleading. Forgers often replicate these marks to make reproductions appear genuine.

- Cross-Referencing: Always cross-reference marks with reliable sources and examine the entire item for consistency. Look for other signs of authenticity, such as materials, construction techniques, and wear patterns, to support the validity of the marks.

B. Lack of Context

- Contextual Clues: Focusing solely on marks without considering the item's overall context can lead to misjudgment. For example, a piece of furniture may have a legitimate maker's mark but show signs of being a later reproduction if the materials or construction techniques do not match the period.

- Holistic Assessment: Take a holistic approach by considering all aspects of the item, including its provenance, physical characteristics, and historical context.

2. Falling for Reproductions and Fakes

A. Spotting High-Quality Reproductions

- Close Imitations: Some reproductions are so well-made that they can easily deceive even experienced collectors. These reproductions may use authentic materials and skilled craftsmanship but lack the historical authenticity of true antiques.

- Subtle Differences: Educate yourself on the differences between originals and reproductions. Pay attention to subtle details, such as the quality of the finish, signs of artificial aging, and discrepancies in style or construction that do not align with the supposed period.

B. Avoiding Online Scams

- Online Risks: The internet has made it easier to buy and sell antiques, but it has also increased the risk of encountering scams. Be cautious when purchasing from online marketplaces, especially if the seller lacks a solid reputation or the item is priced too attractively.

- Due Diligence: Always request detailed photos, ask questions about provenance, and consider using escrow services for high-value transactions. If possible, inspect the item in person or seek the opinion of a trusted expert before making a purchase.

3. Emotional Bias in Decision-Making

A. Overvaluing Based on Personal Attachment

- Emotional Investment: It's easy to let emotions cloud your judgment, especially if you have a personal connection to a particular type of item or find something that resonates with you. This emotional attachment can lead to overvaluing the item or overlooking flaws.

- Objective Evaluation: Maintain objectivity by assessing the item based on its merits, historical significance, and market value, rather than personal feelings. Consider getting a second opinion to provide a more balanced perspective.

B. Fear of Missing Out (FOMO)

- Impulse Decisions: The fear of missing out can drive collectors to make hasty decisions, such as overbidding at auctions or buying items without proper research. This urgency can result in overpaying or acquiring items that do not truly enhance your collection.

- Patience Pays Off: Take your time to research and evaluate potential acquisitions. Remember that in the world of collecting, patience often pays off, and there will always be more opportunities.

4. Ignoring Provenance and Documentation

A. Importance of Provenance

- Value of History: Provenance provides a documented history of an item, adding to its authenticity and value. Ignoring or undervaluing provenance can lead to missed opportunities or acquiring items with questionable backgrounds.

- Documentation Review: Always ask for and review any available provenance when considering a purchase. Items with strong, well-documented provenance are generally more valuable and desirable.

B. Verifying Documentation

- Avoiding Forgeries: Not all documentation is genuine. Forged or misleading documents can accompany fake or altered items, leading to costly mistakes.

- Verification Process: Verify all documentation with trusted sources or experts. Look for inconsistencies in dates, names, or events, and compare with known records or databases.

5. Underestimating Restoration Impact

A. Over-Restoration

- Balance in Restoration: While restoration can enhance the appearance and longevity of an antique, over-restoration can diminish its value. Excessive cleaning, replacing original parts, or altering the item's original character can reduce its historical significance.

- Preservation Focus: When considering restoration, aim to preserve as much of the original material and appearance as possible. Consult with a professional conservator who understands the balance between restoration and preservation.

B. Not Recognizing Inappropriate Restoration

- Modern Interference: Inappropriate restoration, such as using modern materials or techniques, can be difficult to detect but significantly affects the value and authenticity of an item.

- Detecting Issues: Learn to recognize signs of improper restoration, such as mismatched materials, inconsistent finishes, or repairs that do not align with the item's period. When in doubt, seek the advice of a restoration expert or appraiser.

Understanding these common pitfalls and how to avoid them is crucial for making informed decisions and building a valuable collection. By approaching each potential acquisition with caution, research, and a critical eye, you can minimize risks and enhance the authenticity and value of your collection. 3.5 Common Pitfalls and How to Avoid Them

Chapter 3 Review: Identifying Antiques and Collectibles

Chapter 3 of *HowExpert Guide to Antiques and Collectibles* is a crucial resource for collectors, offering the essential skills and knowledge required to accurately identify and appraise antiques and collectibles. This chapter provides comprehensive guidance on recognizing authentic items, understanding marks and signatures, distinguishing features by category, using identification tools and techniques, and avoiding common pitfalls.

3.1 Recognizing Authentic Items

- Research and Historical Context: This section emphasizes the importance of thorough research and a solid understanding of historical context when identifying authentic antiques. Knowing the era, region, and typical characteristics of items from a specific time period is key to accurate identification.

- Physical Examination: Collectors are guided on how to physically inspect items for signs of age, wear, and construction techniques that align with the item's purported age. This includes looking for details like hand-crafted elements, patina, and materials used.

- Provenance and Documentation: Provenance—an item's documented history— is highlighted as a critical component in verifying authenticity. The chapter advises collectors to seek out provenance documents and consult experts or use authentication services to confirm the legitimacy of valuable items.

3.2 Common Marks and Signatures

- Understanding Marks: This section covers the importance of maker's marks, hallmarks, and artist signatures as indicators of an item's origin and authenticity. These marks often provide valuable clues about the item's history and value.

- Verification Process: Collectors are encouraged to verify these marks and signatures against trusted references and databases to ensure their accuracy and avoid forgeries. The section also discusses the risks associated with misreading or over-relying on marks without further verification.

3.3 Distinguishing Features by Category

- Category-Specific Features: The chapter delves into the specific distinguishing features of different categories, such as furniture, ceramics, jewelry, art, textiles, and books. For each category, collectors learn to identify key elements like construction techniques, materials, and design styles.

- Informed Decision-Making: By understanding these unique characteristics, collectors can make more informed decisions when acquiring items and avoid the pitfalls of misidentification, which can lead to overpaying or acquiring less valuable items.

3.4 Tools and Techniques for Identification

- Essential Tools: This section outlines the various tools that collectors should use for detailed examination, including loupes, magnifying glasses, UV lights, and scales. These tools help in closely inspecting items for signs of authenticity.

- Advanced Techniques: The chapter also covers the use of chemical testing kits and reference guides for verifying materials and marks. Additionally, it highlights the value of digital tools and online databases, which can provide quick and reliable identification resources.

3.5 Common Pitfalls and How to Avoid Them

- Avoiding Common Mistakes: Collectors are warned against common pitfalls such as over-relying on marks and signatures, falling for reproductions, and letting emotions influence purchasing decisions. The chapter stresses the importance of objectivity in the collecting process.

- Preserving Value: The dangers of ignoring provenance, over-restoring items, and failing to consult experts are also discussed. By following the chapter's advice, collectors can avoid these costly mistakes and focus on building a valuable, authentic collection.

Chapter 3 equips collectors with the practical knowledge and tools needed to confidently identify and evaluate antiques and collectibles. By mastering the skills outlined in this chapter, collectors can enhance the authenticity and value of their collections while avoiding common mistakes that can lead to costly errors. This chapter is essential for anyone serious about collecting, as it provides the foundation for making informed and accurate decisions in the world of antiques and collectibles.

Chapter 4: Valuing Your Collection

Valuing antiques and collectibles accurately is a crucial aspect of collecting, whether you're buying, selling, or simply ensuring that your collection is well-insured. This chapter covers the factors that affect value, different appraisal methods, resources for valuation, understanding market trends, and practical tips for maximizing the value of your collection.

4.1 Factors Affecting Value

Determining the value of antiques and collectibles involves understanding the various factors that contribute to their worth. This section explores the key elements that affect an item's value, helping collectors make informed decisions about their collections.

1. Age and Rarity

A. The Impact of Age

- Historical Significance: The age of an item is often directly correlated with its value. Older items, especially those from significant historical periods, tend to be more valuable because they offer a tangible connection to the past.

- Survival Over Time: Items that have survived for centuries are often seen as more valuable due to their rarity and historical significance.

B. The Role of Rarity

- Limited Production: Rarity is a crucial factor in determining value. Items that were produced in limited quantities or are now scarce are typically more sought after by collectors.

- Scarcity Due to Survival: The rarity of an item can be due to its limited production, the materials used, or the fact that few examples have survived over time. For example, a rare coin or a limited-edition print will generally be more valuable than a mass-produced item from the same period.

2. Condition

A. Importance of Condition

- Premium for Pristine Items: The condition of an item is one of the most critical factors in determining its value. Items in excellent condition with minimal wear, no repairs, or restorations typically command higher prices.

- Devaluation Due to Damage: Even minor damage, such as chips, cracks, or fading, can significantly decrease an item's value, especially if it affects the item's functionality or appearance.

B. Originality and Preservation

- Value of Unaltered Items: Items that remain in their original state, without modifications or repairs, are generally more valuable. Collectors place a premium on originality, as it reflects the item's historical authenticity and integrity.

- Preservation Techniques: Proper preservation techniques, such as appropriate storage and care, can maintain an item's condition over time, preserving its value.

3. Provenance

A. What is Provenance?

- Historical Documentation: Provenance refers to the documented history of an item, including previous ownership, sales records, and any related documentation. An item with a well-documented history is often more valuable, as provenance can confirm its authenticity and significance.

- Connection to Notable Figures: Items with connections to notable individuals, events, or places often have enhanced value due to their historical importance.

B. Verifying Provenance

- Authentic Documentation: Authentic documentation, such as receipts, certificates, or historical records, can enhance an item's provenance and, consequently, its value.

- Risk of Forged Documents: It's important to verify the accuracy and authenticity of provenance documents, as forged or misleading records can artificially inflate an item's perceived value.

4. Market Demand

A. Understanding Market Demand

- Fluctuating Desires: The current demand for specific types of antiques and collectibles can fluctuate based on trends, cultural shifts, or economic conditions. Items that are highly sought after by collectors will typically command higher prices.

- Factors Influencing Demand: Market demand can be influenced by various factors, including popular culture, historical anniversaries, or the rediscovery of a particular artist or period.

B. Impact of Trends

- Rise in Popularity: Trends play a significant role in determining the value of collectibles. For example, certain styles of furniture or specific artists may become more popular over time, leading to increased demand and higher prices for related items.

- Decline in Favor: Conversely, items that fall out of favor with collectors may see a decline in value as demand decreases.

Understanding these factors is essential for accurately valuing your collection and making informed decisions when buying, selling, or insuring your antiques and collectibles. By considering age, rarity, condition, provenance, and market demand, you can better assess the worth of your items and ensure that your collection maintains its value over time.

4.2 Appraisal Methods

Appraising antiques and collectibles accurately is essential for understanding their value, whether for selling, insuring, or simply managing your collection. Various appraisal methods can be used to assess an item's worth, each offering different levels of detail and accuracy. This section explores the most common appraisal methods and how to effectively use them.

1. Professional Appraisals

A. Hiring a Certified Appraiser

- Expert Insight: A professional appraisal is one of the most reliable ways to determine the value of your items. Certified appraisers have the expertise, experience, and access to market data that allow them to provide accurate valuations.

- Specialization: It's crucial to choose an appraiser who specializes in the type of items you need valued, such as fine art, jewelry, or furniture. This specialization ensures that the appraiser is knowledgeable about the specific market trends and nuances related to your items.

B. The Appraisal Process

- Detailed Examination: During the appraisal process, the appraiser will examine the item in detail, considering factors such as condition, rarity, provenance, and market demand.

- Market Research: The appraiser may also research similar items that have recently sold, compare them to your item, and use this information to estimate its value.

- Appraisal Report: After the appraisal, you will receive a written report that outlines the item's description, condition, and estimated value, which can be used for insurance purposes, sale, or estate planning.

2. Comparative Market Analysis

A. Analyzing Recent Sales

- Market Comparison: Comparative Market Analysis (CMA) involves comparing your item to similar items that have recently sold at auctions, online marketplaces, or antique shops. By analyzing these sales, you can estimate the current market value of your item.

- Frequent Trades: This method is particularly useful for items that are frequently traded, such as coins, stamps, or vintage toys, where there is a large amount of sales data available.

B. Factors to Consider

- Condition and Rarity: When conducting a CMA, consider the condition, rarity, and provenance of both your item and the items being compared. Small differences in these factors can lead to significant variations in value.

- Recent Data: It's important to use recent sales data, as market conditions can change rapidly. Prices from several years ago may not accurately reflect the current value of an item.

3. Self-Appraisal

A. Leveraging Your Knowledge

- Collector's Expertise: For collectors with extensive experience and knowledge in a specific area, self-appraisal can be a practical approach. By researching similar items and using reference books, you can estimate the value of your items.

- Objective Assessment: Self-appraisal requires a deep understanding of the market, as well as the ability to objectively assess the condition and uniqueness of the item.

B. Using Reference Materials

- Guides and Books: Reference books, price guides, and online databases are valuable tools for self-appraisal. These resources often include detailed information on specific categories of collectibles, including historical context, production numbers, and price ranges.

- Cross-Referencing: Cross-referencing multiple sources can help you arrive at a more accurate valuation, but it's important to remain objective and not let personal attachment to an item cloud your judgment.

4. Online Valuation Tools

A. Utilizing Valuation Websites

- Digital Estimates: Several websites and apps offer online valuation tools that provide estimates of an item's value based on images and descriptions you upload. These tools use databases of past sales and market trends to generate an estimated value.

- Popular Tools: Examples of online valuation tools include WorthPoint, ValueMyStuff, and Kovels, which provide estimates based on similar items in their databases.

B. Limitations of Online Tools

- General Estimates: While online valuation tools can give you a general idea of an item's value, they may not be as accurate as professional appraisals. The automated nature of these tools means they might not account for unique factors like provenance or subtle differences in condition.

- Starting Point: These tools should be used as a starting point or for lower-value items, with more important or high-value items still requiring a professional appraisal.

5. Auction Appraisals

A. Benefits of Auction Appraisals

- Auctioneer Expertise: Auction houses often provide free appraisals for items they are interested in selling. These appraisals are based on the auctioneer's knowledge of what similar items have sold for at recent auctions.

- Auction Value Estimate: An auction appraisal can give you an estimate of what your item might fetch at auction, which can be useful if you are considering selling.

B. Consignment Considerations

- Variable Outcomes: If you choose to consign your item to an auction house, be aware that the appraisal value is an estimate, and the actual sale price can vary based on bidder interest, market conditions, and the auction setting.

- Fees and Commissions: Auctions also involve fees and commissions that can impact the final amount you receive, so consider these costs when evaluating the appraisal.

Understanding and using the appropriate appraisal methods is essential for accurately valuing your antiques and collectibles. Whether you opt for a professional appraisal, conduct a comparative market analysis, or use online tools, each method offers unique insights into your collection's worth. By choosing the right approach based on the item's value, rarity, and your personal expertise, you can ensure that your collection is accurately appraised and properly valued.

4.3 Resources for Valuation

Accurately valuing antiques and collectibles requires access to reliable resources that provide up-to-date information on market trends, historical context, and pricing. This section explores various resources that collectors can use to appraise their items, from auction results and price guides to online databases and expert consultations.

1. Auction Results and Databases

A. Utilizing Auction House Databases

- Access to Sales Data: Major auction houses, such as Sotheby's, Christie's, and Heritage Auctions, maintain extensive online databases of past auction results. These databases are invaluable for understanding the current market value of similar items.

- Comparative Analysis: By searching for items similar to yours, you can see what they have sold for recently, which helps in estimating the value of your own items. These databases often include detailed descriptions and photographs, providing context and comparison points.

B. Benefits of Auction Data

- Market Trends: Auction results reflect what collectors are currently willing to pay for items, making them a highly accurate indicator of market value.

- Up-to-Date Insights: Regularly checking auction results can help you stay informed about market trends, especially for high-end items or those in niche markets.

2. Price Guides and Reference Books

A. Importance of Price Guides

- Comprehensive Information: Price guides and reference books offer detailed pricing information based on historical sales data and expert knowledge. These guides often cover a wide range of collectibles, from coins and stamps to furniture and fine art.

- Valuation Comparisons: Using price guides allows you to compare your items against similar ones and understand their potential value based on condition, rarity, and other factors.

B. Selecting the Right Reference Books

- Current Editions: It's important to choose the most current editions of price guides and reference books, as market values can fluctuate over time. Some well-known price guides include *Kovels' Antiques & Collectibles Price Guide* and *Miller's Antiques Handbook & Price Guide*.

- Specialized Knowledge: Specialized reference books that focus on specific categories, such as *The Overstreet Comic Book Price Guide* or *Schroeder's Antiques Price Guide*, provide in-depth coverage and are particularly useful for niche collectibles.

3. Online Valuation Tools and Databases

A. Using Online Valuation Tools

- Convenient Estimates: Online valuation tools like WorthPoint, ValueMyStuff, and Kovels.com provide quick estimates of your item's value based on similar items in their extensive databases. These tools allow you to upload photos and descriptions to get a valuation estimate.

- Ease of Use: These online resources are convenient for obtaining a rough estimate of value, especially when you need a quick assessment or are dealing with lower-value items.

B. Limitations of Online Tools

- General Estimates: While online tools are useful for general valuations, they may not account for unique factors like provenance or subtle differences in condition that could significantly affect an item's value.

- Starting Point: These tools should be used as a starting point, with more detailed or high-value items still requiring professional appraisal or consultation with experts.

4. Expert Consultations

A. Consulting with Appraisers

- Professional Insight: Professional appraisers offer detailed valuations based on their expertise and knowledge of the market. Consulting with an appraiser is particularly important for high-value items or when precise valuation is needed for insurance or sale purposes.

- Strategic Advice: Appraisers can also provide insight into the best methods for selling your items and offer advice on how to maximize their value.

B. Accessing Museum and Academic Resources

- Expert Knowledge: Museums, historical societies, and academic institutions often have experts in various fields who can offer insights into the historical and cultural significance of your items. While they may not provide formal appraisals, their expertise can help you better understand the context and value of your collection.

- Public Resources: Some museums and universities also offer public resources, such as collections databases and research libraries, that can aid in your valuation efforts.

5. Online Marketplaces and Forums

A. Monitoring Online Marketplaces

- Real-Time Data: Websites like eBay, Etsy, and Ruby Lane are popular platforms for buying and selling antiques and collectibles. By monitoring listings and completed sales on these sites, you can gauge the current market value of similar items.

- Variable Prices: Keep in mind that prices on these platforms can vary widely depending on the seller, item condition, and demand, so use this data as part of a broader valuation strategy.

B. Participating in Collectors' Forums

- Community Insights: Online forums and communities dedicated to specific types of collectibles can be a valuable resource for valuation advice. Experienced collectors often share their knowledge, discuss market trends, and provide feedback on potential valuations.

- Shared Knowledge: Participating in these communities allows you to connect with others who share your interests and gain insights that may not be available through traditional valuation methods.

By leveraging these resources, you can gain a comprehensive understanding of the value of your antiques and collectibles. Whether you're using auction results, consulting price guides, or engaging with online tools and experts, these resources provide the information you need to make informed decisions about your collection.

4.4 Understanding Market Trends

The value of antiques and collectibles is not static; it fluctuates based on various market trends and external factors. Understanding these trends is crucial for making informed decisions about buying, selling, or holding onto your items. This section explores how to track and interpret market trends that impact the value of your collection.

1. Tracking Trends

A. Monitoring Auction Results

- Real-Time Insights: Auction houses provide real-time data on what collectors are willing to pay for items, making them an excellent source for tracking market trends. Regularly reviewing auction results helps you understand which categories are gaining popularity and which are declining.

- Pattern Recognition: Look for patterns in auction results, such as increasing prices for certain types of items or a rise in the number of bids for specific categories, which can indicate growing demand. This data can guide your decisions on when to buy or sell.

B. Following Dealer and Retail Sales

- Market Sentiment: Antique dealers and retail shops also offer insights into market trends. By observing the pricing and turnover of items in these settings, you can gauge what is currently in demand.

- Firsthand Exposure: Visiting antique fairs, markets, and shops provides firsthand exposure to trends, allowing you to see which items are being prominently displayed and sold. Dealers often adjust prices based on current market conditions, providing clues about emerging trends.

2. Cultural and Economic Influences

A. Impact of Pop Culture and Media

- Cultural Shifts: Popular culture, including movies, television shows, and social media, can significantly influence the demand for certain collectibles. For example, a movie featuring a particular style of furniture or jewelry can spark renewed interest in those items, driving up their value.

- Trend Monitoring: Stay attuned to cultural trends, as these can quickly shift collector interest and affect market values. Items associated with current or nostalgic pop culture trends often see a spike in demand, making them more valuable in the short term.

B. Economic Factors

- Economic Cycles: Economic conditions, such as inflation, interest rates, and consumer confidence, directly impact the collectibles market. In times of economic uncertainty, high-end luxury items like fine art and rare antiques may experience a decline in value as buyers become more conservative.

- Boom Periods: Conversely, during economic booms, there is often an increase in disposable income, leading to higher demand for luxury and collectible items. Understanding the broader economic context can help you anticipate shifts in market demand and adjust your collection strategy accordingly.

3. Seasonal Variations

A. Seasonality in Collecting

- Holiday-Driven Demand: Certain types of collectibles experience seasonal demand fluctuations. For example, holiday-themed items, such as Christmas ornaments or Halloween decorations, typically see increased interest and higher prices leading up to the respective holidays.

- Strategic Timing: Understanding the seasonality of your items can help you time your buying and selling activities to maximize value. Selling at the peak of seasonal demand can result in higher prices, while buying off-season may offer opportunities for bargains.

B. Timing the Market

- Maximizing Returns: Timing your sales or purchases to coincide with favorable market conditions is crucial for maximizing returns. For instance, selling during a period of high demand or when a particular category is trending can lead to better prices.

- Off-Peak Opportunities: Conversely, buying during off-peak times, when demand is lower, can provide opportunities to acquire items at reduced prices. Being patient and waiting for the right moment can significantly impact the profitability of your collection.

4. Long-Term Trends

A. Historical Value Trends

- Cyclical Nature: Some collectibles follow long-term value trends that evolve over decades. Understanding these trends requires knowledge of the item's history and its market performance over time.

- Investment Strategies: For example, certain categories of art or furniture may go through cycles of popularity, with periods of high demand followed by a decline and eventual resurgence. Recognizing these patterns can inform long-term investment strategies and help you make decisions that will benefit your collection in the future.

B. Emerging Markets

- Identifying Growth Areas: New markets for collectibles can emerge as tastes and interests evolve. For example, items that were once considered mundane or too modern, such as mid-century furniture or vintage electronics, can become highly collectible as they age and gain historical significance.

- Early Adoption: Staying ahead of emerging trends allows you to invest in items before they become widely recognized as valuable, potentially leading to significant returns. Keeping an eye on younger generations' interests can also provide clues to future collectible markets.

5. Researching and Staying Informed

A. Using Market Reports and Publications

- Industry Insights: Industry publications, market reports, and specialized magazines provide valuable insights into current trends and forecasts. These resources often feature expert analysis, interviews with industry leaders, and data on sales and market performance.

- Ongoing Education: Subscribing to these publications helps you stay informed about shifts in the market and emerging trends that could affect the value of your collection. Continuous learning is key to staying ahead in the collecting world.

B. Engaging with Collector Communities

- Knowledge Sharing: Online forums, social media groups, and collector clubs are excellent platforms for discussing market trends with other collectors. Engaging with these communities allows you to share knowledge, gather opinions, and get a sense of the collective sentiment regarding specific items or categories.

- Networking Opportunities: Networking with other collectors can also lead to opportunities to buy, sell, or trade items based on shared insights into market trends. Building relationships within the collector community can provide a wealth of information and opportunities that might not be available elsewhere.

Understanding market trends is essential for making strategic decisions about your collection. By keeping an eye on auction results, staying informed about cultural and economic influences, and timing your transactions according to seasonal and long-term trends, you can maximize the value of your antiques and collectibles.

4.5 Tips for Maximizing Value

Maximizing the value of your antiques and collectibles requires strategic planning, proper care, and an understanding of market dynamics. Whether you're looking to sell or simply maintain the value of your collection, this section provides practical tips to help you achieve the best possible return on your investment.

1. Proper Storage and Care

A. Protecting Your Items from Damage

- Control the Environment: The condition of your items plays a significant role in their value. To preserve their condition, store your antiques and collectibles in a controlled environment that is free from excessive humidity, temperature fluctuations, and direct sunlight.

- Use Appropriate Storage Materials: Use materials such as acid-free paper for documents and textiles, padded cases for delicate items, and climate-controlled storage for sensitive materials like wood or paper.

B. Regular Maintenance

- Prevent Deterioration: Regularly clean and inspect your items to prevent the buildup of dust, dirt, or mold, which can cause deterioration over time. However, be careful to use cleaning methods that are safe for the specific materials of your collectibles.

- Avoid Over-Cleaning: Avoid using harsh chemicals, as these can damage the item's surface or patina, potentially reducing its value.

2. Selling at the Right Time

A. Timing the Market

- Sell When Demand is High: Understanding market trends and seasonality can help you time your sales to maximize value. Sell items when demand is high, such as during peak seasons or when a particular category is trending.

- Monitor Market Conditions: Monitor auction results and market reports to identify the best times to sell, and be patient if market conditions are not currently favorable.

B. Avoiding Fire Sales

- Don't Rush the Sale: Avoid selling items quickly or under pressure, as this can lead to accepting lower offers. Take the time to research and find the right buyer who appreciates the value of your item and is willing to pay a fair price.

- Consider Auction Consignment: If necessary, consider consigning your items to an auction house, where competitive bidding can help drive up the final sale price.

3. Marketing and Presentation

A. High-Quality Photography

- Use Clear and Detailed Images: When selling items online or in auctions, high-quality photographs are essential. Clear, well-lit images that show the item from multiple angles can significantly increase buyer interest.

- Highlight Key Features: Use a neutral background, proper lighting, and close-up shots of important details, such as marks, signatures, or unique features, to enhance the presentation of your items.

B. Detailed Descriptions

- Provide Comprehensive Information: Provide detailed and accurate descriptions of your items, including information about their condition, provenance, and any distinguishing features.

- Be Honest About Flaws: Honesty is key; accurately describe any flaws or restorations to build trust with potential buyers and avoid disputes after the sale.

4. Building a Strong Provenance

A. Documenting Your Items

- Keep Thorough Records: Keep thorough records of your items, including purchase receipts, appraisals, and any historical documentation. Provenance adds credibility to your collection and can significantly increase an item's value.

- Gather Additional Documentation: Whenever possible, gather additional documentation, such as photographs, letters, or articles that connect the item to a particular event, period, or individual.

B. Highlighting Provenance in Sales

- Feature Provenance Prominently: When selling items, make sure to prominently feature their provenance in the listing or auction catalog. Provenance can be a key selling point, especially for high-value or historically significant items.

- Provide Verified Documents: Provide copies of all relevant documents to potential buyers, and consider having the provenance verified by a third party to further enhance credibility.

5. Networking and Building Relationships

A. Connecting with Other Collectors

- Build a Strong Network: Networking with other collectors, dealers, and experts can open up opportunities to buy, sell, or trade items at favorable terms. Building relationships within the collecting community can also provide access to private sales, exclusive events, and insider knowledge about market trends.

- Engage in the Community: Join collector clubs, attend fairs and auctions, and participate in online forums to expand your network and stay connected with the market.

B. Leveraging Expert Advice

- Consult with Specialists: Consult with appraisers, conservators, and dealers who specialize in your area of collecting. Their expertise can help you make informed decisions about buying, selling, and maintaining your collection.

- Identify Hidden Value: Expert advice can also help you identify hidden value in your collection, such as overlooked items or potential restoration opportunities that could increase value.

Maximizing the value of your antiques and collectibles involves more than just buying and selling at the right time. Proper care, strategic marketing, strong provenance, and networking within the collecting community all play vital roles in ensuring that your collection retains or even increases its value over time. By following these tips, you can enhance the appeal of your items and achieve the best possible return on your investment.

Chapter 4 Review: Valuing Your Collection

Chapter 4 of *HowExpert Guide to Antiques and Collectibles* offers critical insights into the valuation process, helping collectors accurately assess the worth of their items and strategically enhance their collection's value. This chapter delves into the factors that affect value, various appraisal methods, key resources for valuation, understanding market trends, and practical tips for maximizing value.

4.1 Factors Affecting Value

- Age and Rarity: Items that are older and rarer generally have higher value. Collectors are guided to understand how the scarcity and age of an item contribute significantly to its market price.

- Condition: The condition of an item is crucial, with pieces in excellent condition commanding higher prices. This section emphasizes the importance of preserving items in their best possible state.

- Provenance: Provenance, or the documented history of an item, is highlighted as a factor that can significantly boost value, particularly if the item is connected to notable individuals or historical events.

- Market Demand: Market demand is a dynamic factor that can fluctuate based on cultural influences, trends, and economic conditions. Understanding this helps collectors make informed decisions about buying or selling.

4.2 Appraisal Methods

- Professional Appraisals: Professional appraisals are recommended for obtaining reliable valuations, as they are based on expert knowledge and comprehensive market data.

- Comparative Market Analysis: This method allows collectors to estimate an item's value by comparing it to similar items that have recently sold, providing a practical approach to self-appraisal.

- Self-Appraisal: For knowledgeable collectors, self-appraisal using reference books and online tools can be effective, though it requires a deep understanding of the market and item specifics.

- Online Valuation Tools: While convenient and quick, online valuation tools are noted for providing estimates that may lack the accuracy and depth of a professional appraisal.

4.3 Resources for Valuation

- Auction House Databases and Price Guides: These resources are essential for collectors who want to understand current market values and track historical pricing trends.

- Online Valuation Tools and Expert Consultations: This section also covers the use of online tools and consultations with experts to gain a broader perspective on an item's value.

- Collector Communities and Online Marketplaces: Engaging with collector communities and monitoring online marketplaces are highlighted as valuable ways to gain insights into market trends and pricing.

4.4 Understanding Market Trends

- Monitoring Auction Results and Sales: Collectors are encouraged to keep an eye on auction results and dealer sales to stay informed about market trends.

- Economic Factors and Seasonal Variations: The impact of economic conditions and seasonal variations on demand and value is discussed, helping collectors time their transactions strategically.

- Recognizing Trends: Understanding both long-term and emerging trends allows collectors to decide whether to hold onto items or sell them based on market dynamics.

4.5 Tips for Maximizing Value

- Proper Storage and Care: Emphasized as crucial for preserving the condition and thus the value of items, proper storage and care are fundamental practices for collectors.

- Timing Sales: Selling at the right time, particularly when market demand is high, can significantly increase the prices achieved for items.

- Effective Marketing: High-quality photography and detailed descriptions are essential for effective marketing, ensuring that items are presented in the best possible light to potential buyers.

- Building Provenance and Networking: Establishing strong provenance and networking with other collectors can enhance the value and marketability of a collection, making it more appealing to buyers.

Chapter 4 provides collectors with the essential tools and strategies needed to accurately value their antiques and collectibles, maximize their worth, and navigate the complexities of the market. By understanding the key factors that influence value, employing the right appraisal methods, utilizing available resources, and staying informed about market trends, collectors can make informed decisions that enhance both the personal and financial value of their collections.

Chapter 5: Preserving and Caring for Antiques

Preserving and caring for antiques is crucial to maintaining their value, historical significance, and aesthetic appeal. Proper care involves understanding how to store, clean, and handle these items to prevent damage and deterioration over time. This chapter covers the best practices for preserving and caring for your antiques, including proper storage techniques, cleaning tips, damage prevention strategies, and the nuances between restoration and preservation.

5.1 Proper Storage Techniques

Storing antiques correctly is crucial to preserving their condition and value. The right storage environment and materials can prevent damage from environmental factors and ensure that your items remain in excellent condition for years to come. This section outlines the best practices for storing various types of antiques.

1. Climate Control

A. Temperature and Humidity

- Maintain Stable Conditions: Maintaining a stable temperature and humidity level is essential for preserving antiques. Fluctuations in temperature and humidity can cause materials to expand and contract, leading to cracks, warping, or mold growth.

- Optimal Environment: Aim to store your antiques in a climate-controlled environment where the temperature remains between 65-70°F (18-21°C) and the relative humidity is kept between 45-55%. Avoid storing items in basements, attics, or garages, where conditions can be unpredictable.

B. Air Circulation

- Prevent Mold and Mildew: Good air circulation is important for preventing mold and mildew, especially in textiles, paper, and wood.

- Enhance Airflow: Use fans or dehumidifiers in storage areas to keep air moving and reduce moisture buildup. Ensure that items are not packed too tightly, allowing air to circulate freely around each piece.

2. Protective Materials

A. Acid-Free Storage

- Prevent Deterioration: Acid-free paper, boxes, and tissue are essential for storing items like documents, textiles, and photographs. Acid in regular paper can cause yellowing and deterioration over time, so it's important to use materials specifically designed for archival storage.

- Use Archival Quality: Wrap delicate items in acid-free tissue paper and store them in archival-quality boxes to prevent damage from light, dust, and environmental pollutants.

B. Padded Storage Solutions

- Protect Fragile Items: For fragile items like ceramics, glassware, and small decorative objects, use padded storage solutions to protect them from bumps and vibrations.

- Cushion with Care: Use foam inserts, bubble wrap, or padded cases to cushion these items. Ensure that the padding does not apply too much pressure, which could cause breakage or deformation.

3. Light Protection

A. Avoiding Direct Sunlight

- Prevent Fading and Discoloration: Exposure to direct sunlight can cause fading, discoloration, and deterioration, particularly in textiles, paintings, and wood.

- Minimize Light Exposure: Store antiques away from windows or cover them with UV-protective glass or curtains to minimize light exposure. For items on display, consider using UV-filtering film on windows or placing them in areas with indirect lighting.

B. Using UV-Protective Materials

- Shield Against Harmful Rays: When displaying or storing items in lit areas, use UV-protective materials, such as UV-filtering glass or acrylic, to shield them from harmful rays.

- Protect Small Items: UV-protective cases are also available for small items like photographs, textiles, or paper documents, providing an additional layer of protection against light damage.

4. Specialized Storage for Different Materials

A. Wood and Furniture

- Prevent Cracking and Warping: Wood is sensitive to changes in humidity and temperature, which can cause it to crack or warp. Store wooden furniture and items in a stable environment and use covers to protect them from dust.

- Avoid Pressure Marks: Avoid placing heavy objects on top of wooden furniture, as this can cause pressure marks or scratches over time.

B. Textiles and Clothing

- Avoid Creases and Stress: Store textiles and clothing items flat or rolled to avoid creases and stress on the fabric. Use acid-free tissue paper between layers to prevent fibers from breaking down.

- Ensure Breathability: Keep textiles in breathable, acid-free boxes or muslin bags to protect them from dust and pests. Avoid plastic covers, as they can trap moisture and lead to mold growth.

C. Metals and Jewelry

- Reduce Tarnishing: Metals like silver, gold, and bronze can tarnish if exposed to moisture and air. Store metal items in dry, padded containers, and consider using anti-tarnish strips or cloths to reduce tarnishing.

- Prevent Scratches: For jewelry, use individual pouches or compartments to prevent pieces from scratching each other. Store in a dry, cool environment to avoid moisture buildup.

5. Avoiding Common Storage Mistakes

A. Overcrowding

- Avoid Accidental Damage: Avoid overcrowding storage spaces, as this can lead to items being accidentally damaged when moved or accessed.

- Provide Adequate Space: Ensure that each item has enough space to breathe and be handled safely. Use shelves, racks, or drawers to organize items and prevent them from being stacked on top of each other.

B. Improper Handling

- Handle with Care: Always handle antiques with care when placing them in storage. Use both hands to support heavy or fragile items, and wear gloves when necessary to prevent oils from your skin from transferring to the item.

- Label Clearly: Label storage boxes clearly so that items can be easily identified without unnecessary handling, reducing the risk of accidental damage.

Proper storage techniques are essential for maintaining the condition and value of your antiques. By controlling the environment, using protective materials, and handling items with care, you can ensure that your collection remains in pristine condition for generations to come.

5.2 Cleaning and Maintenance Tips

Regular cleaning and maintenance are essential for preserving the beauty and longevity of your antiques. However, antiques require special care to avoid damaging their delicate surfaces and materials. This section provides tips on how to clean and maintain your antiques properly, ensuring they remain in excellent condition.

1. Regular Dusting

A. Using the Right Tools

- Dust Regularly: Dusting your antiques regularly helps prevent the buildup of dirt and grime that can cause long-term damage. Use soft, lint-free cloths, such as microfiber or cotton, to gently dust surfaces without scratching them.

- Use Soft Brushes: For intricate or delicate items, such as carvings or filigree, use a soft-bristle brush or a can of compressed air to remove dust from hard-to-reach areas.

B. Avoiding Feather Dusters

- Prevent Snagging: While feather dusters are commonly used for dusting, they can snag on small or intricate parts of antiques, potentially causing damage. Instead, opt for a microfiber duster or a soft cloth that won't catch on the item's surface.

2. Gentle Cleaning Solutions

A. Choosing the Right Cleaners

- Select Mild Solutions: When more thorough cleaning is needed, choose cleaning solutions that are appropriate for the specific material of the antique. For example, use a mild soap and water solution for ceramics and glass, while wooden furniture may benefit from a specialized wood cleaner or conditioner.

- Test Before Use: Always dilute cleaning solutions according to the manufacturer's instructions and test them on a small, inconspicuous area of the item before applying them to the entire surface.

B. Avoiding Harsh Chemicals

- Protect Surfaces: Avoid using harsh chemicals, such as bleach, ammonia, or commercial cleaners, as these can strip away finishes, cause discoloration, or degrade the material over time.

- Use Gentle Polishes: For metal items, avoid using abrasive polishes that can remove patina, which is often a desirable characteristic that adds to the item's value. Instead, opt for a gentle polish designed specifically for antique metals.

3. Specific Cleaning Techniques for Different Materials

A. Wood

- Dust and Polish: For wooden furniture, dust regularly with a soft cloth and occasionally use a high-quality furniture polish or wax to protect the wood's finish. Avoid using water or wet cloths on wooden surfaces, as moisture can cause the wood to swell or warp.

- Clean Carvings Gently: When cleaning intricate wood carvings, use a soft brush to remove dust and dirt from crevices. Avoid using sharp objects that could scratch or damage the wood.

B. Metal

- Clean with Care: Clean metal antiques with a soft cloth to remove fingerprints and dust. For tarnished silver or brass, use a polish that is specifically formulated for antiques, as these are less abrasive and will help preserve the item's original finish.

- Preserve Patina: Be cautious when polishing, as over-polishing can remove the patina that gives antique metals their character and value.

C. Ceramics and Glass

- Use Mild Solutions: Clean ceramics and glass with a mild soap and water solution, using a soft cloth or sponge to gently wipe the surface. Avoid submerging delicate items in water, as this can cause damage to painted or glazed surfaces.

- Dry Thoroughly: Rinse thoroughly with clean water and dry with a lint-free cloth to prevent water spots. For items with intricate designs or fragile parts, consider using a soft brush to clean hard-to-reach areas.

D. Textiles

- Avoid Water Damage: For textiles, such as antique clothing or tapestries, avoid washing them in water, as this can cause colors to bleed or fabrics to shrink. Instead, consider dry cleaning for delicate or valuable items, using a professional service that specializes in antiques.

- Store Carefully: Store textiles in a dry, dark place, and use acid-free tissue paper to help prevent creasing. If cleaning is necessary, gently vacuum the textile through a screen to remove dust without damaging the fabric.

4. Regular Maintenance Practices

A. Inspecting for Damage

- Check Regularly: Regularly inspect your antiques for signs of damage, such as cracks, chips, loose joints, or pest infestations. Early detection allows you to address issues before they worsen, preserving the item's condition.

- Focus on Vulnerable Areas: Pay special attention to areas that are prone to wear, such as the legs of furniture, the handles of ceramics, or the seams of textiles.

B. Rotating Display Items

- Prevent Wear: If you have items on display, consider rotating them periodically to prevent one area from becoming excessively worn or faded due to exposure to light or handling.

- Distribute Stress Evenly: Rotating your collection also helps distribute any potential environmental stress evenly across different items, reducing the risk of damage.

C. Keeping Detailed Records

- Document Care: Maintain a log of your cleaning and maintenance activities, noting the date, methods used, and any observations about the item's condition. This record can be invaluable for future reference, especially when it comes to preserving provenance and history.

- Track Maintenance: Detailed records also help in assessing the long-term effects of your maintenance practices, allowing you to make informed decisions about future care.

Regular cleaning and maintenance, when done correctly, are essential for preserving the condition and value of your antiques. By using the right tools, gentle cleaning solutions, and specific techniques for different materials, you can ensure that your collection remains in pristine condition. Regular inspections and careful handling further contribute to the longevity of your antiques, allowing you to enjoy them for years to come.

5.3 Preventing Damage and Deterioration

Preventing damage and deterioration is key to preserving the value and beauty of your antiques. Various environmental and physical factors can contribute to the degradation of antiques over time, so it's essential to implement strategies that protect your items from harm. This section outlines best practices for preventing damage and ensuring the longevity of your collection.

1. Environmental Control

A. Managing Temperature and Humidity

- Control the Environment: Fluctuations in temperature and humidity can cause significant damage to antiques. Wood can warp or crack, metals can corrode, and textiles can become brittle or moldy.

- Maintain Stability: Maintain a stable environment with a temperature of around 65-70°F (18-21°C) and relative humidity between 45-55%. Use humidifiers or dehumidifiers as needed to control moisture levels, especially in areas prone to dampness.

B. Protecting from Light Exposure

- Minimize UV Damage: Prolonged exposure to light, particularly ultraviolet (UV) light, can cause fading, discoloration, and deterioration in materials like textiles, paper, and paintings.

- Use Protective Measures: Keep antiques out of direct sunlight and use UV-protective glass or acrylic for framed items. Consider installing UV-filtering window films or using curtains to reduce light exposure in rooms where antiques are displayed.

2. Physical Protection

A. Proper Handling Techniques

- Handle with Care: Improper handling is a common cause of accidental damage to antiques. Always handle items with clean, dry hands, or wear cotton gloves to prevent oils and dirt from transferring to the surface.

- Support Delicate Items: Support delicate items with both hands and avoid lifting them by vulnerable parts, such as handles or rims. For large or heavy items, use appropriate lifting techniques or enlist the help of others to prevent strain or accidental drops.

B. Preventing Scratches and Abrasions

- Use Padding: Place soft pads or felt under the feet of furniture and other heavy items to prevent scratches on floors and surfaces.

- Protect Surfaces: Use protective coverings, such as glass tops or padded cloths, on surfaces where antiques are displayed to prevent scratches and scuffs from everyday use or accidental contact.

C. Securing Fragile Items

- Stabilize Delicate Pieces: Secure fragile items, such as porcelain, glass, or delicate sculptures, in display cases or on stable shelves. Ensure that the shelving is sturdy and level to prevent items from tipping over.

- Anchor Small Items: Consider using museum gel or wax to anchor small, delicate items in place, reducing the risk of accidental bumps or vibrations causing them to fall.

3. Pest and Mold Prevention

A. Protecting Against Pests

- Prevent Infestations: Pests such as moths, beetles, and rodents can cause significant damage to textiles, wood, and paper. Regularly inspect your antiques for signs of pest activity, such as droppings, holes, or sawdust.

- Use Deterrents: Use pest deterrents like cedar blocks, mothballs, or natural repellents, and store vulnerable items in sealed containers or cabinets. For severe infestations, consider consulting a professional pest control service that specializes in antiques.

B. Preventing Mold and Mildew

- Control Moisture: Mold and mildew thrive in damp, poorly ventilated areas, and can cause irreparable damage to antiques. Store items in dry, well-ventilated spaces and avoid basements, attics, or other areas prone to moisture.

- Act Quickly: If you notice any signs of mold or mildew, such as musty odors or visible growth, address the issue immediately by improving ventilation, reducing humidity, and cleaning affected areas with appropriate methods.

4. Regular Inspections and Maintenance

A. Routine Checks for Damage

- Inspect Regularly: Regularly inspect your antiques for signs of wear, damage, or deterioration. Look for cracks, chips, loose joints, or signs of pest activity.

- Address Issues Early: Early detection of issues allows you to take corrective action before the damage worsens. Consider keeping a checklist to ensure that you inspect each item thoroughly and regularly.

B. Professional Maintenance Services

- Consult Experts: For valuable or delicate items, consider enlisting the help of professional conservators or restorers who specialize in antiques. These experts can perform more complex maintenance tasks, such as repairing loose joints, treating metal corrosion, or stabilizing fragile textiles.

- Avoid DIY Mistakes: Professional maintenance is particularly important for high-value items, as improper DIY repairs can often do more harm than good.

C. Rotating and Repositioning Items

- Distribute Wear Evenly: To prevent uneven wear and fading, rotate items that are on display. This practice helps distribute exposure to light, dust, and handling across different parts of your collection, reducing the risk of localized damage.

- Relieve Stress: Periodically reposition furniture or large items to prevent stress on joints or surfaces that remain under constant pressure.

5. Safe Display Practices

A. Choosing the Right Display Location

- Avoid Environmental Stress: Place antiques in locations that minimize exposure to environmental stressors, such as direct sunlight, heat sources, or areas with high humidity. Avoid displaying items near windows, radiators, or fireplaces.

- Use Protective Cases: Use display cases with built-in UV protection and climate control for particularly sensitive items, such as textiles, manuscripts, or delicate ceramics.

B. Protecting High-Traffic Areas

- Secure in Public Spaces: If your antiques are displayed in high-traffic areas, such as hallways or living rooms, take extra precautions to protect them from accidental bumps or spills. Consider placing valuable items in display cases or on high shelves out of reach of children and pets.

- Ensure Stability: Ensure that display stands and cases are stable and secure, reducing the risk of items being knocked over.

Preventing damage and deterioration is essential for preserving the condition and value of your antiques. By managing environmental factors, handling items with care, and implementing protective measures, you can safeguard your collection from common hazards and enjoy your antiques for many years to come.

5.4 Restoration vs. Preservation

When it comes to caring for antiques, collectors often face the decision of whether to restore an item to its former glory or to preserve it in its current state. Both approaches have their merits and drawbacks, and the right choice depends on the item's condition, historical significance, and your goals as a collector. This section explores the differences between restoration and preservation, helping you make informed decisions about the care of your antiques.

1. Understanding Restoration

A. What is Restoration?

- Restoration Defined: Restoration involves repairing or refurbishing an antique to bring it back to its original appearance or function. This process may include tasks such as reupholstering furniture, refinishing wood, repairing broken parts, or cleaning and polishing metal surfaces.

- Goal of Restoration: The goal of restoration is to make the item look as it did when it was first made, which can enhance its visual appeal and, in some cases, its market value.

B. Benefits of Restoration

- Enhancing Appeal: Restoring an item can make it more attractive and functional, potentially increasing its desirability to buyers if you decide to sell it.

- Stabilizing the Item: Restoration can also help to stabilize an item, preventing further deterioration or making it safe for use or display.

C. Risks of Restoration

- Potential Value Reduction: Restoration can sometimes reduce the value of an antique, particularly if the work is not done sympathetically or if it involves replacing original materials with modern substitutes.

- Over-Restoration: Over-restoration, where too much of the original character is removed or altered, can diminish the historical integrity of the item, making it less appealing to serious collectors.

2. Focusing on Preservation

A. What is Preservation?

- Preservation Defined: Preservation focuses on maintaining the current condition of an antique and preventing further deterioration, without attempting to alter or restore its appearance.

- Goal of Preservation: This approach emphasizes the importance of retaining the item's historical integrity, including any signs of age, wear, or past repairs that are part of its history.

B. Benefits of Preservation

- Maintaining Authenticity: Preservation maintains the originality and authenticity of an antique, which is often more desirable to collectors and museums.

- Retaining Historical Value: By preserving the item as it is, you retain its historical value, ensuring that future generations can appreciate it in its authentic state.

C. Challenges of Preservation

- Living with Imperfections: Preserving an item in its current condition may mean accepting and living with imperfections, such as scratches, dents, or fading, rather than attempting to make it look new again.

- Ongoing Maintenance: Preservation requires careful maintenance and environmental control to ensure that the item does not deteriorate further over time.

3. *Making Informed Decisions*

A. Assessing the Item's Value and Significance

- Consider the Item's Importance: Before deciding whether to restore or preserve an item, consider its historical significance, rarity, and market value. High-value items with significant provenance or cultural importance are often better candidates for preservation rather than restoration.

- Restoration for Sentimental Items: For items with sentimental value but less historical or monetary significance, restoration might be a more appropriate choice, especially if you intend to use or display the item regularly.

B. Consulting with Experts

- Seek Professional Guidance: If you're unsure whether to restore or preserve an item, consult with a professional conservator or appraiser who specializes in antiques. They can provide guidance on the best course of action based on the item's condition, materials, and historical context.

- Understand the Impact: Experts can also help you understand the potential impact of restoration on the item's value and offer recommendations for preservation techniques that will protect the item without altering its character.

C. Balancing Aesthetics and Integrity

- Combining Approaches: In some cases, a combination of restoration and preservation may be the best approach. For example, you might choose to restore functional aspects of an item, such as repairing a chair so it can be used safely, while preserving its original finish and patina.

- Striking a Balance: Striking a balance between improving the item's appearance and maintaining its historical integrity is key to making informed restoration and preservation decisions.

4. Choosing the Right Approach for Your Collection

A. Preservation for Historical and Rare Items

- Focus on Preservation: For items with significant historical value, rare artifacts, or pieces with well-documented provenance, preservation is often the preferred approach. Maintaining the item's originality and historical integrity ensures its continued value and relevance.

- Specialized Care: These items may require specialized care, including controlled storage conditions and minimal handling, to preserve their condition.

B. Restoration for Functional and Decorative Items

- Consider Restoration: For antiques that you intend to use or display regularly, restoration can be a practical option. Restoring the item can make it more visually appealing and functional while still allowing you to enjoy its historical significance.

- Sympathetic Restoration: However, it's important to work with skilled restorers who understand the importance of sympathetic restoration, using techniques and materials that match the original as closely as possible.

C. Documentation of Restoration and Preservation Efforts

- Maintain Records: Whether you choose restoration, preservation, or a combination of both, it's essential to document any work done on the item. This documentation should include details about the materials and techniques used, as well as before-and-after photographs.

- Preserve Provenance: Detailed records can help maintain the item's provenance and provide valuable information for future caretakers or collectors.

Choosing between restoration and preservation is a critical decision that can impact the value and integrity of your antiques. By understanding the benefits and risks of each approach and consulting with experts when needed, you can make informed choices that protect your collection and preserve its historical significance for years to come.

5.5 Handling Antiques Safely

Handling antiques with care is crucial to preventing accidental damage and preserving their condition. Whether you are moving, cleaning, or displaying your antiques, proper techniques and precautions are necessary to protect these valuable items. This section provides guidelines for safely handling antiques to ensure their longevity.

1. Proper Handling Techniques

A. Clean Hands and Gloves

- Importance of Clean Hands: Always handle antiques with clean, dry hands to prevent transferring oils, dirt, or moisture to the items. Wearing cotton gloves is recommended, especially for delicate materials like textiles, paper, or metals, where skin oils can cause damage over time.

- Avoiding Residue: Avoid using latex or rubber gloves, as these can sometimes leave residues on certain materials or cause allergic reactions.

B. Supporting Fragile Items

- Proper Support: When lifting or moving fragile items, always support them from underneath with both hands. Never lift items by handles, rims, or other protruding parts that may be weak or prone to breaking.

- Assistance for Larger Items: For larger or heavier items, enlist the help of another person to ensure safe handling. Use appropriate lifting techniques to avoid straining yourself or the item.

C. Avoiding Excessive Handling

- Minimizing Risk: Limit handling of fragile or valuable items as much as possible. Frequent handling increases the risk of accidental damage and wear.

- Careful Inspection: When items need to be moved or inspected, do so carefully and deliberately, taking time to ensure a secure grip and stable environment.

2. Moving and Transporting Antiques

A. Preparing for Transport

- Route Planning: Before moving antiques, especially large items like furniture or mirrors, plan the route and ensure that doorways, hallways, and elevators are clear of obstacles.

- Packing Delicate Items: For small, delicate items, wrap them individually in soft, padded materials such as bubble wrap, foam, or blankets. Place them in sturdy boxes or crates that provide adequate protection against bumps and vibrations.

B. Using Professional Movers

- Hiring Specialists: For valuable or fragile items, consider hiring professional movers who specialize in antiques. They have the experience and equipment necessary to handle delicate items safely and securely.

- Insurance and Instructions: Ensure that the movers are fully insured and understand the specific needs of your antiques, such as climate control during transport or special handling instructions.

C. Securing Items During Transport

- Stabilizing in Vehicles: When transporting antiques in a vehicle, secure them using straps or padding to prevent movement. Items should be placed on a flat, stable surface and cushioned to absorb shocks during transit.

- Packing Small Items: For smaller items, pack them tightly in boxes with padding between them to prevent shifting. Label the boxes as "Fragile" to ensure careful handling.

3. Safe Display Practices

A. Stable Display Surfaces

- Choosing the Right Surface: Display antiques on stable, level surfaces that can support their weight without risk of tipping or collapse. Use stands, mounts, or cases designed specifically for displaying delicate items like ceramics, glassware, or small sculptures.

- Avoiding High Shelves: Avoid placing heavy items on high shelves or narrow ledges where they could be easily knocked over.

B. Protecting Against Environmental Hazards

- Light and Heat Protection: Display items away from direct sunlight, heat sources, and areas with high humidity to prevent damage from environmental factors.

- Using Protective Cases: Use display cases with built-in UV protection and climate control for particularly sensitive items. These cases also provide a barrier against dust, dirt, and accidental contact.

C. Preventing Accidental Damage

- High-Traffic Areas: In high-traffic areas, consider placing valuable items out of reach of children, pets, or crowded spaces to reduce the risk of accidental damage.

- Securing Display Items: If you must display items in busy areas, secure them with museum gel or wax to prevent them from being easily knocked over. These products provide a discreet way to anchor items to display surfaces without causing damage.

4. Handling Specific Types of Antiques

A. Furniture

- Lifting and Moving: When moving furniture, always lift it off the ground rather than dragging it to prevent damage to both the furniture and the floor. Lift from the base, not the top, to avoid putting stress on joints or veneers.

- Disassembly for Transport: If disassembly is required for transport, carefully label each part and keep all screws, bolts, and other hardware in a labeled bag to ensure proper reassembly.

B. Textiles and Clothing

- Handling with Care: Handle textiles and clothing with extreme care, as these materials can be delicate and prone to tearing or stretching. Support the entire garment when lifting it, and avoid hanging heavy or fragile textiles, as this can cause the fabric to sag or stretch over time.

- Folding for Storage: When folding textiles for storage or display, use acid-free tissue paper to prevent creases and minimize stress on the fabric.

C. Ceramics and Glass

- Supporting the Base: Always handle ceramics and glass with both hands, supporting the base to prevent stress on fragile parts. Avoid gripping items too tightly, as this can cause pressure points that may lead to cracks.

- Handling Detachable Parts: For items with lids or detachable parts, remove these pieces before handling the item as a whole to prevent them from falling or becoming dislodged.

D. Metal Objects

- Preventing Tarnish: Handle metal objects with clean, dry hands or gloves to prevent tarnishing from skin oils. Be mindful of sharp edges or points on certain metal items, such as tools or weapons, to avoid injury.

- Handling Polished Metals: When handling silver or other polished metals, hold items by less visible areas to prevent fingerprints on polished surfaces.

5. Training and Education

A. Educating Household Members

- Importance of Training: Ensure that everyone in the household understands the importance of handling antiques with care. Educate family members, house staff, or guests on proper handling techniques and the significance of preserving these items.

- Setting Boundaries: If you have children or pets, consider setting boundaries for areas where valuable antiques are displayed or stored.

B. Regular Review of Handling Practices

- Ongoing Training: Periodically review your handling practices and update them as needed to ensure the continued safety of your antiques. Stay informed about best practices for specific types of items by consulting experts, reading relevant literature, or attending workshops on antique care.

- Reinforcing Vigilance: Encourage everyone involved in the care and handling of your antiques to stay vigilant and mindful of the risks, reinforcing the importance of careful and deliberate handling at all times.

Handling antiques safely is a vital part of preserving their condition and value. By following proper handling techniques, securing items during transport, and taking precautions when displaying them, you can protect your collection from accidental damage and ensure that these cherished items are preserved for future generations to enjoy.

Chapter 5 Review: Preserving and Caring for Antiques

Chapter 5 of *HowExpert Guide to Antiques and Collectibles* offers essential guidance on preserving and caring for your antiques to ensure their longevity and maintain their value. This chapter covers best practices for proper storage, cleaning, preventing damage, understanding restoration versus preservation, and safe handling techniques.

5.1 Proper Storage Techniques

- Stable Environment: Maintaining a stable environment with controlled temperature and humidity is crucial to prevent damage from environmental factors. Fluctuations can cause materials like wood, metal, and fabric to expand, contract, or deteriorate.

- Protective Materials: Using acid-free and padded storage materials is recommended to protect delicate items from dust, moisture, and physical damage. These materials prevent chemical reactions that could degrade the items over time.

- Light Exposure: Avoiding exposure to direct sunlight is key to preserving the color and integrity of antiques. Items should be stored or displayed in low-light conditions, and UV-protective materials should be used when necessary to shield items from harmful rays.

5.2 Cleaning and Maintenance Tips

- Regular Dusting: Dusting regularly with soft, lint-free cloths or brushes helps prevent dirt buildup without scratching delicate surfaces. This routine maintenance is essential for keeping items in pristine condition.

- Gentle Cleaning Solutions: When cleaning, it's important to use gentle, non-abrasive solutions tailored to the specific material. Harsh chemicals can cause irreversible damage, so choosing the right cleaning products is critical.

- Maintenance and Rotation: Performing regular inspections and maintenance, such as rotating display items, ensures even wear and reduces the risk of long-term damage. Keeping detailed records of cleaning and care activities also helps track the history of each item's condition.

5.3 Preventing Damage and Deterioration

- Environmental Control: Controlling environmental factors such as temperature, humidity, and light exposure is vital for protecting antiques from deterioration. Consistent conditions help preserve the materials and extend the life of the items.

- Careful Handling: Handling items with care, using both hands and avoiding excessive touching, minimizes the risk of accidental damage. Proper handling techniques are a simple but effective way to protect valuable pieces.

- Pest Control and Ventilation: Implementing pest control measures and storing items in well-ventilated areas helps prevent mold, mildew, and pest infestations, which can cause significant damage to antiques over time.

5.4 Restoration vs. Preservation

- Restoration Considerations: Restoration can improve the appearance and functionality of an item but may reduce its historical value if not done carefully. Collectors are advised to weigh the benefits and risks before proceeding with restoration.

- Preservation Focus: Preservation aims to maintain the item's current condition, retaining its historical integrity and value. This approach is often preferred for items of significant historical importance.

- Expert Consultation: Before deciding between restoration and preservation, consulting with experts is recommended. Documenting any work done is also crucial for maintaining the item's provenance and value.

5.5 Handling Antiques Safely

- Proper Handling Techniques: Handling antiques with clean, dry hands or cotton gloves is essential to prevent oils and dirt from transferring to delicate surfaces. Supporting fragile items from underneath with both hands reduces the risk of damage.

- Safe Transport and Display: When transporting or displaying items, using padded materials and securing them properly helps prevent movement or tipping, which can cause damage.

- Education and Practice: Educating household members on proper handling techniques and regularly reviewing and updating handling practices ensure that everyone involved in caring for the collection is equipped to do so safely.

Chapter 5 equips collectors with the knowledge and skills needed to care for their antiques effectively. By following the guidelines for storage, cleaning, damage prevention, and handling, collectors can protect their valuable items and preserve their beauty and historical significance for generations to come. This chapter is a vital resource for anyone serious about maintaining the condition and value of their collection.

Chapter 6: Buying Antiques and Collectibles

Buying antiques and collectibles is an exciting aspect of collecting, but it requires knowledge, strategy, and careful consideration to ensure you're making wise investments. This chapter guides you through the process of finding and purchasing antiques, offering tips on where to look, how to negotiate, and what to consider when evaluating sellers and participating in auctions.

6.1 Where to Find Antiques

Finding the right places to purchase antiques is the first step in building a valuable and meaningful collection. Whether you're searching for rare items, specific pieces, or simply exploring what's available, knowing where to look can make all the difference. This section outlines the most effective and popular places to find antiques.

1. Antique Shops and Galleries

A. Specialty Shops

- Curated Selections: Antique shops and galleries are dedicated spaces where you can find a curated selection of antiques. These shops often specialize in specific categories, such as furniture, art, jewelry, or books, allowing you to focus on your particular area of interest.

- Expert Knowledge: Shop owners and staff are usually knowledgeable about the items they sell, making these shops a valuable resource for both learning and purchasing. You can ask questions, learn about the provenance of items, and sometimes even negotiate prices.

B. Local and Regional Stores

- Unique Finds: Exploring local antique shops in your area can yield unexpected treasures. Smaller, locally-owned shops often carry unique items with regional significance, which can add a personal touch to your collection.

- Building Relationships: Regular visits to these stores can help you develop relationships with the owners, who might offer you first access to new arrivals or special deals.

2. Flea Markets and Estate Sales

A. Flea Markets

- Diverse Offerings: Flea markets are bustling venues where vendors sell a wide variety of items, including antiques and collectibles. These markets can range from small, local events to large, well-known markets that attract vendors from across the country.

- Bargaining Opportunities: The informal atmosphere of flea markets often allows for haggling, so be prepared to negotiate. However, it's important to carefully inspect items for authenticity and condition, as flea markets can also have reproductions or damaged goods.

B. Estate Sales

- Direct Access: Estate sales, typically held after the owner of a property has passed away or is downsizing, are excellent opportunities to purchase antiques directly from private collections. These sales often include a wide range of items, from furniture and art to smaller collectibles like jewelry and silverware.

- Competitive Pricing: Prices at estate sales can be more competitive than in shops or galleries, especially if the sellers are motivated to liquidate the estate quickly. Arriving early gives you the best chance to find valuable items before they're picked over.

3. Antique Fairs and Shows

A. Regional and National Shows

- Wide Variety: Antique fairs and shows are events that bring together multiple dealers and vendors, offering a wide variety of antiques under one roof. These events are held at regional and national levels, attracting collectors, dealers, and enthusiasts.

- Networking Opportunities: Attending these shows allows you to see a large number of items in person, compare prices, and network with other collectors. Many fairs also feature expert appraisers, giving you the opportunity to have items evaluated or to gain insights into specific pieces.

B. Themed or Specialty Fairs

- Focused Collections: Some antique fairs and shows focus on specific themes or categories, such as vintage toys, art deco, or Victorian-era pieces. These specialized events can be particularly valuable if you're looking for items within a specific niche.

- Expertise Access: Themed fairs often attract vendors with deep expertise in their area, providing you with a richer educational experience and access to rare or unique items.

4. Online Marketplaces

A. eBay and Etsy

- Global Reach: Online platforms like eBay and Etsy offer a vast selection of antiques and collectibles from sellers around the world. These sites are convenient for browsing a wide range of items from the comfort of your home.

- Buyer Caution: However, buying online requires caution. Always check seller reviews, request additional photos, and ask questions about the item's condition and provenance before making a purchase. The lack of physical inspection makes it crucial to ensure the reliability of the seller.

B. Dedicated Antique Websites

- Curated Collections: Several websites specialize in antiques, offering curated collections and more detailed listings than general online marketplaces. Sites like Ruby Lane, 1stDibs, and Chairish cater specifically to antique buyers and sellers, providing a higher level of curation and expertise.

- Stricter Standards: These platforms often have stricter standards for sellers, which can give buyers more confidence in the authenticity and quality of the items.

C. Online Auctions

- High-Value Finds: Online auction sites like Sotheby's, Christie's, and Heritage Auctions have embraced the digital age, offering online bidding for high-value antiques. These platforms allow you to participate in auctions from anywhere in the world, giving you access to rare and valuable items that might not be available locally.

- Auction Savvy: As with traditional auctions, it's important to research items thoroughly, set a budget, and understand the auction terms, including buyer's premiums and shipping costs.

5. Private Collectors and Dealers

A. Building Relationships with Dealers

- Trusted Sources: Establishing relationships with reputable dealers can be an excellent way to access high-quality antiques. Dealers often have extensive knowledge of the market and can help you find specific items or advise you on potential purchases.

- Exclusive Access: Working with a trusted dealer also gives you access to items that may not be available to the general public, as some pieces are sold privately before reaching broader markets.

B. Networking with Private Collectors

- Insider Information: Networking with other collectors can lead to private sales, trades, or the sharing of information about where to find certain items. Collectors often have deep knowledge of specific areas and can offer insights or connections that are not available through public channels.

- Community Engagement: Joining collectors' clubs, attending conventions, and participating in online forums are effective ways to build these relationships and stay informed about opportunities in the market.

Finding antiques requires a combination of exploration, networking, and research. Whether you're visiting local shops, attending fairs, or browsing online, knowing where to look and how to navigate these venues will enhance your chances of discovering valuable additions to your collection.

6.2 Tips for Successful Negotiation

Negotiating the price of antiques and collectibles is both an art and a science. Whether you're at an antique shop, a flea market, or bidding in an auction, effective negotiation can help you secure valuable items at fair prices. This section provides practical tips for negotiating successfully when purchasing antiques.

1. Do Your Research

A. Understand the Item's Value

- Research Thoroughly: Before entering any negotiation, research the item you're interested in. Understand its historical significance, condition, rarity, and market value. This knowledge gives you a solid foundation to negotiate from and helps you avoid overpaying.

- Utilize Multiple Resources: Use online resources, price guides, and auction results to get a sense of what similar items have sold for recently. This data will help you gauge the fairness of the asking price.

B. Know the Market Trends

- Stay Informed on Trends: Familiarize yourself with current market trends for the type of antique you're interested in. If demand for certain items is high, sellers may be less willing to negotiate, but knowing when an item is out of favor can give you leverage.

- Consider Seasonality: Keep an eye on seasonal trends as well; certain antiques may be more in demand at specific times of the year.

2. Start with a Lower Offer

A. Leave Room for Negotiation

- Strategic Starting Offer: Begin your negotiation with an offer lower than the asking price, but within a reasonable range. This approach leaves room for the seller to counteroffer and allows you to work towards a mutually agreeable price.

- Justify Your Offer: Make your initial offer based on your research, ensuring it reflects the item's value and condition. Be prepared to justify your offer with facts, but remain respectful and open to discussion.

B. Use the "Bundling" Technique

- Bundle Purchases: If you're interested in multiple items from the same seller, consider bundling them together in your negotiation. Sellers are often more willing to offer a discount when multiple items are purchased together.

- Propose a Combined Offer: Propose a total price for the group of items that is lower than the sum of their individual prices, emphasizing the convenience and efficiency of completing a single transaction.

3. Be Prepared to Walk Away

A. Set Your Budget

- Define Your Limit: Before you start negotiating, determine the maximum amount you're willing to pay for the item and stick to it. Having a firm budget in mind prevents you from overspending in the heat of negotiation.

- Be Ready to Walk Away: If the seller is unwilling to meet your price, be prepared to walk away. Sometimes, expressing a willingness to leave can prompt the seller to reconsider their offer.

B. Keep Emotions in Check

- Avoid Emotional Decisions: It's easy to become emotionally attached to an item, especially if it's something you've been searching for. However, letting emotions drive your decision-making can lead to overpaying.

- Focus on Value: Stay focused on the value of the item and your budget. If the price doesn't make sense, it's okay to walk away and continue your search elsewhere.

4. Build Rapport with Sellers

A. Establish a Connection

- Engage Positively: Building a good rapport with the seller can make negotiations smoother and more enjoyable. Engage in friendly conversation, ask about the item's history, and show genuine interest in the seller's expertise.

- Foster Trust: A positive relationship can make the seller more willing to negotiate and may even lead to better deals in the future.

B. Show Respect and Fairness

- Negotiate Fairly: Approach negotiations with respect and fairness. Acknowledge the seller's perspective and be willing to compromise when necessary.

- Avoid Lowball Offers: Avoid making overly lowball offers that could insult the seller or damage the relationship. Instead, aim for a price that reflects the item's value while being fair to both parties.

5. Use Tactics to Gain Leverage

A. Highlight Flaws or Imperfections

- Use Flaws as Leverage: If the item has any flaws or imperfections, use them as leverage during negotiation. Pointing out damage, wear, or missing parts can justify a lower offer, especially if repairs will be needed.

- Diplomatic Approach: Be diplomatic when discussing flaws, focusing on the practical implications rather than criticizing the item.

B. Mention Competing Offers or Prices

- Compare Prices: If you've seen similar items at lower prices elsewhere, mention this to the seller as part of your negotiation strategy. This can encourage the seller to offer a more competitive price.

- Be Honest: However, be honest in your comparisons—falsely claiming to have found a better deal can backfire if the seller calls your bluff.

6. Close the Deal Gracefully

A. Confirm the Final Price

- Clear Agreement: Once you've reached an agreement, clearly confirm the final price with the seller. Make sure both parties understand the terms of the deal, including any additional costs like shipping or taxes.

- Get Documentation: If purchasing from a shop or online platform, request a receipt or written confirmation of the transaction.

B. Express Gratitude

- Thank the Seller: Thank the seller for their time and for working with you on the negotiation. A gracious attitude can leave a positive impression, which may benefit you in future dealings.

- Build a Positive Reputation: Building a reputation as a fair and respectful buyer can lead to more opportunities and better deals down the line.

Successful negotiation is a key skill in building a valuable collection of antiques and collectibles. By researching thoroughly, staying within your budget, building rapport with sellers, and using effective negotiation tactics, you can secure items at fair prices and enhance your collecting experience.

6.3 Auction Houses, Markets, and Online Platforms

When buying antiques and collectibles, the venue you choose to purchase from can significantly impact your experience, the price you pay, and the quality of the items you acquire. Auction houses, markets, and online platforms each offer unique advantages and challenges. This section explores these different buying venues, helping you decide which is best for your needs.

1. Auction Houses

A. Types of Auction Houses

- Variety of Auction Houses: Auction houses range from prestigious international names like Sotheby's and Christie's to smaller, regional establishments. While the former often handle high-end, rare items, the latter can be more accessible to everyday collectors and may offer a wider variety of affordable pieces.

- Specialization: Some auction houses specialize in specific types of antiques, such as fine art, furniture, or jewelry, allowing you to focus on areas of particular interest.

B. The Auction Process

- Understanding Auctions: Participating in an auction requires understanding the process, including registration, bidding increments, and the auctioneer's signals.

Most auction houses offer previews before the sale, allowing you to inspect items in person.

- Additional Costs: Be aware of additional costs, such as the buyer's premium (a percentage of the hammer price added to your final bill), taxes, and shipping fees. These can significantly increase the total cost of your purchase.

C. Advantages of Auction Houses

- Access to Rare Items: Auctions provide access to rare and high-quality items that may not be available through other channels. The competitive nature of auctions can lead to lower prices if there is less interest in a particular item.

- Confidence in Authenticity: Auction houses often provide detailed provenance and condition reports, giving you confidence in the authenticity and value of the items you're bidding on.

D. Challenges of Auction Houses

- Intimidating Environment: The fast-paced environment of an auction can be intimidating for newcomers, and it's easy to get caught up in the excitement, leading to overbidding.

- Need for Preparation: Bidders need to be well-prepared, with a clear budget and a firm understanding of the items' values, to avoid making impulsive decisions.

2. Antique Markets and Flea Markets

A. Exploring Antique Markets

- Variety and Discovery: Antique markets are venues where multiple dealers gather to sell a wide range of items, from furniture and art to small collectibles. These markets can vary in size, with some held regularly and others as annual events.

- Negotiation Opportunities: Markets are ideal for browsing and discovering unexpected treasures. Prices can be more flexible, with room for negotiation, especially toward the end of the day when sellers are eager to make sales.

B. Flea Markets

- Eclectic Mix of Goods: Flea markets offer a more eclectic mix of goods, including antiques, vintage items, and general second-hand goods. While it requires a keen eye to sift through the offerings, flea markets can yield unique finds at lower prices than traditional antique markets.

- Bargain Hunting: The atmosphere at flea markets is typically informal, and bargaining is expected. However, buyers need to be cautious about authenticity and condition, as flea markets may not have the same level of vetting as auction houses or antique shops.

C. Advantages of Markets

- Variety and Volume: The variety and volume of items available at markets make them excellent places for both beginners and experienced collectors to explore.

- Direct Negotiation: The opportunity to negotiate prices directly with sellers can lead to bargains, especially if you have strong negotiation skills and knowledge of the items.

D. Challenges of Markets

- Varying Conditions: Market conditions can vary, and not all sellers are experts in the items they offer. This makes it essential for buyers to do their homework and carefully inspect items before purchasing.

- Environmental Factors: Weather and other environmental factors can affect outdoor markets, so it's important to plan accordingly.

3. Online Platforms

A. eBay and Etsy

- Popular Marketplaces: eBay and Etsy are two of the most popular online marketplaces for antiques and collectibles. They offer a wide range of items, from rare finds to more common pieces, and cater to buyers at all budget levels.

- Convenience and Flexibility: These platforms allow you to search for specific items, compare prices, and purchase from sellers around the world. Auctions, fixed-price listings, and "Buy It Now" options provide flexibility in how you shop.

B. Dedicated Antique Websites

- Curated Selections: Websites like Ruby Lane, 1stDibs, and Chairish focus specifically on antiques and high-end collectibles. These platforms offer a curated selection of items, often with more detailed descriptions, better photos, and higher seller standards than general online marketplaces.

- High-End and Rare Items: These sites are particularly useful for finding rare or high-value items, with the added benefit of more rigorous vetting of sellers and items.

C. Online Auctions

- Global Access: Many traditional auction houses now offer online bidding, making it possible to participate in auctions from anywhere. Sites like Sotheby's, Christie's, and Heritage Auctions provide online catalogs, bidding interfaces, and live-streamed auctions.

- Convenience with Caution: Online auctions can be convenient, but they also require a good understanding of the process, including how to place bids, how to account for additional costs like shipping, and how to verify the condition and authenticity of items remotely.

D. Advantages of Online Platforms

- Global Reach: Online platforms offer convenience and access to a global market, allowing you to find specific items that may not be available locally.

- Transparency and Comparison: The ability to compare prices and read reviews or seller feedback provides additional transparency and helps you make informed decisions.

E. Challenges of Online Platforms

- Lack of Physical Inspection: The main challenge of buying online is the inability to inspect items in person before purchase. This makes it crucial to request detailed photos, ask questions, and verify the seller's reputation.

- Shipping Costs and Risks: Shipping costs and the risk of damage during transit are additional considerations when purchasing antiques online.

Auction houses, markets, and online platforms each offer unique opportunities and challenges for buying antiques and collectibles. By understanding the characteristics of each venue, you can choose the one that best suits your needs, whether you're looking for high-end items at auction, bargains at a flea market, or the convenience of online shopping.

6.4 Evaluating Sellers and Sources

Evaluating the sellers and sources you purchase antiques and collectibles from is crucial to ensuring that you acquire authentic, high-quality items at fair prices. This section provides guidelines for assessing the credibility of sellers and the reliability of their sources, whether you're buying in person or online.

1. Researching Seller Reputation

A. Checking Reviews and Ratings

- Review Importance: When buying from online platforms or auction houses, start by checking the seller's reviews and ratings. Feedback from previous buyers can provide valuable insights into the seller's reliability, customer service, and the accuracy of their item descriptions.

- Assessing Feedback: Pay attention to both the quantity and quality of reviews. A seller with numerous positive reviews is generally more trustworthy than one with only a few or mixed feedback. Look for consistent comments about the authenticity and condition of items, as well as the seller's communication and shipping practices.

B. Investigating Seller Background

- Background Inquiry: For in-person purchases, ask the seller about their background, experience, and expertise in the field of antiques. Reputable sellers should be willing to share their history in the business, including how they acquire their items and their areas of specialization.

- Stability Indicators: If the seller operates a physical store or has a longstanding presence at antique fairs, this can indicate a stable and trustworthy business. Be wary of sellers who are vague or evasive about their background or where their items come from.

2. *Verifying Authenticity and Provenance*

A. Requesting Documentation

- Importance of Documentation: Authenticity is a major concern when purchasing antiques. Always ask the seller for documentation that verifies the item's authenticity and provenance. This may include certificates of authenticity, previous sales records, appraisals, or detailed descriptions of the item's history.

- Independent Verification: For high-value items, consider consulting with an independent expert or appraiser who can verify the item's authenticity before you finalize the purchase.

B. Examining Provenance

- Provenance Significance: Provenance refers to the documented history of an item's ownership, which can significantly impact its value. Items with well-documented provenance, especially those with connections to notable historical figures or events, are often more valuable.

- Detailed Review: Ask the seller for any available provenance details and review them carefully. Be cautious of items with unclear or incomplete provenance, as these can be difficult to authenticate and may not hold their value as well.

C. Understanding Restoration and Repairs

- Restoration Transparency: Ask the seller about any restoration or repairs that have been done to the item. Honest sellers should disclose this information upfront. While some restoration can enhance an item's value, excessive or poor-quality restoration can detract from its authenticity and worth.

- Visual Inspection: Inspect the item closely for signs of restoration, such as mismatched materials, uneven finishes, or modern components. If possible, compare the item to others of the same period or style to assess whether the restoration has been done sympathetically.

3. *Evaluating the Condition of Items*

A. Inspecting for Damage or Wear

- Thorough Inspection: Carefully inspect the item for any signs of damage, wear, or deterioration. Common issues include cracks, chips, scratches, fading, or corrosion, depending on the material.

- Material-Specific Checks: For textiles, check for moth holes, stains, or weakening of the fabric. For furniture, examine joints, veneers, and surfaces for stability and condition. Use a magnifying glass if necessary to spot small imperfections.

B. Assessing Restoration Impact

- Restoration's Role: Determine whether any restoration or repairs have affected the item's value. While minor repairs may be acceptable, extensive restoration can reduce an item's authenticity and appeal.

- Seek Professional Input: If you're uncertain about the extent or quality of restoration, seek advice from a professional restorer or appraiser before making a purchase.

C. Considering Condition in Price Negotiation

- Leverage Condition: Use the item's condition as a factor in price negotiation. If the item has significant damage or wear, or if the restoration has been extensive, you may be able to negotiate a lower price.

- Realistic Valuation: Be realistic about the cost of any necessary repairs or restoration when determining how much you're willing to pay.

4. Assessing the Seller's Policies

A. Understanding Return Policies

- Return Policy Insight: Before making a purchase, especially online, review the seller's return policy. A flexible return policy indicates confidence in the item's authenticity and quality. It also provides you with a safety net if the item does not meet your expectations.

- Caution with Strict Policies: Sellers with strict or no-return policies should be approached with caution, particularly for high-value items. Ensure that you fully understand the conditions under which a return is allowed and any associated costs.

B. Clarifying Payment and Shipping Terms

- Payment Terms: Clarify the payment terms before committing to a purchase. Understand whether the seller requires full payment upfront, offers payment plans, or accepts various payment methods (e.g., credit cards, bank transfers).

- Shipping Considerations: If purchasing online, inquire about the shipping process. Ensure that the seller uses secure, insured shipping methods, especially for fragile or high-value items. Ask about the timeline for shipping and any additional costs that may apply.

C. Ensuring Transparency and Communication

- Communication is Key: A reputable seller should be transparent about all aspects of the transaction, including item details, pricing, and policies. Clear and consistent communication is key to a successful buying experience.

- Red Flags: Be cautious of sellers who are slow to respond, avoid answering questions directly, or provide vague or conflicting information. Good communication is a sign of professionalism and reliability.

5. Building Long-Term Relationships with Sellers

A. Establishing Trust with Regular Sellers

- Long-Term Benefits: Developing a relationship with a trusted seller can be beneficial in the long run. Repeat customers often receive better service, early access to new items, and sometimes discounts.

- Loyalty Pays Off: Be loyal to sellers who consistently provide high-quality items and excellent customer service. Over time, this relationship can lead to insider knowledge about upcoming sales, rare finds, and exclusive deals.

B. Networking and Referrals

- Expanding Your Network: Don't hesitate to ask reputable sellers for referrals to other dealers or sources, especially if they specialize in different types of antiques. Networking within the community can open doors to new opportunities and valuable connections.

- Engage in Community: Attend events, join collectors' clubs, and participate in online forums to expand your network of reliable sellers and sources.

Evaluating sellers and sources is an essential step in ensuring that you purchase authentic and high-quality antiques. By researching seller reputations, verifying authenticity, assessing item conditions, and understanding seller policies, you can make informed decisions and build a trustworthy network of sources for your collection.

6.5 Understanding Auction Etiquette

Participating in auctions is an exciting way to acquire antiques and collectibles, but it requires a good understanding of auction etiquette to navigate the process successfully. Knowing the unwritten rules and expectations can help you bid confidently, avoid common pitfalls, and leave a positive impression on auction houses and other participants. This section covers the key aspects of auction etiquette.

1. Preparing for the Auction

A. Researching the Auction Catalog

- Thorough Review: Before attending an auction, thoroughly review the auction catalog. This will give you an overview of the items being sold, including descriptions, estimates, and any provenance details.

- Item Selection: Mark the items you're interested in and note their lot numbers. Research their value and historical significance to set a realistic budget for each item.

B. Attending Previews and Inspections

- In-Person Inspection: Most auctions offer a preview period where potential buyers can inspect items in person. Take advantage of this opportunity to examine the condition of items closely, verify their authenticity, and ask questions about their history.

- Remote Inspection: If you're unable to attend the preview in person, request additional photos or condition reports from the auction house. This is especially important for high-value items where details can significantly impact value.

C. Registering to Bid

- Registration Process: Register as a bidder before the auction begins. This typically involves providing identification and, in some cases, a refundable deposit. You'll receive a bidder's number or paddle, which you'll use to place bids during the auction.

- Online and Phone Bidding: If you're bidding online or by phone, ensure you complete the registration process in advance and understand the procedures for placing bids remotely.

2. Conducting Yourself During the Auction

A. Arriving on Time

- Punctuality Matters: Arrive at the auction venue on time, or log in early if you're participating online. Auctions often follow a strict schedule, and arriving late could mean missing out on key lots you're interested in.

- Settling In: Being punctual also allows you to get settled and familiarize yourself with the auctioneer's style and the bidding process.

B. Understanding the Auctioneer's Signals

- Auctioneer's Cadence: Pay close attention to the auctioneer's signals and cadence. Auctioneers often speak quickly and use a variety of gestures to acknowledge bids, announce increments, and signal when a lot is about to close.

- Clarifications: If you're unsure about the current bid or the bidding increments, don't hesitate to ask for clarification. Auctioneers are accustomed to answering questions and want to ensure all bidders are on the same page.

C. Bidding Respectfully and Responsibly

- Clear Bidding: When placing a bid, do so clearly and confidently by raising your paddle or using the appropriate online bidding mechanism. Avoid making gestures that could be mistaken for a bid, such as nodding or scratching your face.

- Serious Bidding: Only bid if you're serious about purchasing the item. Bidding frivolously can disrupt the auction and annoy other participants. Stick to your budget and avoid getting caught up in the excitement, which can lead to overbidding.

D. Respecting Other Bidders

- Courteous Conduct: Be respectful of other bidders during the auction. Avoid engaging in distracting conversations, using your phone, or making comments about items or bids.

- Fair Competition: Remember that auction bidding can be competitive, but it should remain courteous. Avoid trying to intimidate other bidders or manipulate the process to your advantage.

3. Winning the Bid

A. Acknowledging the Auctioneer

- Winning Confirmation: If you win a lot, acknowledge the auctioneer with a nod or a small gesture to confirm the winning bid. The auctioneer will announce your bidder number and the final hammer price.

- Understanding Additional Fees: Make sure you understand any additional fees, such as the buyer's premium and taxes, which will be added to the final price.

B. Finalizing the Purchase

- Payment Process: After the auction, promptly proceed to the payment area to settle your bill. Be prepared to pay in full unless other arrangements have been made with the auction house.

- Item Collection: Collect your items according to the auction house's procedures. If the items need to be shipped, confirm the shipping details and ensure the items are insured during transit.

C. Handling Payment Issues

- Professional Resolution: If any issues arise during payment or collection, address them calmly and professionally with the auction house staff. Auction houses typically have policies in place to handle disputes or concerns, and maintaining a respectful demeanor will help resolve issues more effectively.

- Avoid Public Disputes: Avoid making public complaints or confrontations that could disrupt the auction or harm your reputation with the auction house.

4. Post-Auction Etiquette

A. Following Up with the Auction House

- Post-Auction Communication: After the auction, it's good practice to follow up with the auction house if you have any questions or need further documentation for your purchased items. This could include requests for provenance details, condition reports, or shipping updates.

- Missed Lots: If you were unable to win a lot you were interested in, consider contacting the auction house to inquire if the item is still available or if they can notify you of similar items in future auctions.

B. Building Relationships for Future Auctions

- Positive Relationship Building: Developing a positive relationship with auction house staff can be beneficial for future auctions. Consistently demonstrating good etiquette and reliability as a bidder can lead to early access to catalogs, invitations to special events, and opportunities for private sales.

- Networking with Bidders: Networking with other bidders can also be valuable, as they may share information about upcoming auctions, market trends, or items of mutual interest.

Understanding auction etiquette is essential for participating confidently and effectively in auctions. By preparing thoroughly, bidding responsibly, and respecting both the auction process and other participants, you can enhance your experience and increase your chances of securing valuable antiques and collectibles.

Chapter 6 Review: Buying Antiques and Collectibles

Chapter 6 of *HowExpert Guide to Antiques and Collectibles* offers invaluable guidance for collectors on the process of buying antiques and collectibles. This chapter covers essential topics such as where to find items, effective negotiation strategies, the intricacies of purchasing from different venues, evaluating sellers, and understanding auction etiquette.

6.1 Where to Find Antiques

- Antique Shops and Galleries: These venues offer curated selections with knowledgeable staff, making them ideal for finding specific items or categories. The expertise available at these locations can help collectors make informed purchases.

- Flea Markets and Estate Sales: These are excellent places to discover unique and affordable treasures, often with opportunities for negotiation. Flea markets and estate sales offer a more hands-on, exploratory experience where bargains can often be found.

- Antique Fairs and Shows: Bringing together multiple dealers, these events offer a wide variety of items in one location, making them perfect for both browsing and networking. Collectors can compare items and prices across vendors, which can lead to better deals.

- Online Marketplaces: Platforms like eBay, Etsy, and specialized antique websites provide convenience and access to a global market. However, these platforms require careful vetting of sellers to ensure authenticity and avoid scams.

6.2 Tips for Successful Negotiation

- Researching Value and Trends: Before entering negotiations, it's crucial to research the item's value and current market trends. This knowledge gives collectors a strong foundation for making offers and negotiating effectively.

- Strategic Offers: Starting with a lower offer allows room for negotiation, and being prepared to walk away helps maintain budget discipline. Understanding the item's worth and market demand can guide negotiations.

- Building Rapport with Sellers: Establishing a connection with sellers can facilitate better deals. Tactics like highlighting flaws or mentioning competing offers can also help in securing a lower price.

6.3 Auction Houses, Markets, and Online Platforms

- Auction Houses: These venues provide access to rare and high-quality items, but buyers need to understand the bidding process, including potential additional costs like buyer's premiums and taxes.

- Antique and Flea Markets: These markets are great for finding a diverse range of items, often with direct price negotiations. The personal interaction with sellers can lead to unique discoveries and deals.

- Online Platforms: While convenient and offering a vast selection, online platforms require caution. Buyers must verify the authenticity of items and consider shipping costs and risks, particularly for fragile or high-value items.

6.4 Evaluating Sellers and Sources

- Checking Reviews and Ratings: It's essential to verify the reputation of sellers by checking reviews, ratings, and background information. This helps ensure that collectors are dealing with reputable sources.

- Verifying Authenticity and Provenance: Collectors should inspect the condition of items and request documentation to confirm authenticity and provenance, which is crucial for avoiding fakes or overpaying for damaged goods.

- Understanding Seller Policies: Knowing the return and payment terms of sellers is critical, especially for high-value purchases. Clear communication about these terms helps avoid disputes and ensures a smooth transaction.

6.5 Understanding Auction Etiquette

- Preparing for Auctions: Collectors should research the auction catalog and attend previews to familiarize themselves with the items up for bid. This preparation helps in making confident bids and avoiding overpaying.

- Bidding Respectfully: Understanding auctioneer signals and adhering to auction house procedures are key to successful participation. Respectful and strategic bidding builds credibility with the auction house and other bidders.

- Building Relationships: Positive interactions with auction houses and fellow bidders can lead to better opportunities in future auctions. Networking within the auction community can also provide access to exclusive items and insider knowledge.

Chapter 6 equips collectors with the essential knowledge and skills needed to navigate the buying process for antiques and collectibles effectively. By understanding where to find items, how to negotiate, and the importance of evaluating sellers and adhering to auction etiquette, collectors can make informed decisions and build their collections with confidence. This chapter is crucial for anyone looking to successfully acquire valuable and authentic pieces in the competitive world of antiques and collectibles.

Chapter 7: Selling Antiques and Collectibles

Selling antiques and collectibles can be a rewarding way to share your treasures with others while potentially making a profit. However, the process requires careful preparation, accurate pricing, and strategic marketing to ensure you achieve the best possible outcomes. This chapter guides you through the essential steps of selling your antiques, from preparing items for sale to negotiating with buyers.

7.1 Preparing Items for Sale

Preparing your antiques and collectibles for sale is a critical step that can significantly impact their appeal to buyers and the final price you receive. Proper preparation involves cleaning, documenting, and presenting your items in the best possible light. This section covers the key steps to ensure your items are ready for the market.

1. Thorough Cleaning and Maintenance

A. Cleaning Techniques for Different Materials

- Appropriate Cleaning Methods: Begin by cleaning your items to remove dust, dirt, and grime that may have accumulated over time. Use cleaning methods appropriate for the material—mild soap and water for ceramics, specialized polish for metals, and a soft cloth for wood.

- Avoiding Harsh Chemicals: Avoid using harsh chemicals or abrasive materials that could damage the item's surface or diminish its value. For delicate or valuable items, consider professional cleaning or restoration services to ensure the best results.

B. Addressing Minor Repairs

- Minor Repairs: If your item has minor damages, such as loose joints on furniture or small chips in ceramics, consider repairing them before selling. Properly executed repairs can enhance the item's appeal and increase its value.

- Weighing Restoration Risks: Be cautious with extensive repairs or restorations, as these can sometimes reduce an item's authenticity and market value. Always weigh the potential benefits of repair against the importance of preserving the original condition.

2. Documenting Condition and Provenance

A. Writing Detailed Descriptions

- Accurate Condition Documentation: Accurately document the condition of your item, noting any flaws, wear, or restorations. This transparency builds trust with potential buyers and helps set realistic expectations.

- Descriptive Details: Include a detailed description of the item's features, materials, and any unique characteristics. Highlight any marks, signatures, or labels that verify its authenticity.

B. Providing Provenance and History

- Presenting Provenance: If available, gather and present any provenance information that documents the item's history, including previous ownership, auction records, or connections to notable figures or events.

- Enhancing Value with Provenance: Provenance can significantly enhance an item's value, particularly for rare or historically significant pieces. If you lack formal documentation, share any anecdotal history or context that might interest buyers.

3. Photography Tips for Online Listings

A. Setting Up the Perfect Shot

- Lighting and Background: High-quality photos are essential for attracting buyers, especially for online sales. Use natural lighting to bring out the item's true colors and details. Avoid harsh, direct light, which can cast unflattering shadows or reflections.

- Neutral Background: Place the item against a neutral background to keep the focus on it. A plain white or black backdrop often works best, depending on the item's color.

B. Capturing Important Details

- Multiple Angles and Close-Ups: Take multiple photos from various angles, including close-ups of important details like marks, signatures, or any unique features.

- Transparency in Photography: If the item has any flaws, be sure to photograph them clearly to maintain transparency with potential buyers. This honesty can help avoid disputes and returns later on.

C. Editing and Presentation

- Photo Editing: Use photo editing tools to adjust brightness, contrast, and color balance, ensuring the images are clear and accurate. Avoid excessive editing that could misrepresent the item's true condition.

- Logical Photo Sequence: Present the photos in a logical sequence, starting with a full view of the item and followed by detailed shots. This approach helps buyers get a comprehensive understanding of the item.

4. Preparing for In-Person Sales

A. Displaying Items at Markets or Fairs

- Attractive Arrangement: When selling at antique markets or fairs, presentation is key. Arrange your items attractively, using clean, well-lit displays that highlight their best features.

- Protection of Valuables: Consider using display cases for smaller, valuable items to protect them from handling and theft. Clearly label each item with its price and any relevant details.

B. Creating an Inviting Sales Space

- Tidy and Accessible Space: Ensure your sales space is welcoming and easy to navigate. Keep the area tidy and free from clutter, making it easy for potential buyers to view and handle items.

- Additional Information: Offer additional information about each item, such as printed descriptions or a catalog, to help buyers make informed decisions.

C. Being Ready to Answer Questions

- Knowledgeable Selling: Be prepared to answer questions about the items, including their history, condition, and any repairs or restorations. Knowledgeable sellers are more likely to earn buyers' trust and close sales.

- Providing Documentation: Have any relevant documentation, such as provenance records or certificates of authenticity, readily available for buyers to review.

Proper preparation is essential for maximizing the appeal and value of your antiques and collectibles when selling. By cleaning, documenting, and presenting your items effectively, you can attract more interest, build buyer confidence, and achieve better sales outcomes.

7.2 Setting the Right Price

Determining the right price for your antiques and collectibles is crucial to attracting buyers and ensuring you receive a fair return on your investment. Pricing too high can deter potential buyers, while pricing too low can undervalue your items. This section provides strategies for setting a competitive and realistic price.

1. Researching Market Value

A. Analyzing Comparable Sales

- Comparative Analysis: Begin by researching the prices of similar items that have recently sold. Look at auction results, online marketplace listings, and dealer prices to gather a range of data.

- Focus on Key Factors: Focus on items that are comparable in terms of age, condition, provenance, and rarity. This research will give you a benchmark for what buyers are willing to pay.

B. Utilizing Price Guides and Resources

- Consulting Price Guides: Refer to antique price guides and online resources that offer valuation estimates for various types of collectibles. These guides can provide a general sense of market trends and item values.

- Cross-Referencing Data: Keep in mind that these resources often provide broad estimates, so use them in conjunction with your research on specific comparable sales.

2. Considering Condition and Rarity

A. Adjusting for Condition

- Impact of Condition: The condition of your item plays a significant role in its value. Items in mint or excellent condition generally command higher prices than those with visible wear, damage, or repairs.

- Realistic Pricing: Be realistic about how the condition impacts the price. While minor imperfections might only slightly reduce the value, significant flaws should be reflected in a lower asking price.

B. Assessing Rarity and Demand

- Evaluating Rarity: Rare items or those in high demand are likely to fetch higher prices. Consider the scarcity of the item and whether it is sought after by collectors.

- Justifying Higher Prices: If your item is one of only a few available on the market, or if it has unique features that distinguish it from similar pieces, you can justify a higher price.

3. Setting a Competitive Price

A. Finding the Sweet Spot

- Competitive Pricing: Aim to set a price that is competitive within the current market while still providing a fair return. If you price your item too high, it may sit unsold for an extended period. If you price it too low, you risk undervaluing it.

- Negotiation Buffer: Consider starting with a slightly higher price than your minimum acceptable amount. This approach gives you room to negotiate with buyers while still achieving your desired outcome.

B. Factoring in Selling Costs

- Including Selling Costs: When setting your price, factor in any costs associated with selling the item, such as auction house fees, online platform commissions, shipping, and insurance. These expenses can significantly impact your net profit.

- Ensuring Profitability: Ensure that your pricing strategy accounts for these costs, so you don't end up losing money on the sale.

4. Flexibility and Negotiation

A. Being Open to Offers

- Encouraging Offers: Indicate whether you're open to offers in your listing or during negotiations. Flexibility in pricing can attract more buyers and lead to quicker sales.

- Pre-determined Lowest Price: Decide in advance the lowest price you're willing to accept, and be prepared to negotiate. A willingness to engage in price discussions can create a positive rapport with buyers and increase the likelihood of a sale.

B. Considering Time and Market Conditions

- Adapting to Circumstances: If you need to sell the item quickly, you may need to price it more aggressively. Conversely, if you're in no rush, you can afford to wait for the right buyer willing to meet your price.

- Market Awareness: Pay attention to market conditions, such as economic trends or seasonal demand, which can influence buyers' willingness to pay certain prices.

5. Seeking Professional Appraisal

A. When to Get an Appraisal

- High-Value Items: For high-value or rare items, it may be worthwhile to seek a professional appraisal. An appraiser can provide an expert assessment of your item's value based on its condition, rarity, and market demand.

- Auction and Collector Sales: Appraisals are particularly useful when selling through auction houses or to collectors who require documented proof of value.

B. Using Appraisal Information in Pricing

- Guiding Price Setting: Use the appraisal as a guideline for setting your price. While appraisals can provide a value range, the final price should also consider current market conditions and your specific selling goals.

- Sharing Appraisal with Buyers: Be prepared to share the appraisal with potential buyers as part of your item's documentation, especially if it supports a higher asking price.

Setting the right price for your antiques and collectibles requires careful research and consideration. By analyzing market trends, assessing the condition and rarity of your items, and being open to negotiation, you can establish a price that attracts buyers and maximizes your return.

7.3 Best Selling Venues and Platforms

Choosing the right venue or platform to sell your antiques and collectibles is crucial for reaching the right audience and achieving the best possible price. Different selling venues cater to different types of buyers and offer varying levels of exposure, convenience, and costs. This section explores the most effective venues and platforms for selling your items.

1. Auction Houses

A. Traditional Auction Houses

- High-End Auctions: Established auction houses like Sotheby's, Christie's, and Bonhams are ideal for high-value, rare, or unique items. These venues attract serious collectors and investors willing to pay premium prices for exceptional pieces.

- Competitive Bidding: Auction houses provide a competitive environment that can drive up prices, especially for items in high demand. However, sellers should be aware of the fees and commissions charged by auction houses, which can be substantial.

B. Regional and Local Auction Houses

- Local Market Focus: For less high-profile items, regional or local auction houses can be a better option. These venues often cater to a more localized market and may specialize in specific types of antiques or collectibles.

- Cost-Effective Selling: Selling through a regional auction house can be more cost-effective, with lower fees and a more tailored approach to marketing your items.

C. Online Auction Platforms

- Global Reach: Online auction platforms like eBay, Invaluable, and LiveAuctioneers provide access to a global audience, making them an excellent option for sellers looking to reach buyers beyond their local market.

- Flexible Listings: These platforms offer flexibility in terms of listing duration, starting prices, and reserve prices. However, they also require sellers to manage shipping and handle customer inquiries directly.

2. Antique Shops and Consignment Stores

A. Selling Directly to Antique Shops

- Quick Transactions: Selling directly to antique shops is a straightforward option for those looking to sell quickly without the hassle of managing sales themselves. Shop owners typically purchase items outright, often for resale in their store.

- Lower Returns: While this option provides immediate payment, sellers should expect to receive a lower price than they might achieve through other venues, as the shop owner needs to make a profit on the resale.

B. Consignment Stores

- Showcasing Items: Consignment stores offer a middle ground between direct sales and auctions. Items are displayed in the store, and you receive payment once the item sells, minus a consignment fee.

- Delayed Payment: This option allows your item to be showcased to potential buyers without requiring upfront payment. However, it may take time for your item to sell, and the consignment fee will reduce your overall profit.

3. *Online Marketplaces*

A. eBay

- Wide Audience: eBay is one of the most popular online marketplaces for antiques and collectibles, offering a vast global audience. It provides options for both auction-style listings and fixed-price sales.

- Platform Fees: Sellers benefit from eBay's established platform and extensive reach but should be aware of listing fees, final value fees, and PayPal transaction fees. Managing buyer inquiries and shipping logistics is also part of the process.

B. Etsy

- Niche Market: Etsy is known for its focus on handmade, vintage, and unique items, making it a great platform for selling antiques with a creative or artisanal appeal. The site's user base includes collectors who appreciate well-crafted or unusual items.

- Seller Tools: Like eBay, Etsy charges listing and transaction fees. It also offers a seller-friendly interface with tools for marketing and promoting your listings.

C. Specialized Antique Websites

- Curated Listings: Websites like Ruby Lane, 1stDibs, and Chairish cater specifically to antiques and high-end collectibles, attracting serious collectors and buyers looking for curated, high-quality items.

- Stricter Requirements: These platforms often have stricter seller requirements and higher fees but provide a more focused and upscale market. Sellers benefit from the credibility and trust these platforms have built with their audience.

4. Flea Markets and Antique Fairs

A. Local Flea Markets

- Broad Appeal: Flea markets are excellent venues for selling a variety of antiques and collectibles, particularly items that are lower in value or appeal to a broad audience. The informal setting allows for direct interaction with buyers and immediate sales.

- Haggling Culture: Sellers need to be prepared for haggling and should ensure their items are well-displayed to attract attention in the bustling market environment.

B. Antique Fairs and Shows

- Targeted Audience: Antique fairs and shows attract a more specialized audience of collectors and enthusiasts. These events are ideal for selling higher-value items or those with particular historical or artistic significance.

- Networking Opportunities: Renting a booth at an antique fair involves costs, but the opportunity to connect with serious buyers in person can lead to successful sales and valuable networking opportunities.

5. Private Sales and Dealer Networks

A. Selling to Dealers

- Convenient Transactions: Selling directly to dealers can be a quick and convenient option, especially for those with established relationships in the antiques community. Dealers are often willing to purchase items for immediate resale, though they will typically offer less than market value.

- Speed vs. Profit: This option is best for sellers looking to offload items quickly without the time investment of other selling methods.

B. Private Sales

- Higher Returns: Private sales involve negotiating directly with individual buyers, often through networking or referrals. This method can result in higher prices since there are no intermediaries taking a commission.

- Time-Intensive: However, private sales require strong negotiation skills and may take longer to find the right buyer. Building a network of collectors and enthusiasts can facilitate private sales and lead to repeat business.

Choosing the right venue or platform for selling your antiques and collectibles depends on the type of item, its value, and your selling goals. Whether you opt for auction houses, online marketplaces, or direct sales to dealers, understanding the advantages and challenges of each venue will help you maximize your success and achieve the best possible outcomes.

7.4 Marketing Your Collection

Effectively marketing your antiques and collectibles is crucial for attracting potential buyers and ensuring a successful sale. Whether you're selling online or in person, a well-thought-out marketing strategy can significantly enhance visibility, generate interest, and ultimately increase the value of your items. This section outlines key strategies for marketing your collection.

1. Crafting an Effective Listing

A. Writing Detailed Descriptions

- Comprehensive Details: A compelling and detailed description is essential for capturing the interest of potential buyers. Include all relevant information about the item, such as its age, origin, materials, and any unique features.

- Highlighting History: Emphasize the item's history and provenance if available, as this can add significant value. Be honest about the condition, noting any flaws or restorations, to build trust with buyers.

B. Utilizing Keywords for SEO

- Optimizing for Search: Incorporate relevant keywords into your listing to improve search engine optimization (SEO) and increase the chances of your item appearing in search results. Use terms that potential buyers are likely to search for, such as the item's category, style, period, and material.

- Avoiding Overuse: Steer clear of keyword stuffing, which can make your listing difficult to read and may lead to penalties from search engines. Focus on creating a natural flow of information that appeals to both search engines and buyers.

C. High-Quality Photographs

- Visual Appeal: High-quality images are crucial for online listings. Ensure your photos are well-lit, sharp, and show the item from multiple angles. Include close-ups of any important details, such as marks, signatures, or unique features.

- Neutral Backgrounds: Use a neutral background to keep the focus on the item, and avoid distractions in the frame. Consider using photo editing tools to enhance clarity and color accuracy, but avoid over-editing that misrepresents the item's true condition.

2. Utilizing Social Media and Online Communities

A. Promoting on Social Media Platforms

- Expanding Reach: Social media platforms like Instagram, Facebook, and Pinterest are powerful tools for reaching a broad audience. Share images and stories about your items, and use relevant hashtags to increase visibility among collectors and enthusiasts.

- Engagement Strategies: Create engaging content, such as videos or live streams, to showcase your collection in more detail. Regularly interact with your followers by responding to comments, answering questions, and participating in relevant groups or discussions.

B. Engaging with Online Communities

- Networking Opportunities: Join online forums, groups, and communities focused on antiques and collectibles. These platforms are excellent for networking with potential buyers, sharing knowledge, and promoting your items.

- Building Credibility: Be an active participant by contributing valuable insights, answering questions, and sharing your expertise. This helps establish your credibility and makes other members more likely to consider your items when they're looking to buy.

C. Leveraging Influencers and Collaborations

- Influencer Marketing: Partnering with influencers or collaborating with well-known figures in the antiques and collectibles community can help you reach a larger audience. Consider offering a commission or a discount in exchange for them promoting your items.

- Collaborative Opportunities: Collaborations can also include guest blog posts, interviews, or features on popular collector websites or magazines, further increasing your visibility.

3. Promoting Through Traditional Channels

A. Advertising in Collector Magazines and Journals

- Targeted Advertising: Traditional print media, such as collector magazines, journals, and newsletters, remain valuable channels for reaching serious collectors and enthusiasts. Place ads or feature your items in publications that cater to your specific niche.

- Sharing Expertise: Write articles or share your expertise in these publications to build your reputation and attract interest in your collection.

B. Participating in Antique Fairs and Shows

- Direct Marketing: Attending antique fairs, shows, and exhibitions allows you to market your collection directly to a targeted audience. These events provide opportunities to network with other collectors, dealers, and potential buyers.

- Professional Presentation: Consider setting up a booth or display to showcase your items, and prepare informative brochures or catalogs that visitors can take with them.

C. Networking with Dealers and Collectors

- Building Relationships: Building relationships with dealers, collectors, and other professionals in the antiques community can lead to word-of-mouth referrals and private sales opportunities. Attend industry events, join local collector clubs, and participate in workshops to expand your network.

- Collaborative Sales: Offering to consign items through established dealers or collaborating on sales can also help you reach a wider audience.

4. Offering Incentives and Promotions

A. Limited-Time Offers and Discounts

- Creating Urgency: Create urgency and attract buyers by offering limited-time promotions, discounts, or special deals. This can be particularly effective during peak buying seasons or when you're looking to quickly sell a specific item.

- Clear Communication: Clearly communicate the terms of the promotion, including any deadlines, to encourage immediate action.

B. Bundling Items

- Increased Value: Consider offering items as part of a bundle or set, especially if they belong to a related category or collection. Bundling can increase the perceived value of the items and make the offer more appealing to buyers.

- Efficient Sales: Price the bundle attractively to incentivize buyers to purchase multiple items at once, which can help you clear inventory more efficiently.

C. Loyalty Programs and Repeat Buyer Discounts

- Encouraging Repeat Business: Encourage repeat business by offering loyalty programs or discounts to buyers who purchase multiple items or return for future purchases.

- Tailored Promotions: Track your buyers' preferences and tailor promotions to their interests, increasing the likelihood of repeat sales.

5. Monitoring and Adjusting Your Strategy

A. Tracking Sales and Feedback

- Continuous Improvement: Regularly monitor the performance of your listings, social media posts, and promotional activities. Track metrics such as views, inquiries, sales, and feedback to understand what's working and what needs improvement.

- Informed Adjustments: Use buyer feedback to refine your marketing strategy, adjusting your descriptions, pricing, or promotional tactics as needed.

B. Adapting to Market Trends

- Staying Informed: Stay informed about current market trends, including shifts in buyer preferences, demand for certain categories, and pricing fluctuations. Adjust your marketing efforts to align with these trends, ensuring your items remain competitive and appealing.

- Experimenting with New Approaches: Be willing to experiment with new marketing channels, techniques, or partnerships to find the most effective ways to reach your target audience.

Marketing your antiques and collectibles effectively is essential for attracting buyers and maximizing your sales potential. By crafting detailed listings, leveraging social media and traditional channels, offering incentives, and continuously refining your strategy, you can successfully market your collection and achieve the best possible results.

7.5 Negotiating Sales

Negotiating sales is an art that requires skill, patience, and a clear understanding of both the value of your items and the needs of your buyers. Effective negotiation can help you secure the best possible price for your antiques and collectibles while maintaining positive relationships with buyers. This section provides strategies for negotiating sales successfully.

1. Being Open to Offers

A. Flexibility in Pricing

- Encouraging Engagement: Indicate in your listings or during discussions with potential buyers that you are open to offers. This approach encourages buyers to engage with you, knowing that there may be room for negotiation.

- Considering Reasonable Offers: Be prepared to consider offers that are slightly below your asking price, especially from serious buyers who show genuine interest in the item. Flexibility can lead to quicker sales and satisfied customers.

B. Setting a Minimum Acceptable Price

- Establishing Boundaries: Determine the lowest price you are willing to accept before entering negotiations. This helps you avoid underselling your item and ensures that you are comfortable with the final price.

- Adapting as Needed: Keep this minimum price in mind during negotiations, but be open to adjusting it if circumstances change, such as discovering additional costs or learning more about the buyer's situation.

2. Communicating Effectively

A. Clear and Professional Communication

- Maintaining Clarity: Maintain clear and professional communication throughout the negotiation process. Respond to inquiries promptly, provide detailed information, and be transparent about the item's condition, history, and any other relevant details.

- Using Respectful Language: Use polite language and maintain a respectful tone, even if the negotiation becomes challenging. Professionalism can build trust and increase the likelihood of a successful sale.

B. Listening to the Buyer's Needs

- Understanding Motivations: Take the time to understand the buyer's needs and motivations. Are they looking for a specific item to complete a collection, or are they concerned about the price?

- Tailoring Your Strategy: By listening carefully, you can tailor your negotiation strategy to address the buyer's concerns, making them more likely to agree to your terms.

C. Justifying Your Price

- Providing Context: Be prepared to justify your asking price by explaining the item's value, rarity, condition, and any recent comparable sales. Providing this context helps the buyer see the fairness in your price.

- Using Supporting Evidence: Use facts and evidence, such as provenance documents, appraisals, or historical data, to support your position. This can make your argument more persuasive and reduce the buyer's inclination to push for a lower price.

3. Handling Counteroffers

A. Evaluating Counteroffers

- Assessing Fairness: When a buyer makes a counteroffer, evaluate it carefully. Consider how it compares to your minimum acceptable price and whether it reflects the market value of the item.

- Considering Adjustments: If the counteroffer is reasonable, consider accepting it or making a slight adjustment to reach a mutually agreeable price. If it's too low, counter with a price closer to your original asking price while remaining open to further discussion.

B. Keeping the Negotiation Positive

- Maintaining Positivity: Even if a counteroffer is lower than expected, keep the negotiation positive. Avoid dismissive or negative reactions, as this can discourage the buyer from continuing the conversation.

- Expressing Appreciation: Express appreciation for the buyer's offer and explain your reasoning for the price you're proposing. A positive attitude can foster a collaborative negotiation atmosphere.

4. Closing the Sale

A. Finalizing the Terms

- Clarifying Details: Once a price is agreed upon, clearly outline the terms of the sale, including payment methods, shipping or delivery arrangements, and any return policies. Ensure both parties understand and agree to these terms before proceeding.

- Providing Formal Documentation: If selling online, provide the buyer with a formal invoice that includes all relevant details. For in-person sales, confirm the payment method and arrange a convenient time for the exchange.

B. Ensuring Secure Payment

- Choosing Secure Methods: Use secure payment methods to protect both yourself and the buyer. For online sales, platforms like PayPal or credit card payments offer protection for both parties. For in-person transactions, consider cash or certified checks.

- Considering Escrow Services: Be cautious with large transactions and consider using an escrow service for particularly high-value items to ensure that both payment and delivery are handled securely.

C. Following Up with the Buyer

- Ensuring Satisfaction: After the sale, follow up with the buyer to ensure they are satisfied with their purchase. This can include confirming receipt of the item, addressing any concerns, or simply thanking them for their business.

- Building Relationships: Positive post-sale communication can lead to repeat business, referrals, and a strong reputation within the collecting community.

5. Handling Difficult Negotiations

A. Staying Calm Under Pressure

- Maintaining Composure: Some negotiations may become difficult, especially if the buyer is particularly demanding or insistent on a lower price. Stay calm and composed, and avoid letting emotions dictate your responses.

- Taking Breaks: Take breaks if needed to regroup and consider your next steps. Remaining professional and level-headed can help de-escalate tense situations.

B. Knowing When to Walk Away

- Recognizing Limits: Not every negotiation will result in a sale. If the buyer's offers are consistently below your acceptable range or if the negotiation becomes too challenging, be prepared to walk away.

- Leaving the Door Open: Politely decline the offer and express that you're open to future discussions if the buyer's circumstances change. Walking away can sometimes prompt the buyer to reconsider and return with a better offer.

Negotiating sales effectively is a key skill for successfully selling antiques and collectibles. By being open to offers, communicating clearly, handling counteroffers strategically, and closing the sale securely, you can achieve favorable outcomes and build lasting relationships with buyers.

Chapter 7 Review: Selling Antiques and Collectibles

Chapter 7 of *HowExpert Guide to Antiques and Collectibles* provides a detailed roadmap for collectors looking to sell their antiques and collectibles. It covers crucial steps such as preparing items for sale, setting the right price, selecting the best venues, marketing your collection, and negotiating effectively to maximize your sales potential.

7.1 Preparing Items for Sale

- Cleaning and Maintenance: Properly cleaning and maintaining items is essential to enhance their appeal to potential buyers. This involves using appropriate methods for different materials, ensuring that items are presented in their best condition.

- Documenting Condition: Thorough documentation of each item's condition, including clear and detailed descriptions, is crucial. Providing provenance or historical details adds value and credibility to your listings.

- High-Quality Photography: Taking high-quality photographs is a key aspect of preparing items for sale. Using a neutral background and natural lighting helps to showcase the item's features effectively, making it more attractive to buyers.

7.2 Setting the Right Price

- Market Research: Setting the right price begins with thorough market research. Analyzing comparable sales, consulting antique price guides, and considering the condition and rarity of the item are all essential steps.

- Competitive Pricing: A competitive price reflects the item's value while allowing room for negotiation. This balance is important to attract buyers while still aiming for a fair profit.

- Considering Costs: When setting the price, it's important to factor in selling costs such as auction fees, shipping expenses, and any other associated costs to ensure profitability.

7.3 Best Selling Venues and Platforms

- Choosing the Right Venue: The choice of selling venue should align with the type of item being sold. Options include prestigious auction houses for high-value items, regional auctions, antique shops, or online marketplaces like eBay and Etsy.

- Venue Considerations: Each venue has its advantages and challenges, including the type of audience it attracts, selling fees, and the level of exposure provided. Understanding these factors helps in selecting the most suitable platform for your items.

- Exploring Alternatives: Beyond traditional venues, options like consignment stores, flea markets, and private sales offer additional flexibility and may better suit certain selling goals.

7.4 Marketing Your Collection

- Crafting Listings: Effective marketing begins with creating detailed and engaging listings. Well-written descriptions paired with high-quality photos help attract potential buyers.

- Promotional Channels: Utilizing a mix of social media, online communities, and traditional channels like collector magazines broadens the reach of your marketing efforts, increasing the chances of a successful sale.

- Incentives for Buyers: Offering incentives such as discounts, limited-time offers, or bundles can entice buyers and stimulate sales, especially in competitive markets.

7.5 Negotiating Sales

- Setting a Minimum Price: Before entering negotiations, it's crucial to set a minimum acceptable price to ensure that sales remain within your desired profit range.

- Effective Communication: Successful negotiation involves clear and respectful communication with buyers. Justifying your price with facts and remaining open to offers can lead to favorable outcomes.

- Handling Counteroffers: Responding positively to counteroffers and finalizing the sale with clear terms helps in building trust. Following up with buyers after the sale can also lead to lasting relationships and potential future sales.

Chapter 7 equips collectors with the knowledge and strategies needed to effectively sell antiques and collectibles. By focusing on thorough preparation, competitive pricing, selecting the right selling venues, effective marketing, and skillful negotiation, sellers can maximize their sales potential and achieve successful outcomes. This chapter is essential for anyone looking to navigate the complexities of selling in the antiques and collectibles market with confidence and professionalism.

Chapter 8: Historical Context and Case Studies

Understanding the historical context and stories behind antiques and collectibles adds depth to the collecting experience and can significantly enhance the value of your items. This chapter delves into the fascinating histories of famous antiques, offers lessons from notable collectors, presents case studies of unique finds, explores the impact of historical events on collecting, and provides guidance on researching your antiques.

8.1 Famous Antiques and Their Stories

The stories behind famous antiques are often as valuable as the items themselves. These tales of discovery, ownership, and historical significance not only enhance the appeal of these treasures but also offer fascinating insights into the cultures and eras from which they originated. In this section, we explore some of the most renowned antiques and the captivating stories that accompany them.

1. The Fabergé Eggs

A. Origins and Craftsmanship

- Symbol of Opulence: The Fabergé Eggs, created by the House of Fabergé in Russia, are among the most famous and luxurious items in the world of antiques. Commissioned by the Russian Tsars Alexander III and Nicholas II as Easter gifts for their wives, these eggs are celebrated for their intricate design, precious materials, and exquisite craftsmanship.

- Hidden Surprises: Each egg contains a hidden surprise, such as a miniature portrait, a mechanical bird, or a model of a palace, symbolizing the opulence and creativity of the Russian Imperial Court.

B. The Fate of the Eggs

- Lost Treasures: Of the 50 Imperial Fabergé Eggs made, several were lost during the Russian Revolution, leading to a global hunt for these missing treasures.

- Ongoing Search: Some have been recovered in the most unexpected places, such as private collections or obscure auctions. The story of the Fabergé Eggs continues to captivate collectors and historians alike, as efforts to locate the missing eggs and preserve the known ones are ongoing.

2. The Hope Diamond

A. Legendary Origins and Curse

- Mystical Gem: The Hope Diamond, one of the most famous gemstones in the world, is renowned not only for its stunning blue hue but also for the legends of misfortune that surround it.

- A Storied Past: Originally mined in India, the diamond has passed through the hands of kings, merchants, and collectors, each leaving their mark on its storied history. The diamond is said to carry a curse, bringing misfortune and tragedy to its owners.

B. Journey to the Smithsonian

- Gift to the Nation: After passing through numerous owners, the Hope Diamond was donated to the Smithsonian Institution by jeweler Harry Winston in 1958, where it has become one of the most popular exhibits.

- Enduring Allure: The diamond's journey from the courts of France to its current home in the Smithsonian is a testament to its enduring allure and the mysteries that continue to surround it.

3. The Rosetta Stone

A. Discovery and Historical Impact

- Key to Ancient Egypt: The Rosetta Stone, discovered in 1799 by French soldiers during Napoleon's campaign in Egypt, is a granodiorite stele inscribed with a decree issued in 196 BC. What makes this artifact extraordinary is that the decree is written in three scripts: Greek, Demotic, and Hieroglyphic.

- Unlocking History: The stone provided the key to deciphering Egyptian hieroglyphs, a breakthrough that unlocked the history and culture of ancient Egypt for the modern world.

B. Role in Egyptology

- Cornerstone of Egyptology: The Rosetta Stone's contribution to the field of Egyptology cannot be overstated. It became the cornerstone for scholars like Jean-François Champollion, who successfully translated the hieroglyphs, forever changing our understanding of ancient civilizations.

- Preserved Legacy: Today, the Rosetta Stone is housed in the British Museum, where it remains one of the most visited and revered artifacts.

4. The Amber Room

A. The Lost Jewel of Prussia

- Eighth Wonder of the World: The Amber Room, often referred to as the "Eighth Wonder of the World," was a chamber decorated in amber panels, gold leaf, and mirrors. Originally constructed in the 18th century for the Prussian King Frederick I, it was later gifted to Tsar Peter the Great of Russia.

- War-Time Mystery: During World War II, the room was looted by Nazi forces and transported to Königsberg, where it was lost in the chaos of the war's end. Its current whereabouts remain a mystery, fueling numerous searches and theories over the decades.

B. Efforts to Recreate and Recover

- Recreation: In the years following the war, several attempts were made to locate the Amber Room, but it remains one of the greatest unsolved mysteries of World War II.

- Modern Tribute: A replica of the Amber Room was completed in 2003 and installed in the Catherine Palace near St. Petersburg, Russia, but the original's fate continues to intrigue historians, treasure hunters, and collectors.

5. The Sutton Hoo Treasure

A. Discovery and Significance

- Anglo-Saxon Wealth: The Sutton Hoo treasure, discovered in 1939 in Suffolk, England, is one of the most significant archaeological finds in British history.

The burial site, dating back to the 7th century, contained a ship and a wealth of Anglo-Saxon artifacts, including a helmet, shield, and gold jewelry.

- Royal Burial: The treasure is believed to be the grave goods of a king, possibly Rædwald of East Anglia, and provides invaluable insights into early medieval England.

B. Impact on British Archaeology

- Challenging Perceptions: The discovery of the Sutton Hoo treasure revolutionized our understanding of the Anglo-Saxon period, challenging previous notions of the "Dark Ages" as a time of cultural and economic decline.

- Cultural Heritage: The artifacts from Sutton Hoo are now housed in the British Museum, where they continue to draw visitors and inspire further study of Britain's ancient past.

Famous antiques like the Fabergé Eggs, the Hope Diamond, and the Rosetta Stone not only represent incredible craftsmanship but also carry stories that have shaped history. Their journeys through time, the people who owned them, and the legends that surround them add layers of meaning and value, making them treasured not just for their material worth, but for the narratives they embody.

8.2 Lessons from Notable Collectors

The world of antiques and collectibles is enriched by the experiences and wisdom of notable collectors who have dedicated their lives to the pursuit of rare and valuable items. These individuals offer invaluable lessons on how to approach collecting with passion, strategy, and a keen eye for detail. In this section, we'll explore the strategies, philosophies, and key takeaways from some of the most renowned collectors in history.

1. Strategic Collecting: J. Paul Getty

A. Focused Specialization

- Building Expertise: J. Paul Getty, one of the wealthiest men in history and a legendary art collector, emphasized the importance of specialization in building a meaningful collection. Rather than collecting indiscriminately, Getty focused on specific categories that deeply interested him, such as European paintings, Greek and Roman antiquities, and Renaissance art.

- Lesson: Specializing in a particular area of interest allows collectors to develop deep knowledge and expertise, leading to more informed and strategic acquisitions. This focus helps in building a cohesive and valuable collection that tells a story.

B. Negotiation and Patience

- Shrewd Acquisition: Getty was known for his shrewd negotiation skills and his patience in acquiring pieces at the right price. He often waited for years to purchase a particular item, using market fluctuations and seller circumstances to his advantage.

- Lesson: Patience and negotiation are key to successful collecting. Rather than rushing into purchases, collectors should be willing to wait for the right opportunity to acquire items at a fair price, maximizing their investment.

2. Building a Legacy: Isabella Stewart Gardner

A. Creating a Personal Vision

- Curating with Passion: Isabella Stewart Gardner, an American art collector and philanthropist, was passionate about creating a collection that reflected her personal tastes and vision. She meticulously curated her collection, which includes masterpieces from artists like Rembrandt, Vermeer, and Botticelli, and displayed them in her museum in Boston, arranged according to her unique aesthetic.

- Lesson: Collecting is a deeply personal endeavor, and building a collection that reflects your individual tastes and interests can create a legacy that resonates with others. Gardner's collection remains a testament to her vision and continues to inspire visitors to her museum.

B. Preserving and Sharing

- Ensuring Longevity: Gardner was not only focused on acquiring art but also on preserving it for future generations. She established the Isabella Stewart Gardner

Museum, ensuring that her collection would be preserved and accessible to the public long after her death.

- Lesson: Collectors should think beyond their lifetime and consider how their collections can be preserved and shared with others. Establishing trusts, donating to museums, or creating private foundations are ways to ensure that a collection's legacy endures.

3. The Power of Passion: Henry Clay Frick

A. Passion-Driven Collecting

- Love for Craftsmanship: Henry Clay Frick, an American industrialist and art patron, collected with an intense passion for the works he loved. His collection, which includes Old Master paintings, fine furniture, and decorative arts, reflects his deep appreciation for beauty and craftsmanship.

- Lesson: Passion is a driving force in collecting. Collectors who pursue items that resonate with them on a personal level are more likely to build collections that are both meaningful and valuable. Passionate collecting also leads to a more enjoyable and fulfilling experience.

B. Combining Art and Architecture

- Harmonizing Display: Frick's approach to collecting extended beyond individual pieces to the environment in which they were displayed. He commissioned the construction of The Frick Collection in New York, where art and architecture harmonize to enhance the viewing experience.

- Lesson: The presentation of a collection is as important as the collection itself. Thoughtfully displaying items in a way that complements their aesthetic can significantly enhance the enjoyment and value of a collection.

4. Risk-Taking and Innovation: Peggy Guggenheim

A. Championing Modern Art

- Embracing the New: Peggy Guggenheim, an American art collector and bohemian, was known for her adventurous spirit and willingness to take risks in her collecting. She was an early supporter of avant-garde artists like Jackson

Pollock, Marcel Duchamp, and Max Ernst, acquiring their works before they became widely recognized.

- Lesson: Innovation and risk-taking are essential for collectors who want to be ahead of the curve. By supporting emerging artists or investing in underappreciated genres, collectors can shape the future of the art world and potentially see significant appreciation in the value of their collection.

B. Creating a Cultural Hub

- Cultural Integration: Guggenheim's collection was not just about acquiring art; it was about creating a vibrant cultural hub. Her Venetian palace, where she displayed her collection, became a gathering place for artists, intellectuals, and cultural figures.

- Lesson: A collection can be more than just a personal treasure trove; it can be a living, breathing part of the cultural landscape. Engaging with the art community and sharing your collection with others can elevate its significance and impact.

5. The Importance of Ethics: Andrew Mellon

A. Ethical Acquisition

- Upholding Integrity: Andrew Mellon, a U.S. Secretary of the Treasury and art collector, was deeply committed to ethical collecting. He focused on acquiring art through legitimate channels and was conscious of the provenance of the items he purchased.

- Lesson: Ethical considerations are paramount in collecting. Ensuring that items are acquired legally and with clear provenance not only protects the collector from legal issues but also upholds the integrity of the collection.

B. Philanthropy and Public Access

- Public Contribution: Mellon's commitment to the public good led him to donate his extensive art collection to the nation, forming the core of the National Gallery of Art in Washington, D.C.

- Lesson: Collectors have the opportunity to contribute to the public good by making their collections accessible to others. Whether through donations, loans, or public exhibitions, sharing a collection can enrich the cultural heritage of a community or nation.

The experiences of notable collectors like J. Paul Getty, Isabella Stewart Gardner, Henry Clay Frick, Peggy Guggenheim, and Andrew Mellon offer valuable lessons for anyone interested in building a meaningful and successful collection. By focusing on specialization, patience, passion, ethical acquisition, and legacy-building, collectors can create collections that not only reflect their personal interests but also contribute to the broader cultural landscape.

8.3 Case Studies of Unique Finds

The world of antiques and collectibles is filled with stories of unique finds that have captured the imagination of collectors and scholars alike. These discoveries, often made by chance or through dedicated searching, highlight the excitement and unpredictability of collecting. In this section, we explore several case studies of remarkable finds, examining the circumstances of their discovery, their significance, and the impact they had on the world of antiques.

1. The Staffordshire Hoard

A. Discovery by an Amateur Detectorist

- Persistence Rewarded: The Staffordshire Hoard, the largest collection of Anglo-Saxon gold and silver metalwork ever found, was discovered in 2009 by Terry Herbert, an amateur metal detectorist, in a farmer's field in Staffordshire, England. Herbert's discovery was the result of years of metal detecting, highlighting how persistence and passion can lead to extraordinary finds.

B. Significance and Impact

- Anglo-Saxon Legacy: The hoard consists of over 3,500 items, including sword fittings, helmet fragments, and religious artifacts, all dating back to the 7th century. It provides invaluable insights into the craftsmanship, warfare, and culture of the Anglo-Saxon period. The Staffordshire Hoard has since been studied extensively, reshaping our understanding of early medieval England. The items are now displayed in museums, drawing interest from the public and scholars alike.

C. The Role of Collaboration in Preservation

- Shared Heritage: Following its discovery, the Staffordshire Hoard was jointly acquired by the Birmingham Museum and Art Gallery and the Potteries Museum & Art Gallery, ensuring that it remains accessible to the public and preserved for future generations.

- Lesson: This case study underscores the importance of collaboration between collectors, museums, and historians in preserving and interpreting significant finds.

2. The Sutton Hoo Ship Burial

A. The Remarkable Find

- Buried Treasure: In 1939, archaeologists uncovered an Anglo-Saxon ship burial at Sutton Hoo in Suffolk, England. The site contained a wealth of artifacts, including a ceremonial helmet, weapons, jewelry, and a magnificent shield, believed to be the grave goods of a king, possibly Rædwald of East Anglia. The burial site was discovered on the estate of Edith Pretty, who had long suspected that the mounds on her land concealed something significant. Her decision to involve professional archaeologists led to one of the most important archaeological finds in British history.

B. Historical and Cultural Importance

- Anglo-Saxon Insights: The Sutton Hoo ship burial has provided invaluable insights into the early medieval period, shedding light on the wealth, power, and cultural connections of the Anglo-Saxon elite. The artifacts from Sutton Hoo are now housed in the British Museum, where they continue to be studied and admired, contributing to our understanding of this pivotal era in British history.

C. The Legacy of the Discovery

- Enduring Influence: The discovery of Sutton Hoo has had a lasting impact on the field of archaeology and the public's interest in early medieval history. It has inspired further research and exploration of similar burial sites across Europe.

- Lesson: This case study highlights the importance of professional expertise in uncovering and preserving historical treasures, as well as the lasting legacy that such discoveries can create.

3. The Lost Leonardo: Salvator Mundi

A. Rediscovery and Authentication

- A Masterpiece Unveiled: The painting *Salvator Mundi*, attributed to Leonardo da Vinci, was rediscovered in 2005 at a small regional auction in the United States, where it was sold for a relatively modest sum, as it was thought to be a copy. After extensive restoration and authentication efforts by experts, it was identified as an original work by Leonardo da Vinci, one of the few known to exist in private hands.

B. The Controversy and Auction

- Debate and Value: The painting's authenticity has been the subject of debate among scholars, with some questioning whether it was indeed painted by Leonardo. Despite the controversy, *Salvator Mundi* was auctioned by Christie's in 2017 for a record-breaking $450.3 million, making it the most expensive painting ever sold. This case illustrates the complexities and challenges involved in the authentication and valuation of high-profile art.

C. The Impact on the Art Market

- Market Dynamics: The sale of *Salvator Mundi* has had a significant impact on the art market, highlighting both the allure and the risks associated with collecting high-value art. The painting's story has captivated the public, sparking discussions about art, authenticity, and value.

- Lesson: This case study demonstrates the potential for incredible discoveries in the world of art, as well as the importance of careful research, expert authentication, and the role of market forces in determining value.

4. The Codex Leicester

A. A Scientific Treasure

- Leonardo's Legacy: The *Codex Leicester*, a 72-page manuscript by Leonardo da Vinci, is one of the most famous scientific journals in history. The codex contains Leonardo's observations on a wide range of subjects, including astronomy, geology, and the movement of water. The manuscript was rediscovered in the 18th century and has since passed through the hands of several prominent collectors, including Thomas Coke, Earl of Leicester, who gave it its name.

B. The Bill Gates Acquisition

- Modern Patronage: In 1994, the *Codex Leicester* was purchased by Bill Gates for $30.8 million, making it one of the most expensive books ever sold. Gates has since made the manuscript accessible to the public through digital reproductions and has loaned it to museums around the world. The acquisition of the codex by a modern technology mogul underscores the enduring value of historical documents and their relevance to contemporary audiences.

C. The Value of Intellectual Heritage

- Inspiring Generations: The *Codex Leicester* is not just a valuable artifact; it represents the intellectual heritage of one of history's greatest minds. Its contents continue to inspire scientists, historians, and the general public, demonstrating the lasting impact of Leonardo's genius.

- Lesson: This case study highlights the importance of preserving and sharing intellectual treasures, ensuring that they remain accessible to future generations.

5. *The Dead Sea Scrolls*

A. Discovery and Initial Reaction

- Ancient Scriptures Uncovered: The Dead Sea Scrolls, a collection of ancient Jewish manuscripts, were discovered in the 1940s by Bedouin shepherds in the Qumran caves near the Dead Sea. These scrolls, dating back to the 3rd century BCE, include some of the oldest known manuscripts of the Hebrew Bible. The discovery of the scrolls was initially met with skepticism, but subsequent research confirmed their authenticity and significance.

B. The Impact on Biblical Scholarship

- Scriptural Insights: The Dead Sea Scrolls have had a profound impact on biblical scholarship, providing insights into the development of the Hebrew Bible and the religious practices of the Second Temple period. The scrolls are now housed in the Shrine of the Book in Jerusalem, where they continue to be studied and admired by scholars and visitors alike.

C. The Ongoing Study and Preservation

- Collaborative Efforts: The preservation and study of the Dead Sea Scrolls have involved international collaboration, with scholars working to piece together fragmented texts and translate their contents.

- Lesson: This case study emphasizes the importance of careful preservation, scholarly collaboration, and the ongoing study of ancient texts to unlock their full historical and cultural significance.

The case studies of unique finds like the Staffordshire Hoard, the Sutton Hoo ship burial, *Salvator Mundi*, the *Codex Leicester*, and the Dead Sea Scrolls demonstrate the thrill and significance of discovering historical treasures. These finds not only add to our knowledge of the past but also inspire future generations of collectors, historians, and scholars. Whether discovered by chance or through diligent searching, these treasures continue to captivate the world with their stories and impact.

8.4 The Impact of Historical Events on Collecting

Historical events have profoundly shaped the world of antiques and collectibles, influencing the availability, value, and movement of items across the globe. Wars, revolutions, economic shifts, and cultural changes have all left their mark on what is collected, how it is valued, and who owns it. In this section, we explore the impact of key historical events on collecting, examining how they have altered the landscape of antiques and collectibles.

1. Wars and Conflicts

A. Looting and Displacement

- Cultural Losses: Wars and conflicts, such as World War II, have led to widespread looting and displacement of cultural treasures. The Nazi regime, for example, systematically looted art and cultural artifacts from occupied territories, resulting in the displacement of thousands of items. Many of these pieces were never recovered, while others surfaced in private collections or on the art market, often under controversial circumstances.

B. Recovery Efforts Post-Conflict

- Restoring Heritage: After wars, recovery efforts are crucial in restoring looted or displaced items to their rightful owners. The Monuments Men, a group of Allied soldiers and civilians during World War II, were instrumental in recovering and returning art stolen by the Nazis. Their work laid the foundation for modern practices in art recovery and restitution, emphasizing the importance of provenance research and ethical collecting.

2. Revolutions and Regime Changes

A. Russian Revolution and Imperial Treasures

- Imperial Dispersal: The Russian Revolution of 1917 led to the downfall of the Romanov dynasty and the dispersal of the Russian Imperial collection. Many treasures from the Hermitage Museum and other royal collections were sold by the Soviet government to raise funds, ending up in private collections and museums around the world. These sales made Russian imperial items highly sought after but also raised complex ethical questions about acquiring items sold under duress.

B. Impact of the Chinese Cultural Revolution

- Cultural Destruction and Smuggling: The Chinese Cultural Revolution (1966-1976) had a devastating effect on China's cultural heritage, with many antiques, religious artifacts, and historical relics destroyed or defaced in an effort to eradicate the "Four Olds." However, the revolution also led to the smuggling of valuable Chinese artifacts out of the country, where they were preserved in private collections and museums abroad. Today, there is a growing movement to repatriate these items to China, reflecting broader efforts to reclaim cultural heritage.

3. Economic Booms and Busts

A. Roaring Twenties and the Great Depression

- Market Fluctuations: The economic boom of the 1920s, known as the Roaring Twenties, saw significant growth in the art and antiques market. Wealthy individuals and institutions invested heavily in collecting, leading to a surge in demand for fine art, decorative arts, and antiques. However, the stock market crash of 1929 and the subsequent Great Depression dramatically impacted the market, with many collectors forced to sell their collections at a loss.

B. Post-War Economic Expansion

- Middle-Class Collecting: The economic expansion following World War II led to renewed interest in collecting, particularly among the burgeoning middle class. This period saw the rise of mass-produced collectibles and a growing interest in historical items reflecting nostalgia for pre-war and Victorian eras. The prosperity of these years also fueled the growth of the antiques trade, with dealers, auction houses, and fairs flourishing.

4. Cultural Shifts and Movements

A. Arts and Crafts Movement's Influence

- Craftsmanship Over Mass Production: The Arts and Crafts Movement of the late 19th and early 20th centuries was a response to the industrialization of society and the mass production of goods. Advocates like William Morris emphasized the importance of craftsmanship, quality materials, and the beauty of handcrafted items. This cultural shift significantly impacted collecting, as people began seeking items representing the movement's values.

B. Mid-Century Modern Revival

- Design Renaissance: The mid-20th century saw the rise of Mid-Century Modern design, characterized by clean lines, organic forms, and a focus on functionality. This design movement has recently experienced a resurgence in popularity, leading to renewed interest in collecting Mid-Century Modern furniture, lighting, and accessories. Cultural shifts in taste and design preferences often lead to changes in what is collected, as items that were once out of fashion become desirable again.

C. Popular Culture's Impact on Collecting

- Media-Driven Trends: Popular culture significantly influences collecting trends. For example, the success of the television show *Mad Men* sparked renewed interest in 1960s design, leading to a surge in demand for vintage clothing, accessories, and home decor from that era. Similarly, the release of movies or documentaries about historical events or figures can drive interest in related antiques and collectibles.

5. Globalization and the International Art Market

A. Expansion of the Global Market

- Cross-Border Collecting: Globalization has had a profound impact on the antiques and collectibles market, making it easier for items to be bought, sold, and transported across borders. The rise of online auctions and international dealers has expanded the market, allowing collectors to access items from around the world. However, globalization also raises concerns about the ethical implications of collecting items from other cultures, particularly in cases where these items may have been acquired through colonialism or other exploitative practices.

B. Repatriation Movement

- Returning Cultural Heritage: In recent years, there has been a growing movement for the repatriation of cultural artifacts to their countries of origin. This movement has led to the return of significant items, such as the Benin Bronzes to Nigeria and Aboriginal artifacts to Australia, and continues to shape the ethical landscape of collecting. Collectors should be mindful of the origins of the items they acquire and consider the ethical implications of their ownership.

Historical events have left an indelible mark on the world of antiques and collectibles, shaping what is collected, how it is valued, and who owns it. By understanding the impact of wars, revolutions, economic cycles, cultural shifts, and globalization on collecting, collectors can make more informed and ethical decisions, contributing to the preservation and appreciation of cultural heritage.

8.5 How to Research Your Antiques

Researching antiques is a crucial step in understanding their history, provenance, and value. Whether you're a seasoned collector or just starting out, thorough research can provide insights that enhance your appreciation and help you make informed decisions. In this section, we will explore effective strategies and resources for researching antiques, from identifying key characteristics to verifying authenticity and tracing provenance.

1. Identifying Key Characteristics

A. Understanding Materials and Craftsmanship

- Clues to Origin and Age: The materials and craftsmanship of an antique can provide valuable clues about its origin, age, and authenticity. Pay close attention to the type of wood, metal, or fabric used, as well as the construction techniques and finishing details. For example, hand-forged nails, dovetail joints, or hand-painted decorations can indicate the item's age and authenticity.

- Tip: Use reference books or online databases to compare your item with known examples, focusing on the materials and craftsmanship that are characteristic of a particular period or maker.

B. Recognizing Maker's Marks and Signatures

- Identifying Origins: Many antiques feature maker's marks, signatures, or hallmarks that can help identify their origin and authenticity. These marks can include the name or initials of the maker, a symbol representing a workshop, or a hallmark indicating the metal content of silver or gold items.

- Tip: Researching these marks in specialized reference books or online databases can provide critical information about the item's history and value. Be sure to verify the mark's authenticity, as forgeries are not uncommon in the antiques market.

2. Verifying Authenticity

A. Consulting Experts and Appraisers

- Expert Insights: When in doubt, consulting an expert or a professional appraiser can be invaluable in verifying the authenticity of an antique. Experts can provide insights based on their experience and specialized knowledge, and appraisers can offer an objective assessment of an item's value and provenance.

- Tip: Seek out experts or appraisers who specialize in the type of antique you are researching, whether it be furniture, fine art, or jewelry. Their expertise can help you avoid costly mistakes and ensure that you're dealing with a genuine item.

B. Utilizing Scientific Methods

- Scientific Verification: In some cases, scientific methods such as radiocarbon dating, dendrochronology, or spectrographic analysis can be used to verify the age and authenticity of an antique. These methods can provide precise information about the materials and construction, helping to confirm or refute the item's purported origin.

- Tip: While scientific testing can be expensive, it may be worth the investment for high-value items where authenticity is in question. Always use reputable laboratories and experts for such analyses.

3. Tracing Provenance

A. Researching Ownership History

- Historical Ownership: Provenance, or the history of an item's ownership, is a key factor in determining its value and significance. Researching an antique's provenance involves tracing its ownership history, which can sometimes be found in auction records, sales receipts, or estate inventories.

- Tip: Start by gathering any documentation that came with the item, such as receipts or certificates of authenticity. Then, consult auction catalogs, museum records, or archives to trace the item's previous owners and confirm its provenance.

B. Investigating Historical Context

- Understanding Context: Understanding the historical context in which an antique was created or used can provide deeper insights into its significance. Researching the period, culture, and events surrounding the item's creation can help you understand why it was made and how it was used, adding layers of meaning to your collection.

- Tip: Use historical texts, museum exhibitions, and academic publications to place your antique within its broader historical context. This can enhance your appreciation of the item and potentially increase its value.

4. Using Online Resources

A. Accessing Digital Archives and Databases

- Digital Tools: The internet offers a wealth of resources for antique research, including digital archives, online databases, and auction house records. These resources can provide access to historical documents, images of similar items, and records of past sales, all of which can aid in your research.

- Tip: Some useful online resources include the British Museum's Collections Online, the Smithsonian's Collections Search Center, and online auction platforms like Sotheby's or Christie's. Be sure to cross-reference information from multiple sources to ensure accuracy.

B. Participating in Online Forums and Communities

- Community Knowledge: Online forums and communities dedicated to antiques can be a valuable resource for research. These platforms allow collectors to share information, ask questions, and discuss their findings with others who have similar interests and expertise.

- Tip: Engage with online communities such as forums on antique websites, social media groups, or collector associations. These communities can provide practical advice, help identify items, and connect you with experts who can assist in your research.

5. Consulting Reference Books and Catalogs

A. Utilizing Specialized Reference Books

- In-Depth Research: Reference books are an essential tool for any antique collector. These books provide detailed information on specific types of antiques, including maker's marks, production techniques, and historical context. Having a well-curated library of reference books can greatly enhance your research efforts.

- Tip: Invest in reputable reference books that cover the specific categories of antiques you are interested in. Books by recognized experts or those published by museums often provide the most reliable information.

B. Reviewing Auction Catalogs

- Market Insights: Auction catalogs from major auction houses often include detailed descriptions, provenance information, and images of the items sold.

These catalogs can be invaluable resources for researching similar items, understanding market trends, and assessing the value of your antiques.

- Tip: Collect auction catalogs related to your areas of interest, and use them to compare your items with those that have been previously sold. This can provide insights into both the value and the history of your antiques.

Researching your antiques is an essential part of collecting, providing you with the knowledge to appreciate, value, and care for your items properly. By utilizing a combination of historical research, expert consultation, and modern technology, you can uncover the stories behind your antiques, ensuring they are accurately documented and preserved for future generations.

Chapter 8 Review: Historical Context and Case Studies in Antiques and Collectibles

Chapter 8 of *HowExpert Guide to Antiques and Collectibles* delves into the historical context and provides illuminating case studies within the world of antiques and collectibles. This chapter offers valuable insights into how historical events influence collecting, the lessons learned from legendary collectors, and guidance on researching antiques. Here's a detailed review of the key points covered:

8.1 Famous Antiques and Their Stories

- Fabergé Eggs: Crafted for the Russian Tsars, these exquisite pieces are renowned for their intricate designs and hidden surprises, symbolizing luxury and imperial opulence.

- Hope Diamond: Known for its deep blue hue, the Hope Diamond carries a legend of a curse, adding to its mystique and appeal among collectors.

- Rosetta Stone: This artifact was crucial in deciphering Egyptian hieroglyphs, making it a cornerstone in the study of ancient civilizations and highly valued in the antiquities market.

8.2 Lessons from Notable Collectors

- J. Paul Getty: Advocated for a focused, patient approach to collecting, emphasizing the importance of specialization in building a meaningful collection.

- Isabella Stewart Gardner: Her collection reflects a personal vision, with a strong emphasis on preservation and legacy, serving as a model for collectors who wish to create a lasting impact.

- Henry Clay Frick: His passion for integrating art with architecture is exemplified in The Frick Collection, highlighting the importance of environment in the presentation of a collection.

- Peggy Guggenheim: Known for her bold choices and support of modern art, Guggenheim's approach underscores the value of taking risks and creating cultural hubs.

- Andrew Mellon: Focused on ethical acquisition, Mellon's contributions to the National Gallery of Art emphasize the importance of public access and cultural responsibility.

8.3 Case Studies of Unique Finds

- Staffordshire Hoard: Discovered by an amateur detectorist, this find sheds light on Anglo-Saxon craftsmanship and the historical significance of such discoveries.

- Sutton Hoo Ship Burial: The unearthing of this burial site revealed significant Anglo-Saxon artifacts, reshaping our understanding of early medieval England.

- Salvator Mundi: This rediscovered painting, attributed to Leonardo da Vinci, sparked debates over its authenticity and achieved a record-breaking auction price, illustrating the high stakes of art authentication.

- Codex Leicester: Leonardo da Vinci's scientific journal is a prime example of the value placed on intellectual heritage and the enduring fascination with the Renaissance genius.

- Dead Sea Scrolls: These ancient manuscripts offer profound insights into early biblical texts, highlighting the importance of preservation and the collaborative efforts required in the study of such significant artifacts.

8.4 The Impact of Historical Events on Collecting

- Wars and Conflicts: The chapter discusses the looting and displacement of cultural treasures during wars, emphasizing the importance of recovery efforts and the ethical considerations of post-conflict collecting.

- Revolutions and Regime Changes: These events often lead to the dispersal of imperial treasures, influencing collecting trends and raising ethical questions regarding ownership and repatriation.

- Economic Booms and Busts: Economic cycles, such as the Roaring Twenties and the Great Depression, significantly impact the antiques market, affecting both availability and pricing of collectibles.

- Cultural Shifts: Movements like the Arts and Crafts Movement and the Mid-Century Modern Revival have shaped what is collected, reflecting broader societal trends and tastes.

- Globalization: The expansion of the international art market and the increasing importance of ethical collecting, including the repatriation movement, are highlighted as key trends affecting modern collecting.

8.5 How to Research Your Antiques

- Identifying Key Characteristics: This section guides collectors on how to understand materials, craftsmanship, and recognize maker's marks, which are crucial in identifying and valuing antiques.

- Verifying Authenticity: Consulting experts and utilizing scientific methods for authentication are emphasized as essential steps in confirming the legitimacy of an item.

- Tracing Provenance: Researching the ownership history and investigating the historical context of an item are crucial for establishing its value and authenticity.

- Using Online Resources: Access to digital archives, participation in online forums, and the use of specialized websites are recommended for collectors looking to expand their research capabilities.

- Consulting Reference Books and Catalogs: The chapter advises utilizing specialized books and auction catalogs as valuable resources for detailed research and understanding market trends.

Chapter 8 provides collectors with essential knowledge on the historical context of antiques and collectibles, drawing from notable case studies and the experiences of legendary collectors. It underscores the importance of ethical collecting, thorough research, and understanding the broader historical and cultural influences that shape the collecting world. This chapter equips collectors with the insights needed to make informed decisions and appreciate the deeper significance of the items in their collections.

Chapter 9: Legal and Ethical Considerations

The world of antiques and collectibles is not just about the thrill of discovery and the beauty of historical artifacts; it also involves navigating complex legal and ethical landscapes. As a collector, understanding these considerations is crucial to building and maintaining a reputable and valuable collection. This chapter provides a comprehensive guide to the key legal and ethical issues you must be aware of, from understanding provenance to dealing with fakes and forgeries.

9.1 Understanding Provenance

Provenance is one of the most critical aspects of collecting antiques and collectibles, serving as a documented history that traces an item's ownership and origins. It plays a pivotal role in establishing an item's authenticity, legality, and value. This section delves into the importance of provenance, how to research it, and the best practices for documenting and maintaining it.

1. The Importance of Provenance

A. Authenticity and Verification

- Provenance as a Chain of Custody: Provenance acts as a chain of custody that links an item to its historical origins, verifying its authenticity. For collectors, provenance is the cornerstone of an item's credibility. Without it, even the most beautiful or seemingly authentic piece can be suspect.

- Relying on Provenance for Assurance: Collectors and buyers rely on provenance to ensure that an item is genuine and not a forgery or reproduction. This is particularly important for high-value items, where the financial stakes are higher.

B. Enhancing Value and Marketability

- Adding Value Through History: Provenance can significantly enhance the value of an antique or collectible. Items with documented histories connecting them to notable people, events, or collections are often more desirable and can command higher prices.

- Examples of Enhanced Value: A painting once owned by a famous collector or exhibited in a renowned museum will be valued more than a similar piece with an unknown history. In the art world, provenance can be the difference between a record-breaking sale and a piece that struggles to find a buyer.

C. Legal and Ethical Considerations

- Ensuring Legal Acquisition: Provenance is crucial in ensuring that an item has been acquired legally and ethically. It confirms that the item was not looted, stolen, or illegally exported, which is especially important for items from conflict zones or regions with strict cultural heritage laws.

- Avoiding Legal Challenges: Collectors who unknowingly purchase items with dubious provenance may face legal challenges, including the potential seizure of the item. Provenance protects collectors from these risks by providing a clear history of ownership.

2. Researching Provenance

A. Gathering Existing Documentation

- Initial Documentation: The first step in establishing provenance is to gather any existing documentation related to the item. This might include sales receipts, certificates of authenticity, auction catalogs, exhibition records, and previous ownership details.

- Tracing the Item's Journey: These documents provide the initial clues about the item's history and are invaluable in tracing its journey through time. For example, a receipt from a reputable auction house can confirm when and where an item was sold.

B. Investigating Ownership History

- Creating a Continuous Chain: To fully establish provenance, it is often necessary to research the ownership history of an item. This involves delving into public records, archives, and databases to trace previous owners and transactions.

- Contacting Previous Owners: In some cases, this may involve contacting previous owners or their descendants to gather additional information. Historical research may also be required to understand the context in which the item was created and how it changed hands over the years.

C. Consulting Experts and Institutions

- Seeking Expert Assistance: Provenance research can be complex, and expert assistance may be required. Art historians, museum curators, and provenance researchers specialize in tracing the histories of items and can provide valuable insights.

- Collaborating with Institutions: Institutions like museums and libraries may hold relevant records, such as exhibition catalogs, donor records, or correspondence, that can help establish provenance. Collaborating with experts can also lend additional credibility to the provenance of an item.

D. Cross-Referencing with Reputable Sources

- Ensuring Accuracy: Cross-referencing the information gathered from various sources is essential to ensure the accuracy and completeness of the provenance. This can involve comparing the item with similar pieces in museum collections, auction records, or academic publications.

- Resolving Inconsistencies: Cross-referencing can help identify inconsistencies or gaps in the provenance, such as periods where the item's whereabouts are unknown or where ownership claims conflict. Resolving these issues is crucial to establishing a clear and credible provenance.

3. Documenting Provenance

A. Creating a Provenance Report

- Detailed Documentation: Once provenance has been established, it is important to document it clearly and systematically. A provenance report should include all relevant details, such as the names of previous owners, dates of ownership, and supporting documentation.

- Narrative and Significance: The report should also include a narrative that explains the significance of the provenance, highlighting any connections to notable individuals, events, or institutions. This report serves as a permanent record that can be passed on to future owners.

B. Maintaining Records and Updating Provenance

- Ongoing Record Maintenance: Provenance is not static; it evolves as an item changes hands. Maintaining and updating provenance records whenever an item is sold, loaned, or transferred is crucial.

- Adding New Information: As new information comes to light, it should be added to the provenance report, along with any additional documentation that supports the item's history. This ensures that the provenance remains intact and reliable.

C. Digital Documentation and Storage

- Secure Digital Storage: In the digital age, storing provenance records securely and making them accessible is vital. Digital documentation allows for easy sharing and backup of provenance information.

- Utilizing Digital Platforms: Consider using digital platforms that specialize in cataloging and managing provenance for collectors. This not only safeguards the information but also makes it more accessible for future research and verification.

Provenance is essential for any serious collector. It provides the foundation for authenticating items, ensuring legal ownership, and enhancing value. By carefully researching, documenting, and maintaining provenance, collectors can protect their investments and contribute to the preservation of cultural heritage.

9.2 Legal Aspects of Buying and Selling

The legal framework surrounding the buying and selling of antiques and collectibles is complex, encompassing various regulations, contracts, and consumer protection laws. Understanding these legal aspects is crucial for both buyers and sellers to ensure that transactions are conducted fairly, transparently, and within the bounds of the law. This section provides a comprehensive guide to key legal considerations in the antiques market, from creating contracts to understanding buyer and seller responsibilities.

1. Contracts and Agreements

A. Importance of Clear Contracts

- Protecting Both Parties: In the world of antiques and collectibles, every transaction should be formalized with a clear, legally binding contract. A well-drafted contract protects both the buyer and the seller by outlining the terms of the sale, including item descriptions, pricing, payment terms, delivery conditions, and any warranties or guarantees.

- Avoiding Disputes: Without a contract, misunderstandings or unmet expectations can lead to disputes. A clear contract helps prevent these issues by ensuring that all parties agree on the transaction's specifics.

B. Key Elements of a Contract

- Item Description: A detailed description of the item being sold, including known defects, restorations, or alterations, is essential.

- Price and Payment Terms: The agreed sale price and the terms of payment, including any deposits or installment plans, should be clearly stated.

- Transfer of Ownership: The contract should specify when ownership of the item transfers from the seller to the buyer, typically upon full payment.

- Warranties and Guarantees: Any warranties or guarantees provided by the seller regarding the item's authenticity, condition, or provenance should be included.

- Dispute Resolution: Provisions for resolving disputes—whether through arbitration, mediation, or court proceedings—should be clearly outlined.

C. Legal Enforceability

- Compliance with Laws: For a contract to be legally enforceable, it must comply with the relevant laws in the jurisdiction where the transaction occurs. This includes adhering to consumer protection laws, ensuring both parties sign the contract, and that all terms are clearly stated and understood.

- Legal Review: In high-value transactions or international sales, having the contract reviewed by a legal professional is advisable to ensure that all legal aspects are covered.

2. *Buyer and Seller Responsibilities*

A. Due Diligence by Buyers

- Verifying Authenticity: Buyers are responsible for conducting due diligence before purchasing an antique or collectible. This involves verifying the item's authenticity, condition, and provenance, and ensuring the seller has legal title to sell it.

- Researching the Item: Investigating the item's history, maker, and market value is crucial to ensure it aligns with the seller's description.

- Inspecting the Item: If possible, buyers should physically inspect the item or request detailed photographs and condition reports to confirm its state.

- Verifying Provenance: Ensuring the item comes with appropriate documentation that traces its ownership history and confirms its authenticity is a key part of the due diligence process.

B. Seller Obligations

- Accurate Disclosure: Sellers are legally obligated to provide accurate and truthful information about the items they are selling. This includes disclosing any known defects, repairs, or restorations that may affect the item's value.

- Authenticity Claims: Sellers should only make claims about an item's authenticity or provenance that can be substantiated with documentation or expert opinion.

- Legal Title: Sellers must confirm that they have clear legal title to the item and the right to sell it. Selling stolen or illegally obtained items can lead to severe legal consequences.

C. Consumer Protection Laws

- Right to Return: In many jurisdictions, consumer protection laws apply to the sale of antiques and collectibles. Buyers may have the right to return items within a certain period if they were misled or if the item is not as described.

- Refund Policies: Sellers may be required to offer refunds or exchanges if the item is found to be defective or not as advertised.

- Transparency: Sellers must provide clear and accurate descriptions of items, including all relevant information that could influence a buyer's decision.

3. International Transactions

A. Cross-Border Legal Considerations

- Import/Export Laws: International transactions introduce additional complexities, such as navigating import/export laws that may restrict certain items or require special permits.

- Currency and Taxation: Issues related to currency exchange rates, international taxes, and duties must be addressed in international sales.

- Jurisdictional Disputes: Determining which country's laws will govern the contract and where any legal disputes will be resolved is essential in cross-border transactions.

B. International Sales Contracts

- Shipping and Insurance: International sales contracts should clearly define who is responsible for shipping, insurance, and any damages that may occur during transit.

- Compliance with Local Laws: Both parties must be aware of and comply with the legal requirements of their respective countries.

- Language and Currency: The contract should specify the language in which it will be interpreted and the currency in which payments will be made.

C. Legal Recourse and Dispute Resolution

- Arbitration Clauses: Including arbitration clauses in the contract can provide a faster, less expensive way to resolve disputes than going to court.

- Choice of Law: The contract should specify which country's laws will govern the transaction and where legal proceedings will take place if necessary.

Understanding the legal aspects of buying and selling antiques and collectibles is essential for protecting your investments and ensuring that transactions are conducted fairly and transparently. By creating clear contracts, fulfilling buyer and seller responsibilities, and navigating the complexities of international transactions, collectors can minimize legal risks and build a reputable and successful collection.

9.3 Ethical Collecting Practices

Ethical considerations are paramount in the world of antiques and collectibles. As custodians of cultural heritage, collectors bear the responsibility of ensuring that their actions do not contribute to the exploitation or degradation of cultural artifacts. Ethical collecting involves understanding the broader impact of acquiring, selling, and preserving items, and making informed decisions that respect the cultural, historical, and legal contexts of the items in question. This section explores the key principles and practices that define ethical collecting.

1. Cultural Sensitivity and Respect

A. Respecting Cultural Heritage

- Understanding Cultural Significance: Collectors must recognize that many antiques and collectibles are not just valuable objects but are deeply connected to the cultural identity and heritage of specific communities. Ethical collecting requires a commitment to respecting the origins of these items and ensuring that their acquisition does not contribute to cultural erosion or exploitation.

- Honoring Traditions: Ethical collectors should honor the traditions and histories associated with the items they collect, acknowledging their cultural importance and the communities from which they originate.

B. Avoiding Illicitly Acquired Items

- Risks of Illegal Acquisition: The market for cultural artifacts has, at times, been tainted by the illegal acquisition and sale of items looted from conflict zones, archaeological sites, or sacred places. Collectors should avoid purchasing items that may have been acquired through illicit means to prevent perpetuating the illegal trade in cultural property and to avoid legal consequences.

- Thorough Provenance Research: Conducting thorough provenance research and verification is essential to ensure that items are legally and ethically obtained. This protects the collector and upholds the integrity of the collection.

C. Supporting Repatriation Efforts

- Correcting Historical Wrongs: In cases where cultural artifacts have been acquired in ways that are now considered unethical or illegal, there is a growing movement to repatriate these items to their countries or communities of origin.

Ethical collectors can support these efforts by being open to returning items that were wrongfully taken and by advocating for the responsible stewardship of cultural heritage.

- Fostering Global Goodwill: Supporting repatriation not only fosters goodwill but also contributes to the global effort to correct historical wrongs, promoting a more ethical and respectful approach to collecting.

2. Sustainability in Collecting

A. Promoting Conservation and Preservation

- Responsibility to Future Generations: Ethical collectors have a responsibility to ensure that the items they acquire are preserved for future generations. This involves taking steps to conserve and care for antiques and collectibles in ways that prevent deterioration and damage.

- Avoiding Harmful Practices: Collectors should avoid purchasing items that contribute to the depletion of endangered species or non-renewable materials, supporting practices that promote the sustainable management of cultural resources.

B. Educating and Raising Awareness

- Role in Public Education: Collectors can play a vital role in educating others about the importance of ethical collecting practices. This includes raising awareness about the impacts of illicit trade, the importance of provenance, and the need for conservation.

- Advocating for Ethical Standards: By sharing their knowledge and advocating for ethical standards, collectors help create a more informed and responsible collecting community.

C. Ethical Sourcing

- Ensuring Legitimacy: Ethical sourcing involves ensuring that the items in your collection are obtained through legal and transparent channels. This includes verifying the seller's credentials, ensuring that all necessary documentation is provided, and avoiding items that cannot be traced back to a legitimate source.

- Supporting a Fair Market: Ethical sourcing protects the collector from potential legal issues and supports a fair and honest market for antiques and collectibles.

3. Legal and Moral Responsibilities

A. Complying with Legal Standards

- Adherence to Laws: Collectors must comply with all relevant laws and regulations governing the acquisition, ownership, and sale of antiques and collectibles. This includes adhering to import and export laws, cultural property regulations, and consumer protection standards.

- Consequences of Non-Compliance: Ignorance of the law is not a defense, and collectors who fail to comply with legal standards may face serious consequences, including fines, confiscation of items, and damage to their reputation.

B. Upholding Moral Integrity

- Personal Code of Conduct: Beyond legal obligations, ethical collecting involves adhering to a personal code of conduct that prioritizes integrity, honesty, and respect. This means being transparent about the provenance and condition of items, avoiding deceptive practices, and ensuring that all transactions are conducted in good faith.

- Building Trusted Relationships: Collectors who uphold high ethical standards are more likely to build trusted relationships within the collecting community and contribute positively to the preservation of cultural heritage.

C. Encouraging Best Practices

- Advocacy and Leadership: Ethical collectors should advocate for best practices within the collecting community. This can include participating in or supporting organizations that promote ethical standards, such as museums, cultural heritage groups, and professional associations.

- Raising Market Standards: By encouraging others to adopt ethical practices, collectors help raise the overall standard of the market and ensure that cultural artifacts are treated with the respect they deserve.

4. The Role of Collectors in Cultural Preservation

A. Stewardship of Cultural Artifacts

- Long-Term Responsibility: Collectors are often seen as stewards of cultural artifacts, with a responsibility to preserve and protect the items in their care. This role involves ensuring that these items are preserved in ways that respect their cultural significance and historical context.

- Contributing to Cultural Heritage: Collectors should consider the long-term impact of their acquisitions and how they can contribute to the preservation of cultural heritage.

B. Collaboration with Institutions

- Partnerships with Museums and Academia: Collaboration with museums, academic institutions, and cultural organizations can enhance the ethical stewardship of collections. By working with these entities, collectors can contribute to research, public education, and the preservation of cultural artifacts.

- Donations and Loans: Donations or loans to museums can ensure that items are preserved and accessible to the public, furthering their educational and cultural value.

C. Supporting Cultural Heritage Initiatives

- Active Involvement in Preservation: Ethical collectors can support initiatives aimed at preserving and protecting cultural heritage, such as conservation projects, repatriation efforts, and educational programs.

- Aligning with Broader Goals: By aligning their collecting practices with broader cultural preservation goals, collectors can make a positive impact on the communities and cultures from which their collections originate.

Ethical collecting is about more than just acquiring beautiful and valuable items; it is about making informed, responsible decisions that respect the cultural, historical, and legal contexts of the items in question. By practicing cultural sensitivity, promoting sustainability, upholding legal and moral responsibilities, and embracing their role as stewards of cultural heritage, collectors can ensure that their collections are not only valuable but also ethically sound and culturally respectful.

9.4 Dealing with Fakes and Forgeries

The antiques and collectibles market is fraught with the risk of encountering fakes and forgeries, ranging from skillfully crafted replicas to outright frauds designed to deceive even seasoned collectors. Understanding how to identify, avoid, and address issues related to fakes and forgeries is essential for any serious collector. This section provides a comprehensive guide to navigating these challenges, ensuring that your collection remains authentic and valuable.

1. Identifying Counterfeits

A. Educating Yourself on Authentic Characteristics

- Understanding Key Features: One of the most effective ways to avoid fakes and forgeries is to educate yourself about the authentic characteristics of the items you collect. This includes knowing the materials, techniques, and stylistic features typical of the period and maker.

- Learning from Authentic Examples: For instance, knowing the specific marks or signatures that genuine pieces bear, the types of materials historically used, and the craftsmanship techniques can help you distinguish between an authentic item and a fake.

B. Recognizing Red Flags

- Unusually Low Prices: Items priced significantly lower than similar authentic pieces may be too good to be true, signaling a possible forgery.

- Inconsistent Provenance: A lack of clear or consistent provenance can be a major warning sign, as authentic items typically have well-documented histories.

- Overly Perfect Condition: Items that appear too perfect for their age, showing no signs of wear or patina, may be modern reproductions rather than genuine antiques.

C. Consulting Reference Materials

- Using Trusted Resources: Reference books, catalogs, and online databases are invaluable tools for comparing items you are considering purchasing with known authentic examples. These resources provide detailed images and descriptions of genuine pieces, helping you spot discrepancies.

- Spotting Variations: Familiarity with the documented variations in authentic items can aid in identifying forgeries that are close but not exact replicas.

2. The Role of Experts

A. Seeking Expert Opinion

- Consulting Specialists: When in doubt, consulting an expert is often the best course of action. Experts, such as appraisers, museum curators, or specialized dealers, have the knowledge and experience to assess the authenticity of an item.

- Objective Evaluations: They can provide an objective evaluation based on their expertise, which is particularly valuable for high-value or rare items where the stakes are higher.

B. Utilizing Scientific Methods

- Advanced Authentication Techniques: Scientific methods can complement visual inspection in verifying the authenticity of an item. Techniques like radiocarbon dating, spectrographic analysis, and thermoluminescence testing can determine the age of materials and their consistency with the claimed period.

- Applications for Various Artifacts: These methods are especially useful for items such as ancient artifacts, paintings, and ceramics, where visual inspection alone may not suffice.

C. Getting a Second Opinion

- Multiple Evaluations: For particularly valuable items, obtaining a second or even third opinion is advisable. Different experts may have varying levels of expertise or access to different information, providing a more comprehensive assessment.

- Enhancing Credibility: Multiple expert opinions can add credibility to the authentication process, which is important if the item is ever resold.

3. Legal Recourse and Consumer Protection

A. Understanding Your Rights

- Legal Remedies: If you discover that an item you purchased is a fake or forgery, it's important to understand your legal rights. Depending on the circumstances of the sale, you may be entitled to a refund, compensation, or other remedies.

- Consumer Protection Laws: Many jurisdictions have consumer protection laws that apply to the sale of antiques and collectibles, offering recourse in cases of fraud or misrepresentation.

B. Addressing the Issue with the Seller

- Initial Steps: The first step in dealing with a suspected fake is to contact the seller. Provide evidence of the forgery, such as expert opinions or scientific test results, and request a refund or resolution.

- Seller's Response: Reputable sellers often work with buyers to resolve issues, as their reputation is also at stake. Some sellers may be unaware of the forgery and will appreciate the opportunity to correct the situation.

C. Legal Action and Dispute Resolution

- Pursuing Legal Remedies: If the seller refuses to cooperate or if the issue cannot be resolved amicably, legal action may be necessary. This could involve filing a lawsuit for fraud or breach of contract.

- Alternative Dispute Resolution: Arbitration or mediation may also be viable options, particularly if these methods are stipulated in the original sales contract. Engaging a lawyer specializing in art and antiques law can help navigate the complexities of such cases.

4. Preventative Measures

A. Building Relationships with Reputable Sellers

- Trust and Reliability: One of the best ways to avoid fakes and forgeries is to build relationships with reputable sellers and dealers. Trusted sellers are more likely to provide authentic items, accurate descriptions, and transparent provenance.

- Long-Term Partnerships: Establishing long-term relationships with these sellers can provide peace of mind and reduce the risk of purchasing fakes.

B. Insisting on Documentation

- Essential Paperwork: Always insist on receiving full documentation with any purchase, including receipts, certificates of authenticity, and detailed provenance records.

- Verification and Future Proofing: This documentation helps verify the authenticity of the item at the time of purchase and supports future sales or appraisals. If a seller is unwilling or unable to provide proper documentation, consider it a red flag.

C. Continuous Education and Awareness

- Staying Informed: The market for antiques and collectibles is constantly evolving, with new techniques for creating forgeries and new discoveries in authentication methods. Continuous education, attending seminars, and keeping up with industry news can help you remain vigilant and better equipped to identify and avoid fakes.

- Adapting to Market Changes: Staying updated on the latest developments in the field ensures that you are aware of the most current threats and opportunities within the market.

Dealing with fakes and forgeries is an unavoidable challenge in the world of antiques and collectibles, but with the right knowledge and precautions, collectors can protect themselves and their investments. By educating yourself on authentic characteristics, consulting experts, understanding your legal rights, and taking preventative measures, you can minimize the risk of falling victim to counterfeit items and ensure that your collection remains genuine and valuable.

9.5 Import and Export Regulations

The global nature of the antiques and collectibles market means that collectors often buy and sell items across international borders. However, this comes with a complex set of import and export regulations that govern the movement of cultural property. These laws are designed to protect cultural heritage, prevent the illicit trade of artifacts, and ensure that transactions are conducted legally and ethically. Understanding and complying with these regulations is essential for collectors who wish to engage in international trade.

1. Navigating Import/Export Laws

A. Understanding Cultural Property Laws

- Protecting Cultural Heritage: Cultural property laws vary significantly from one country to another but generally aim to protect items of historical, artistic, or cultural significance. These laws often restrict the export of certain items, particularly those considered national treasures or part of a country's cultural heritage.

- Avoiding Legal Issues: Collectors must understand the specific laws in both the country of origin and the destination country to avoid legal issues. Ignorance of these laws can result in the seizure of items or legal penalties.

B. Compliance with Export Controls

- Obtaining Export Permits: Many countries require export permits for certain categories of antiques and collectibles, particularly those over a certain age or value. Exporting archaeological artifacts, religious objects, or items made from endangered species may require special permits under national or international laws.

- Ensuring Legal Compliance: Collectors should ensure they obtain all necessary export documentation before moving items across borders, as failing to comply with export controls can result in fines, confiscation of items, or other legal consequences.

C. Import Regulations and Restrictions

- Understanding Import Laws: Import regulations can be as stringent as export controls. Some countries have strict laws regarding the import of cultural property, particularly items that may have been illegally exported from their country of origin.

- Securing Import Permits: Collectors should be aware of these restrictions and ensure they have the necessary import permits, customs declarations, and other documentation to legally bring items into their country.

2. Documentation and Permits

A. Securing Export Licenses

- Legal Export Requirements: Export licenses are often required for the legal export of antiques and collectibles. These licenses, issued by relevant cultural authorities in the country of origin, ensure that items are not being exported illegally.

- Detailed Application Process: The process for obtaining an export license varies depending on the country and the specific item, but generally involves providing detailed information about the item's provenance, age, and significance.

B. Customs Declarations

- Accurate Documentation: When importing items into a new country, it is essential to make accurate customs declarations. This includes providing a detailed description of the item, its value, and its origin.

- Legal Consequences of Misdeclaration: Misdeclaring an item's value or failing to declare it can result in fines, confiscation, or legal action. Working with customs brokers or legal experts ensures that all declarations are accurate and compliant with local laws.

C. CITES and Endangered Species Regulations

- Protecting Endangered Species: Items made from or containing materials from endangered species, such as ivory, tortoiseshell, or certain types of wood, may be subject to additional regulations under the Convention on International Trade in Endangered Species of Wild Fauna and Flora (CITES).

- Compliance with CITES: CITES regulations are designed to prevent the exploitation of endangered species and may prohibit the import or export of certain items without appropriate permits. Collectors should be aware of these regulations and ensure compliance when trading such items.

3. Legal and Ethical Considerations

A. Preventing the Illicit Trade in Cultural Artifacts

- Avoiding the Black Market: The illicit trade in cultural artifacts is a significant global problem, often linked to the looting of archaeological sites, theft from museums, and illegal smuggling operations.

- Ethical Responsibility: Collectors have a responsibility to ensure they are not contributing to this black market by thoroughly researching the provenance of any items they purchase and avoiding items that may have been obtained illegally.

B. Repatriation of Cultural Property

- Supporting Repatriation Efforts: In recent years, there has been a movement toward the repatriation of cultural property, with countries and communities seeking the return of items taken illegally or under duress.

- Ethical Stewardship: Collectors who own such items should be aware of the ethical and legal implications of retaining them and consider participating in repatriation efforts when appropriate.

C. Engaging with Legal Experts

- Navigating Complex Regulations: The complex landscape of import and export regulations often requires assistance from legal experts specializing in cultural property law.

- Legal Guidance: Engaging with these professionals helps collectors understand their legal obligations, obtain the necessary documentation, and avoid costly mistakes.

4. Practical Tips for International Trade

A. Working with Reputable Dealers and Auction Houses

- Ensuring Legal Transactions: When buying or selling antiques and collectibles internationally, it is advisable to work with reputable dealers and auction houses experienced in handling cross-border transactions.

- Navigating Regulations: These professionals assist in navigating import/export regulations, obtaining necessary permits, and ensuring transactions are conducted legally and ethically.

B. Insuring Items During Transit

- Protecting Valuable Items: The risk of damage or loss during transit is a significant concern when shipping valuable antiques and collectibles across borders.

- Adequate Insurance: Collectors should ensure items are adequately insured during transport, covering risks such as theft, damage, or loss.

C. Staying Informed on Regulatory Changes

- Monitoring Changes: Import and export regulations are subject to change, often in response to shifting political landscapes, trade agreements, or new cultural heritage initiatives.

- Adapting to New Regulations: Collectors should stay informed about these changes by consulting legal experts, monitoring industry news, and participating in relevant professional associations.

Understanding and complying with import and export regulations is essential for collectors engaging in international trade of antiques and collectibles. By navigating cultural property laws, securing the necessary documentation, and adhering to ethical practices, collectors can ensure their transactions are legal, responsible, and respectful of cultural heritage.

Chapter 9 Review: Legal and Ethical Considerations in Collecting

Chapter 9 of *HowExpert Guide to Antiques and Collectibles* provides an essential guide to navigating the legal and ethical landscape of the antiques and collectibles market. The chapter is organized into five key sections, each offering practical advice and strategies to help collectors operate within the law while maintaining high ethical standards.

9.1 Understanding Provenance

- Importance of Provenance: Provenance is crucial for verifying an item's authenticity, legal ownership, and value. This section emphasizes that collectors should prioritize provenance to avoid acquiring fakes or items with questionable origins.

- Researching Provenance: Collectors are advised to gather existing documentation, investigate the item's ownership history, and consult experts to establish a credible and continuous chain of ownership. Thorough research is key to building a trustworthy provenance.

- Documenting Provenance: Proper documentation through detailed reports and maintaining up-to-date records is essential for preserving an item's value and authenticity over time. This practice ensures that the provenance remains clear and verifiable for future transactions.

9.2 Legal Aspects of Buying and Selling

- Contracts and Agreements: The importance of clear, legally binding contracts is highlighted to protect both buyers and sellers. These contracts should detail item descriptions, payment terms, and warranties to prevent disputes.

- Buyer and Seller Responsibilities: Buyers must conduct due diligence, and sellers are obligated to disclose accurate information about an item's condition and authenticity. Compliance with legal obligations and consumer protection laws is mandatory.

- International Transactions: This section covers the complexities of cross-border sales, including understanding import/export laws, securing necessary permits, and ensuring compliance with both domestic and international legal standards. Navigating these regulations is critical to avoid legal pitfalls.

9.3 Ethical Collecting Practices

- Cultural Sensitivity and Respect: Collectors are urged to respect the cultural significance of items and avoid acquiring artifacts that may have been illegally obtained or looted. Ethical considerations are paramount in preserving the integrity of collections.

- Sustainability in Collecting: Promoting conservation and ethical sourcing is key to sustainable collecting. Collectors are encouraged to avoid items that contribute to the depletion of endangered species and to ensure that their collections are preserved responsibly.

- Legal and Moral Responsibilities: Upholding both legal standards and moral integrity is essential for maintaining a reputable collection. Collectors should advocate for best practices in the industry and engage with institutions that support cultural preservation.

9.4 Dealing with Fakes and Forgeries

- Identifying Counterfeits: Educating oneself on authentic characteristics and recognizing red flags are critical steps in avoiding fakes. This section advises consulting reference materials and experts to verify the authenticity of items.

- The Role of Experts: Seeking expert opinions and utilizing scientific methods can provide greater assurance of an item's legitimacy. For high-value items, obtaining a second opinion is recommended to confirm authenticity.

- Legal Recourse and Consumer Protection: Understanding one's legal rights and addressing issues with the seller are initial steps when encountering a forgery. If disputes cannot be resolved amicably, legal action may be necessary to protect the buyer's interests.

9.5 Import and Export Regulations

- Navigating Import/Export Laws: Collectors must be aware of cultural property laws, export controls, and import regulations to avoid legal issues when trading internationally. Familiarity with these laws is crucial for legal compliance.

- Documentation and Permits: Securing the appropriate export licenses and making accurate customs declarations are essential for legal compliance. Collectors should also be mindful of CITES regulations when dealing with items made from endangered species.

- Legal and Ethical Considerations: Preventing the illicit trade in cultural artifacts and supporting repatriation efforts are key ethical responsibilities. Collectors are advised to work with legal experts to navigate the complex international regulations effectively.

Chapter 9 equips collectors with the knowledge and strategies necessary to ensure their collecting practices are legally compliant and ethically sound. By understanding the importance of provenance, adhering to legal standards, practicing ethical collecting, and being vigilant against fakes and forgeries, collectors can protect their investments and contribute positively to the preservation of cultural heritage. This chapter is a must-read for any serious collector who aims to maintain a responsible and reputable collection in today's complex market.

Chapter 10: Building and Managing Your Collection

Building and managing a collection of antiques and collectibles is both an art and a science. It requires careful planning, organization, and strategic decision-making to create a collection that not only reflects your personal interests but also holds cultural, historical, and financial value. This chapter delves into the essential aspects of starting, organizing, expanding, securing, and eventually passing on your collection, providing you with the tools to manage your collection effectively and ensure its longevity and impact.

10.1 Starting Your Collection

Starting a collection of antiques and collectibles is an art that combines personal passion with strategic planning. It requires a thoughtful approach to ensure that each acquisition adds value to your collection, aligns with your interests, and contributes to the overarching theme or focus of your collection. This section provides a comprehensive guide to starting a collection, covering key aspects such as defining your focus, conducting in-depth research, and making your initial acquisitions.

1. Defining Your Focus

The first step in building a meaningful collection is to clearly define your focus. This not only guides your future acquisitions but also helps to create a cohesive and purposeful collection.

- A. Choosing a Niche

- Identifying Your Passion: Start by identifying what truly fascinates you. Whether it's a particular historical period, a specific type of artifact, or a unique artistic style, your collection should reflect your personal interests and passions. Focusing on a niche allows you to become an expert in that area, which enhances your ability to identify and acquire valuable items.

- Developing Expertise: Specializing in a particular niche helps you build deep knowledge and expertise. This specialization allows you to recognize subtle details that might be overlooked by general collectors, such as specific maker's marks, production techniques, or historical significance. This expertise not only helps in making informed purchases but also in establishing yourself as a knowledgeable and credible collector within your niche.

- B. Setting Objectives

- Clarifying Your Goals: Clearly defining your goals is essential for guiding your collecting journey. Are you collecting for personal enjoyment, investment purposes, historical preservation, or a combination of these? Understanding your goals will influence your acquisition strategy, the types of items you prioritize, and how you approach the market.

- Guiding Your Strategy: Your objectives will directly impact your collecting strategy. For example, if you're collecting for investment, you might focus on acquiring items with a strong market value or items that are expected to appreciate over time. If your goal is historical preservation, you may prioritize items with significant cultural or historical importance, even if they are not the most expensive or trendy. Setting clear objectives ensures that your collection remains focused and purposeful, avoiding the pitfalls of random or impulsive purchases.

2. Conducting Research

Thorough research is the backbone of successful collecting. It equips you with the knowledge needed to make informed decisions and avoid common pitfalls in the antiques and collectibles market.

- A. Market Analysis

- Understanding Trends: Conducting market research involves understanding the current trends in your area of interest. This includes analyzing pricing patterns, identifying which items are in demand, and recognizing market fluctuations. Staying informed about trends allows you to anticipate shifts in the market and make strategic acquisitions that align with your objectives.

- Identifying Sources: Research also involves identifying reliable sources for your acquisitions. This could include reputable dealers, auction houses, online platforms, or private collectors. Each source has its own advantages and risks, and understanding these will help you navigate the market more effectively. For instance, auctions may offer unique items but can come with competitive bidding, while dealers might offer expertise and authenticity guarantees.

- B. Building Knowledge

- Educating Yourself: Building a strong knowledge base is essential for any collector. This involves learning about the history, materials, and craftsmanship associated with the items you plan to collect. The more you know about the context and creation of the items, the better equipped you'll be to identify genuine pieces and understand their value.

- Leveraging Resources: Use a variety of resources to deepen your understanding of your niche. Attend lectures, workshops, and exhibitions to gain firsthand knowledge and insights from experts. Reading books, academic papers, and catalogs can also provide valuable information that is not readily available online. Networking with other collectors and joining relevant organizations or clubs can further enhance your knowledge and provide opportunities to share insights and experiences.

3. Initial Acquisitions

Your initial acquisitions set the tone for your entire collection. They should be carefully selected to reflect your focus and goals, as well as to establish a strong foundation for future growth.

- A. Starting with Key Pieces

- Acquiring Foundational Items: When starting your collection, focus on acquiring a few key pieces that are representative of your chosen focus. These items should exemplify the quality, style, and historical significance that you want your collection to embody. Foundational pieces not only set the aesthetic and thematic direction for your collection but also serve as benchmarks for future acquisitions.

- Focusing on Significance: Select items that hold historical or cultural significance, as these will likely appreciate in value and add depth to your collection. Significant pieces often have well-documented provenance, which enhances their authenticity and value. Starting with such items establishes your collection as one of quality and importance, even in its early stages.

- B. Verifying Authenticity

- Consulting Experts: Authenticity is crucial in the world of antiques and collectibles. Before making any purchase, it's important to consult with experts who can verify the authenticity of an item. This could involve seeking opinions from appraisers, historians, or specialized dealers. Expert verification helps protect you from the risks of acquiring forgeries or misrepresented items.

- Vetting Sources: Always buy from reputable dealers, auction houses, or other trusted sources that offer guarantees of authenticity. Reputable sources are more likely to provide accurate descriptions and documentation, reducing the risk of acquiring fake or stolen items. Additionally, purchasing from trusted sources helps build your reputation as a serious and ethical collector.

- C. Budgeting and Planning

- Setting a Budget: Establishing a budget for your initial acquisitions is essential. It's easy to become overzealous when starting out, but overspending can limit your ability to expand your collection later. A well-planned budget ensures that you can build your collection sustainably over time.

- Planning for Growth: Consider how your early purchases will fit into the overall growth and value of your collection. Each acquisition should complement and enhance the existing collection, rather than just adding another item. This strategic approach to building your collection ensures that it develops in a cohesive and meaningful way, with each piece contributing to the collection's overall narrative and value.

Starting a collection of antiques and collectibles is a journey that requires a combination of passion, knowledge, and strategic thinking. By defining a clear focus, conducting thorough research, and making informed acquisitions, you can build a collection that not only reflects your interests but also stands the test of time. Whether you are collecting for personal satisfaction, investment, or historical preservation, the steps outlined in this section will help you lay a strong foundation for a successful and fulfilling collecting experience.

10.2 Organizing and Cataloging

After acquiring items for your collection, the next crucial step is to organize and catalog them effectively. Proper organization and meticulous cataloging ensure that your collection is well-maintained, easily accessible, and retains its value over time. This section provides a comprehensive guide to establishing a cataloging system, classifying your collection, and maintaining records.

1. Establishing a Cataloging System

Creating a robust cataloging system is essential for managing your collection efficiently. A well-organized catalog helps you keep track of each item, document its history, and ensure its long-term preservation.

- A. Choosing a Catalog Format

- Digital vs. Physical Catalogs: Decide whether to use a digital catalog, a physical catalog, or both. Digital catalogs are advantageous because they are easily searchable, updateable, and accessible from multiple devices. They are ideal for large collections or items frequently researched. Physical catalogs, on the other hand, offer a tangible record that can be useful for exhibitions, insurance purposes, or passing the collection to future generations. Many collectors maintain both formats to ensure redundancy and ease of access.

- Selecting Software and Tools: If you opt for a digital catalog, choose software specifically designed for collectors. These tools typically offer features such as customizable fields, high-resolution image storage, and the ability to generate detailed reports. They may also include market tracking, provenance records, and insurance documentation, making it easier to manage your collection comprehensively.

- B. Recording Essential Details

- Item Description: Each catalog entry should include a detailed description of the item, covering its physical characteristics, historical significance, and unique features. This should also include dimensions, materials, and the item's condition at the time of acquisition. For items with distinguishing marks, signatures, or labels, make sure these details are documented as they can confirm the item's authenticity.

- Provenance and Acquisition Information: Document the provenance of each item, including previous ownership, place of origin, and any historical context. This information is crucial for high-value items as provenance significantly impacts their value. Additionally, record acquisition details such as the date and place of purchase, seller information, and purchase price. Maintaining accurate records of provenance and acquisition adds credibility and historical depth to your collection.

2. Classifying and Grouping Your Collection

Proper classification and grouping of your collection facilitate easy access and enhance the understanding of relationships between different items.

- A. Organizing by Category

- Grouping by Type or Theme: Organize your collection into categories based on item type, historical period, geographical origin, or thematic relevance. This approach not only makes it easier to locate specific items but also allows you to understand and display the relationships between different pieces in your collection.

- Labeling and Inventory Numbers: Assign each item a unique inventory number and label it accordingly. This number should correspond to the catalog entry, making it easy to cross-reference physical items with their catalog records. Proper labeling is particularly important for large collections, ensuring that no item is misplaced or incorrectly documented.

- B. Storage Solutions

- Choosing Appropriate Storage: Ensure that each item is stored in a manner that protects it from environmental damage, such as temperature fluctuations, humidity, and light exposure. Delicate items, such as textiles, paper, and certain types of wood, may require climate-controlled environments, while others might benefit from specialized display cases or archival-quality storage boxes.

- Accessibility and Safety: Design your storage system to allow easy access to items while ensuring their safety. Items that are frequently handled or displayed should be stored in a way that minimizes the risk of damage, while less frequently accessed items can be securely stored in a way that prioritizes long-term preservation.

3. Maintaining and Updating Records

Maintaining up-to-date records is essential for the ongoing management and valuation of your collection. Regular updates ensure that your catalog reflects the current state and value of your items.

- A. Regular Updates

- Documenting Changes in Condition: Over time, the condition of items may change due to environmental factors, handling, or restoration efforts. Regularly update your catalog to reflect these changes, noting any repairs, restorations, or other alterations that could impact the item's value or historical integrity.

- Adding New Acquisitions: Promptly add new acquisitions to your catalog, ensuring that all relevant details are recorded at the time of purchase. This practice helps maintain a complete and accurate record of your collection.

- B. Backup and Security

- Ensuring Redundancy: For digital catalogs, regularly back up your records to prevent data loss due to technical failures. Consider using cloud storage solutions in addition to physical backups, such as external hard drives or USB storage.

- Securing Physical Records: Store physical catalogs in a secure, climate-controlled environment to prevent damage from environmental factors. Consider keeping a copy in a safe location, such as a fireproof safe, to protect against theft, fire, or other disasters.

Organizing and cataloging your collection is a vital process that requires attention to detail and ongoing commitment. By establishing a comprehensive cataloging system, classifying and storing your items properly, and maintaining up-to-date records, you can ensure that your collection remains well-preserved, easily accessible, and valuable for years to come.

10.3 Expanding and Diversifying Your Collection

Expanding and diversifying your collection is a natural progression as your interests deepen and your knowledge grows. This phase involves strategic acquisitions, exploring new areas of interest, and ensuring that your collection remains dynamic, relevant, and enriched over time. Expanding your collection thoughtfully can enhance its value and significance, while diversification adds depth and breadth to your holdings.

1. Strategic Acquisitions

As your collection grows, it's essential to approach new acquisitions with a strategic mindset. This ensures that each addition complements and enhances the overall collection.

- A. Identifying Gaps in Your Collection

- Assessing Current Holdings: Regularly review your collection to identify any gaps or areas that could be strengthened. For example, you might notice that your collection of 19th-century American furniture is missing key examples of regional styles or specific pieces from renowned makers.

- Targeting Specific Items: Once gaps are identified, target specific items or categories to fill them. This might involve seeking out rare or high-quality pieces that align with your collection's focus. By strategically acquiring these items, you add value and coherence to your collection.

- B. Leveraging Market Opportunities

- Monitoring Market Trends: Stay informed about market trends and fluctuations, which can present opportunities to acquire valuable items at favorable prices. For example, a downturn in a particular collecting category might offer the chance to acquire significant pieces at lower costs.

- Timing Your Acquisitions: Consider the timing of your purchases to maximize value. Acquiring items during periods of low demand or before they become popular can lead to significant appreciation in value over time.

2. Diversifying Your Collection

Diversification involves expanding your collection into new areas or categories that complement your existing focus. This not only adds variety but also reduces risk by spreading your investments across different types of items.

- A. Exploring Related Categories

- Broadening Your Focus: Look for categories that are related to your primary focus but offer new opportunities for collecting. For instance, if your collection centers on Victorian-era furniture, you might diversify by including decorative arts from the same period, such as ceramics, textiles, or metalwork.

- Incorporating Contemporary Items: Diversifying doesn't always mean sticking to the past. Incorporating contemporary or modern items that reflect current trends can add a dynamic element to your collection and attract a broader audience or future buyers.

- B. Balancing Depth and Breadth

- Achieving a Balance: While diversification is valuable, it's important to maintain a balance between depth (a strong focus on a particular area) and breadth (a wide range of items). A well-rounded collection that offers both can appeal to a variety of interests and provide a more comprehensive view of a particular theme or period.

- Avoiding Over-Diversification: Be cautious not to over-diversify, as this can dilute the focus of your collection and make it harder to maintain a cohesive narrative. Each new category should still align with your overall collecting goals and interests.

3. Collaborating and Networking

Expanding and diversifying your collection is not a solo endeavor; it often involves collaboration and networking with other collectors, dealers, and institutions.

- A. Building Relationships with Dealers and Auction Houses

- Cultivating Dealer Relationships: Establishing strong relationships with reputable dealers can provide access to exclusive items, insider knowledge, and better pricing. Dealers who understand your collection's focus can also notify you when items of interest become available.

- Engaging with Auction Houses: Regular participation in auctions is another way to expand your collection. Auction houses often offer rare and high-quality items that are difficult to find elsewhere. Building rapport with auction specialists can also provide you with valuable insights and bidding strategies.

- B. Networking with Other Collectors

- Joining Collectors' Groups: Networking with other collectors through clubs, associations, or online forums can open up new opportunities for acquisitions. Fellow collectors might offer trades, sales, or tips on where to find elusive items.

- Participating in Exhibitions and Shows: Attending and participating in exhibitions, antique fairs, and collectors' shows allows you to see a wide range of items, learn from other collectors, and potentially discover new areas of interest.

4. Planning for Long-Term Growth

As you continue to expand and diversify your collection, it's important to plan for its long-term growth and sustainability.

- A. Setting Long-Term Goals

- Defining Future Objectives: Consider where you want your collection to be in five, ten, or twenty years. Setting long-term goals helps guide your acquisitions and ensures that your collection continues to grow in a meaningful and valuable direction.

- Prioritizing Quality Over Quantity: Focus on acquiring high-quality pieces that will stand the test of time, rather than simply increasing the number of items in your collection. Quality items not only hold their value better but also contribute more significantly to the collection's overall narrative.

- B. Documenting and Preserving New Acquisitions

- Maintaining Records: Ensure that each new acquisition is thoroughly documented and integrated into your cataloging system. This includes recording provenance, acquisition details, and any relevant historical or cultural context.

- Preserving and Protecting: As your collection grows, continue to prioritize the preservation and protection of your items. Implementing proper storage, handling, and conservation practices will help maintain the condition and value of your collection over time.

Expanding and diversifying your collection is an ongoing process that requires careful thought, strategic planning, and a willingness to explore new opportunities. By making informed acquisitions, exploring related categories, networking with other collectors, and planning for the future, you can build a collection that is not only expansive and diverse but also cohesive and valuable.

10.4 Insurance and Security for Your Collection

As your collection grows in value and significance, it becomes increasingly important to protect it from potential risks. Insurance and security measures are essential to ensure that your antiques and collectibles are safeguarded against theft, damage, and other unforeseen events. This section delves into the best practices for insuring and securing your collection, providing a comprehensive guide to protecting your investment.

1. Assessing Insurance Needs

Obtaining adequate insurance coverage is a critical step in protecting your collection. Proper insurance ensures that you are financially protected in the event of loss, damage, or theft.

- A. Valuation for Insurance

- Professional Appraisals: Start by obtaining professional appraisals for each item in your collection. An accurate appraisal provides a clear understanding of the market value of your items, which is essential for determining the appropriate level of insurance coverage. Appraisals should be conducted by qualified experts who specialize in the types of items you collect.

- Regular Updates: The value of antiques and collectibles can fluctuate over time due to market trends, rarity, and condition changes. Regularly updating your appraisals ensures that your insurance coverage remains accurate and reflects the current value of your collection.

- B. Choosing the Right Coverage

- Specialized Insurance Policies: Work with an insurance provider who specializes in antiques and collectibles. Standard homeowners' insurance may not provide sufficient coverage for high-value items, so it's important to obtain a policy specifically designed for collectors. These policies typically offer broader coverage and higher limits for valuable items.

- Comprehensive Coverage Options: Ensure that your policy covers all potential risks, including theft, accidental damage, natural disasters, and transit. Some policies may also offer coverage for loss of value due to damage or restoration. Review the policy terms carefully to understand what is included and any exclusions that may apply.

2. Implementing Security Measures

In addition to insurance, physical and environmental security measures are crucial for protecting your collection from theft, damage, and deterioration.

- A. Physical Security

- Securing the Premises: Invest in high-quality locks, security systems, and surveillance cameras to protect your collection from theft and unauthorized access. Security systems should include alarms, motion detectors, and remote monitoring capabilities. For particularly valuable items, consider storing them in a safe or vault.

- Display and Storage Considerations: If your collection is displayed in your home or a gallery, ensure that items are securely mounted or placed in locked display cases. This prevents accidental damage and discourages theft. For items that are not on display, store them in a secure, climate-controlled environment that minimizes exposure to risks such as humidity, temperature fluctuations, and light.

- B. Environmental Controls

- Climate Control: Antiques and collectibles are often sensitive to environmental conditions. Implementing climate control measures, such as regulating temperature and humidity levels, is essential for preventing deterioration. For example, paper-based items like documents and books should be stored in environments with stable humidity and temperature to avoid mold, warping, or brittleness.

- Light Protection: Exposure to light, especially UV light, can cause fading and degradation of many types of collectibles, including textiles, paintings, and photographs. Use UV-filtering glass or acrylic for display cases, and position items away from direct sunlight. Consider using controlled lighting that minimizes exposure to harmful rays.

3. Disaster Preparedness

Preparing for potential disasters is a critical aspect of protecting your collection. Having a disaster preparedness plan in place can help minimize damage and ensure a swift recovery in the event of an emergency.

- A. Developing an Emergency Plan

- Risk Assessment: Conduct a risk assessment of your collection's location to identify potential hazards such as floods, fires, earthquakes, or severe weather. Understanding the specific risks allows you to tailor your disaster preparedness plan accordingly.

- Creating a Response Strategy: Develop a detailed emergency response plan that includes steps for protecting your collection during a disaster. This plan should outline evacuation procedures, the location of emergency supplies, and a list of high-priority items that require immediate attention. Ensure that all household members or staff are familiar with the plan and know their roles in an emergency.

- B. Securing Backup and Documentation

- Digital Backups: Maintain digital backups of your collection's catalog, including photographs, appraisals, and provenance documents. Store these backups in multiple locations, such as cloud storage and external hard drives, to ensure they are not lost in a disaster.

- Physical Copies: Keep physical copies of important documents, such as insurance policies, appraisals, and provenance records, in a secure location like a fireproof safe. These documents are essential for filing insurance claims and verifying the value of your collection after a disaster.

4. Reviewing and Updating Security and Insurance

As your collection evolves, so too should your approach to security and insurance. Regularly reviewing and updating your measures ensures that your collection remains protected against new risks.

- A. Periodic Reviews

- Reevaluating Coverage: Periodically review your insurance policy to ensure it remains adequate for your collection's current value and composition. Significant acquisitions, changes in market value, or renovations to your property may necessitate updates to your coverage.

- Assessing Security Measures: Regularly assess the effectiveness of your security measures. As technology advances, new security options may become available that offer enhanced protection. Upgrading your security system, adding additional layers of protection, or consulting with security professionals can help you stay ahead of potential threats.

- B. Staying Informed

- Keeping Up with Industry Standards: Stay informed about the latest developments in security technology and insurance products specifically designed for collectors. Attend industry events, read relevant publications, and network with other collectors to share best practices.

- Adapting to Changes: Be prepared to adapt your security and insurance strategies as your collection grows and as new risks emerge. This proactive approach ensures that your collection remains secure and protected, preserving its value and significance for the future.

By implementing comprehensive insurance and security measures, you can safeguard your collection against a wide range of risks. These steps not only protect your financial investment but also ensure that your antiques and collectibles are preserved for future generations to enjoy and appreciate.

10.5 Passing on Your Collection

Passing on your collection is a meaningful way to ensure that your passion for antiques and collectibles continues to be appreciated and preserved by future generations. Whether you decide to leave your collection to loved ones, donate it to an institution, or sell it to another collector, careful planning and documentation are essential. This section outlines the key steps and considerations for passing on your collection effectively.

1. Choosing the Right Recipient

Selecting the appropriate recipient for your collection is a crucial decision that will determine how your items are preserved and appreciated in the future.

- A. Family Members or Heirs

- Identifying Interested Parties: Determine if any family members or heirs share your interest in the collection. If so, discuss your intentions with them and provide guidance on how to care for the items.

- Ensuring Proper Management: Provide instructions on how to maintain, store, and possibly expand the collection. This ensures that your collection is cared for according to your wishes.

- B. Museums or Educational Institutions

- Finding a Suitable Institution: Research museums or educational institutions that align with the theme of your collection. Consider how your items will be displayed, preserved, and potentially used for educational purposes.

- Donation Agreements: Work with the institution to create a donation agreement that specifies how your collection will be handled and any conditions you wish to set.

- C. Selling to Collectors

- Selecting a Buyer: If selling your collection, choose a buyer who will value and preserve the items. This could be a private collector, a specialized dealer, or an auction house.

- Maximizing Value: Consider timing the sale to coincide with market peaks, and ensure that your collection is well-documented and appraised to achieve the best possible price.

2. Legal and Financial Considerations

Ensuring that your collection is passed on legally and in accordance with your wishes requires careful attention to estate planning and financial matters.

- A. Estate Planning

- Including in Your Will: Clearly state your intentions for the collection in your will, specifying who will inherit the items and any conditions for their management or sale.

- Setting Up a Trust: For more complex collections, consider setting up a trust that outlines how the collection should be managed and by whom.

- B. Tax Implications

- Understanding Tax Liabilities: Be aware of potential tax implications for heirs, especially if the collection is valuable. Consult with a tax professional to explore options such as gifting during your lifetime to minimize tax burdens.

- Charitable Deductions: If donating your collection, explore the possibility of tax deductions for charitable contributions. Ensure that the donation meets IRS requirements to qualify for these benefits.

- C. Documentation and Appraisal

- Comprehensive Cataloging: Maintain a detailed catalog of your collection, including descriptions, provenance, and appraised values. This will serve as a crucial reference for legal and financial processes.

- Regular Appraisals: Keep appraisals up to date to reflect any changes in market value. This is important for both estate planning and insurance purposes.

3. Preparing Your Collection for Transfer

Before passing on your collection, it's important to ensure that it is properly documented and that the recipient is prepared to manage it.

- A. Creating a Maintenance Guide

- Instructions for Care: Write a guide that includes detailed instructions on how to care for the collection. This might cover cleaning, storage, and handling procedures specific to the items.

- Resource List: Provide a list of trusted professionals, such as appraisers, conservators, and dealers, who can assist with maintaining or expanding the collection.

- B. Ensuring Proper Transfer

- Legal Transfer of Ownership: Work with a lawyer to ensure that the legal transfer of ownership is executed properly, whether through a will, trust, or sale agreement.

- Documenting the Transfer: Keep copies of all legal documents related to the transfer, including wills, trusts, sales agreements, and donation contracts.

- C. Communicating Your Wishes

- Discussing with Heirs or Institutions: Have open conversations with your heirs or the receiving institution about your intentions and expectations. Clear communication helps prevent misunderstandings and ensures your wishes are respected.

- Finalizing Arrangements: Ensure that all arrangements are finalized, including any financial, legal, or logistical details, to facilitate a smooth transfer of your collection.

By carefully planning and documenting the process of passing on your collection, you can ensure that your treasured items are preserved and appreciated for generations to come. This not only honors your passion for collecting but also contributes to the continued enjoyment and educational value of your collection.

Chapter 10 Review: Passing on Your Collection

Chapter 10, *Passing on Your Collection*, provides a comprehensive guide on how to ensure your antiques and collectibles are preserved and appreciated by future generations. The chapter is divided into three key sections, each offering practical advice and strategies to effectively pass on your collection.

- 10.1 Choosing the Right Recipient

- Family Members or Heirs: Identify family members or heirs who have an interest in your collection. Discuss your intentions with them, providing guidance on how to care for and manage the collection to ensure its continued preservation.

- Museums or Educational Institutions: Research museums or institutions that align with the theme of your collection. Consider donating your collection to ensure it is preserved and appreciated by the public. Establish donation agreements that outline how your collection will be handled.

- Selling to Collectors: If you choose to sell your collection, select a buyer who values and will maintain the integrity of the items. Timing the sale to coincide with market trends can help maximize the value of your collection.

- 10.2 Legal and Financial Considerations

- Estate Planning: Include your collection in your estate plan, specifying who will inherit the items and how they should be managed. Consider setting up a trust to ensure the proper transfer of your collection.

- Tax Implications: Understand the tax implications of passing on your collection, whether through inheritance, donation, or sale. Consulting with a tax professional can help minimize liabilities and maximize benefits for your heirs or chosen institution.

- Documentation and Appraisal: Maintain a detailed catalog of your collection, including descriptions, provenance, and appraised values. Regularly update appraisals to reflect changes in market value, ensuring your collection is accurately documented for legal and financial purposes.

- 10.3 Preparing Your Collection for Transfer

- Creating a Maintenance Guide: Write a comprehensive guide that includes detailed instructions on how to care for and maintain your collection. Provide a list of trusted professionals, such as appraisers and conservators, who can assist in its upkeep.

- Ensuring Proper Transfer: Work with a lawyer to ensure the legal transfer of ownership is correctly executed. Keep copies of all legal documents related to the transfer, including wills, trusts, and sales agreements.

- Communicating Your Wishes: Discuss your intentions and expectations with the chosen recipient, whether they are family members, institutions, or buyers. Clear communication ensures your collection is handled according to your wishes and helps prevent misunderstandings during the transfer process.

Chapter 10 equips collectors with the necessary knowledge to ensure that their collection is passed on thoughtfully and effectively. By carefully selecting the right recipient, addressing legal and financial considerations, and preparing the collection for transfer, collectors can ensure that their passion and legacy continue to be appreciated by future generations.

Chapter 11: Connecting with the Collecting Community

Connecting with the collecting community is one of the most enriching aspects of being a collector. It transforms what could be a solitary pursuit into a dynamic, interactive experience filled with learning, sharing, and growth. This chapter offers a deep dive into the various ways to connect with other collectors, leveraging these connections to enhance your collection and your enjoyment of the hobby.

11.1 Joining Collectors' Clubs and Associations

Joining collectors' clubs and associations is a strategic move that can significantly elevate your collecting experience. These organizations offer a wealth of resources, networking opportunities, and educational benefits that can deepen your knowledge, enhance your collection, and connect you with a community of like-minded individuals.

1. Access to Specialized Knowledge

Membership in collectors' clubs and associations grants you access to specialized knowledge that can greatly enrich your collecting journey.

A. Exclusive Publications and Research

- Curated Content: Collectors' clubs and associations often produce high-quality publications, such as newsletters, journals, and bulletins, providing members with the latest research, market trends, and expert opinions specific to their collecting niche.

- Niche Focus: These publications delve into the intricacies of particular areas of collecting, offering insights and information that are not readily available elsewhere.

- Educational Value: Regular access to tailored content ensures continuous learning, helping collectors refine their expertise and stay at the forefront of their field.

B. Workshops and Seminars

- Expert-Led Sessions: Many clubs organize workshops and seminars led by industry experts, offering hands-on learning experiences covering topics such as authentication, preservation techniques, and market trends.

- Skill Enhancement: These educational sessions enhance the skills of collectors, enabling them to identify valuable pieces, understand the nuances of their collections, and maintain the integrity and value of their items over time.

- Continual Learning: Participation in these events fosters an environment of continual learning, ensuring that collectors remain well-informed and capable of making strategic decisions that enhance the value and significance of their collections.

C. Access to Exclusive Events and Private Collections

- Networking Opportunities: Membership often grants access to exclusive events, such as private viewings, members-only auctions, and networking gatherings, where collectors can connect with like-minded individuals and industry professionals.

- Private Collections: Some clubs offer opportunities to view private collections that are not open to the public. These exclusive viewings provide unique insights into how other collectors curate and care for their collections, offering inspiration and learning opportunities.

- Expert Interaction: These events also allow members to interact directly with experts, gaining personalized advice and insights that can further refine their collecting approach.

2. Networking and Building Relationships

One of the most valuable aspects of joining a collectors' club or association is the opportunity to build meaningful relationships with other collectors and industry professionals.

A. Connecting with Like-minded Collectors

- Shared Passion: Clubs and associations provide a platform to meet others who share your interests, leading to valuable exchanges of information, advice, and opportunities to acquire new items.

- Collaborative Opportunities: Building relationships within these groups can lead to joint acquisitions, collaborative research, and shared collecting experiences.

B. Accessing Insider Information

- Market Insights: Networking with other collectors can provide insider information on market trends, upcoming auctions, and opportunities that aren't widely known.

- Exclusive Deals: Relationships built in these communities often lead to private sales or trades, giving you access to items that may not be available through traditional channels.

C. Expanding Your Influence

- Building a Reputation: Active participation in clubs and associations can help you establish a reputation as a knowledgeable and respected collector, opening doors to more exclusive events and opportunities.

- Leadership Roles: Getting involved in the leadership of these organizations allows you to influence the direction of the club, contribute to its activities, and further enhance your standing in the collecting community.

Joining collectors' clubs and associations is not just about gaining access to resources and events—it's about becoming part of a vibrant community that shares your passion for collecting. These organizations provide a structured environment where you can continuously learn, grow your collection, and build lasting relationships with others who appreciate the art and science of collecting. By actively participating in these groups, you position yourself to gain the knowledge, connections, and opportunities that will elevate your collecting to new heights. Whether you're just starting out or are an experienced collector, being part of these communities can significantly enhance your journey, helping you to build a collection that is both valuable and deeply satisfying.

11.2 Attending Conventions and Fairs

Attending conventions and fairs is a pivotal aspect of engaging with the collecting community. These events offer collectors unparalleled opportunities to acquire rare items, expand their knowledge, and build connections with other collectors and industry professionals. Here's a deep dive into how attending conventions and fairs can enhance your collecting experience.

1. Exploring Opportunities for Acquisition

Conventions and fairs are prime venues for discovering and acquiring new pieces that can add significant value to your collection.

A. Access to Rare and Unique Items

- Exclusive Offerings: Conventions and fairs often feature items that are not available through traditional channels, giving you access to rare and unique pieces that can elevate your collection.

- Diverse Selection: The variety of vendors present at these events ensures a wide range of items, from high-end antiques to niche collectibles, allowing you to explore different aspects of your collecting interests.

- Opportunity to Negotiate: Face-to-face interactions with sellers provide a unique opportunity to negotiate prices and terms, potentially securing valuable items at favorable rates.

B. Discovering New Trends

- Insight into Market Movements: Attending these events allows you to observe emerging trends in the collecting world, helping you stay ahead of market shifts and adjust your collecting strategy accordingly.

- Exposure to New Categories: Fairs and conventions often showcase categories you may not have previously considered, offering inspiration to diversify or expand your collection into new areas.

C. Immediate Access to Expertise

- Direct Interaction with Experts: Many conventions and fairs feature sessions or booths with experts who can provide insights, appraisals, and advice on specific items or categories.

- On-the-Spot Learning: Engage in real-time discussions with sellers and other collectors, gaining knowledge that can directly inform your collecting decisions and strategy.

2. Networking and Community Building

Attending conventions and fairs is not just about acquisitions—it's also a valuable opportunity to network and build relationships within the collecting community.

A. Connecting with Fellow Collectors

- Shared Interests: These events bring together collectors who share similar passions, providing a platform to exchange ideas, stories, and experiences.

- Building Relationships: Networking at these events can lead to long-lasting relationships, offering opportunities for future collaborations, trades, or private sales.

B. Learning from Industry Professionals

- Workshops and Seminars: Many conventions offer workshops and seminars led by industry professionals, providing insights into the latest developments, techniques, and best practices in collecting.

- Gaining Insider Knowledge: Conversations with dealers, experts, and seasoned collectors at these events can offer valuable insider knowledge that might not be readily available elsewhere.

C. Expanding Your Influence

- Establishing a Presence: Regular attendance at key events helps you establish a presence in the collecting community, building your reputation as a serious and knowledgeable collector.

- Opportunities for Leadership: Involvement in event activities, such as speaking engagements or panel discussions, can enhance your visibility and influence within the community.

Attending conventions and fairs is an essential practice for any serious collector. These events offer a unique blend of acquisition opportunities, educational experiences, and networking potential that can significantly contribute to the growth and enrichment of your collection. By actively participating in these gatherings, you not only enhance your collection but also deepen your connection to the vibrant community of collectors, ensuring that your passion for collecting continues to thrive.

11.3 Online Forums and Social Media

Online forums and social media platforms have revolutionized the way collectors connect, share knowledge, and grow their collections. These digital spaces offer endless opportunities to engage with a global community of collectors, stay updated on market trends, and access resources that were once difficult to find. Here's an in-depth look at how online forums and social media can enhance your collecting journey.

1. Expanding Your Knowledge Base

Online platforms are treasure troves of information, where collectors of all levels can learn, share, and grow their expertise.

A. Access to Diverse Perspectives

- Global Community: Online forums and social media groups connect you with collectors from around the world, offering a diverse range of perspectives on items, trends, and collecting strategies.

- Crowdsourced Knowledge: These platforms allow you to tap into the collective knowledge of the community, where members share their experiences, insights, and advice on various aspects of collecting.

B. Staying Updated on Trends

- Real-Time Updates: Social media platforms provide instant access to the latest trends, market shifts, and news in the collecting world, helping you stay informed and make timely decisions.

- Discussion of Emerging Trends: Participate in discussions about emerging trends, allowing you to adjust your collecting strategies or explore new categories before they become mainstream.

C. Access to Educational Resources

- Tutorials and Guides: Many forums and social media groups offer tutorials, guides, and other educational resources that can help you refine your collecting techniques, learn about item authentication, and understand market dynamics.

- Expert Contributions: Engage with content created by experts, such as videos, articles, and webinars, which provide deeper insights into specific niches within the collecting world.

2. *Building and Engaging with a Community*

Online forums and social media are not just about consuming information— they're about building and engaging with a community of like-minded collectors.

A. Networking with Collectors

- Forming Connections: Social media groups and forums allow you to connect with other collectors, forming relationships that can lead to collaborations, trades, or even friendships.

- Participating in Group Discussions: Actively participating in discussions helps you become a valued member of the community, where your contributions are recognized and respected.

B. Sharing Your Collection

- Showcasing Your Items: Use social media to share photos and stories about your collection, gaining feedback and admiration from fellow collectors. This not only builds your reputation but also helps you connect with others who share your interests.

- Learning from Feedback: The feedback you receive from sharing your collection can provide valuable insights, whether it's identifying areas for improvement, discovering new items to add, or learning about the historical context of your pieces.

C. Leveraging Platforms for Buying and Selling

- Access to Marketplace Groups: Many online forums and social media platforms have dedicated marketplace groups where collectors can buy, sell, or trade items directly with one another, often with greater trust and transparency than traditional marketplaces.

- Networking for Private Sales: Building relationships within these communities can lead to private sales or trades, giving you access to items that may not be available through conventional channels.

Engaging with online forums and social media is an essential component of modern collecting. These platforms provide a dynamic environment where you can learn, share, and connect with a global community of collectors. By actively participating in these digital spaces, you can expand your knowledge, grow your collection, and build meaningful relationships that enhance your overall collecting experience.

11.4 Networking with Other Collectors

Networking with other collectors is one of the most valuable strategies for enhancing your collecting experience. Building connections within the collecting community can lead to collaborations, exchanges of knowledge, and access to rare items that might otherwise be out of reach. Here's how effective networking can elevate your collecting journey.

1. Building Valuable Connections

Forming strong relationships with fellow collectors opens up numerous opportunities for growth and enrichment in your collecting endeavors.

A. Establishing Trust and Credibility

- Mutual Respect: Building trust within the collecting community is essential. By consistently demonstrating integrity, honesty, and knowledge, you earn the respect of other collectors, which can lead to more fruitful exchanges and collaborations.

- Credibility through Expertise: Sharing your knowledge and insights with others not only helps build your credibility but also positions you as a go-to person within your niche. This can lead to invitations to exclusive events, opportunities to speak at gatherings, or offers to collaborate on projects.

B. Collaborating on Acquisitions

- Joint Ventures: Networking with other collectors can lead to collaborative acquisitions, where you pool resources to purchase high-value or rare items. This approach can be particularly beneficial when dealing with items that are beyond the reach of a single collector.

- Sharing Knowledge: Collaboration often involves sharing knowledge and insights, helping both parties make informed decisions about potential acquisitions. This mutual support can result in better outcomes and more valuable additions to your collection.

C. Access to Insider Opportunities

- Private Sales and Trades: Strong networks often lead to private sales or trades, where collectors offer items directly to trusted contacts before they hit the broader market. This can give you early access to desirable pieces and the opportunity to acquire them at more favorable terms.

- Exclusive Invitations: Being well-connected within the community can also lead to invitations to private events, auctions, or viewings, where you have the chance to see and acquire items that are not available to the general public.

2. Engaging in Continuous Learning

Networking with other collectors is not just about acquiring items—it's also about continuous learning and staying informed.

A. Sharing Experiences

- Learning from Peers: By engaging with other collectors, you can learn from their experiences, successes, and challenges. This shared knowledge can help you avoid common pitfalls and make more informed decisions in your own collecting journey.

- Expanding Perspectives: Networking exposes you to different perspectives and approaches to collecting, broadening your understanding and helping you explore new areas or refine your existing focus.

B. Participating in Collector Groups

- Joining Clubs and Associations: Participating in collector groups, whether local clubs or online communities, provides a structured environment for networking. These groups often host events, discussions, and activities that encourage interaction and knowledge sharing.

- Attending Meetups and Gatherings: Regularly attending meetups, conventions, and fairs gives you the opportunity to meet other collectors in person, strengthening relationships and facilitating more meaningful exchanges.

C. Mentorship and Guidance

- Finding a Mentor: Building relationships with more experienced collectors can lead to mentorship opportunities, where you receive guidance and advice tailored to your specific interests and goals.

- Becoming a Mentor: As your experience grows, you may find yourself in a position to mentor newer collectors, sharing your knowledge and helping them navigate the complexities of collecting. This role not only enriches your own experience but also strengthens the community as a whole.

Networking with other collectors is a powerful way to enhance your collecting journey. By building strong connections, engaging in continuous learning, and participating in collaborative efforts, you can access opportunities, knowledge, and resources that will significantly enrich your collection. These relationships create a supportive and dynamic environment where both you and your collection can thrive.

11.5 Finding Mentors and Experts

Finding mentors and experts is a crucial step in advancing your knowledge and expertise as a collector. These relationships can provide you with invaluable insights, guidance, and access to resources that can elevate your collecting journey. Here's how to effectively seek out and engage with mentors and experts in the collecting world.

1. The Importance of Mentorship

Mentorship is a powerful tool for personal and professional growth in collecting. A mentor's experience and knowledge can guide you through the complexities of the collecting world, helping you avoid common mistakes and make more informed decisions.

A. Identifying Potential Mentors

- Shared Interests: Look for mentors who share your specific collecting interests. A mentor with expertise in your niche can offer targeted advice and insights that are directly applicable to your collection.

- Proven Experience: Choose mentors who have a proven track record in your area of interest. Their experience in acquiring, managing, and possibly even selling collections can provide you with a wealth of practical knowledge.

- Accessibility and Willingness to Share: A good mentor is someone who is not only knowledgeable but also willing to share their time and expertise. Look for individuals who are approachable and open to mentoring relationships.

B. Building a Mentorship Relationship

- Mutual Respect: A successful mentorship is built on mutual respect. Show genuine interest in your mentor's experiences and insights, and be willing to learn from their successes and challenges.

- Clear Communication: Establish clear communication channels and expectations. Regular check-ins and discussions help ensure that both you and your mentor are benefiting from the relationship.

- Long-Term Commitment: Mentorship is often a long-term relationship. Be prepared to invest time and effort into nurturing this connection, as the benefits will grow over time.

C. Leveraging Mentorship for Growth

- Personalized Guidance: A mentor can provide personalized advice tailored to your specific goals and challenges, helping you make more informed decisions in your collecting journey.

- Access to Networks: Mentors often have extensive networks in the collecting community. Through your mentor, you can gain introductions to other experts, access to exclusive events, and opportunities that might otherwise be out of reach.

- Learning from Experience: The firsthand experiences shared by a mentor—both successes and failures—can provide you with valuable lessons that are not available in books or online resources.

2. Consulting with Experts

Beyond mentorship, consulting with experts can provide you with specialized knowledge that is critical for making informed decisions about your collection.

A. Identifying the Right Experts

- Specialized Knowledge: Seek out experts who have deep knowledge in specific areas of your interest, such as appraisers, historians, or conservators. Their specialized expertise can help you with authentication, valuation, and preservation of your collection.

- Professional Credentials: Look for experts with recognized credentials and a strong reputation in the industry. This ensures that the advice and services you receive are reliable and of high quality.

- Recommendations and Reviews: Utilize recommendations from other collectors or research reviews and testimonials to find trustworthy experts. A well-regarded expert is more likely to provide valuable insights and services.

B. Engaging with Experts

- Clear Objectives: When consulting with an expert, have clear objectives in mind. Whether you need an appraisal, advice on restoration, or historical context, knowing what you want to achieve will make the consultation more effective.

- Professional Interaction: Approach experts with professionalism and respect. Be clear about your needs and expectations, and value the time and expertise they provide.

- Ongoing Relationships: Building an ongoing relationship with trusted experts can be highly beneficial. Regular consultations can help you keep your collection well-maintained, accurately valued, and aligned with your long-term goals.

C. Integrating Expert Advice

- Informed Decision-Making: The insights gained from experts can significantly influence your collecting decisions, helping you avoid costly mistakes and enhancing the overall quality of your collection.

- Enhancing Collection Value: Expert appraisals and advice on preservation can increase the value and longevity of your collection, ensuring that your investments are well-protected.

- Expanding Your Knowledge: Regular interactions with experts contribute to your ongoing education as a collector, deepening your understanding of the items you collect and the broader market.

Engaging with mentors and experts is a critical component of a successful collecting journey. These relationships provide you with the guidance, knowledge, and connections necessary to grow as a collector and enhance the quality and value of your collection. By actively seeking out and building these relationships, you position yourself to achieve greater success and fulfillment in your collecting endeavors.

Chapter 11 Review: Connecting with the Collecting Community

Chapter 11, *Connecting with the Collecting Community*, explores the vital role that relationships and community engagement play in the world of collecting. This chapter outlines various strategies for building connections, gaining knowledge, and enhancing your collecting experience through active participation in the community. Below are the key takeaways:

- 11.1 Joining Collectors' Clubs and Associations

- Access to Specialized Knowledge: Membership in clubs and associations provides access to exclusive publications, workshops, and seminars that offer in-depth insights and expert advice tailored to your collecting niche.

- Networking Opportunities: These organizations offer structured environments for networking with like-minded collectors, which can lead to collaborations, private sales, and long-term relationships that enrich your collecting journey.

- Exclusive Events and Private Collections: Membership often grants access to exclusive events and private collections, allowing you to view rare items and engage directly with experts in your field.

- 11.2 Attending Conventions and Fairs

- Acquisition Opportunities: Conventions and fairs offer unique opportunities to acquire rare and valuable items, often with the chance to negotiate directly with sellers.

- Networking and Community Building: These events are prime venues for connecting with fellow collectors, learning from industry professionals, and expanding your influence within the collecting community.

- Learning and Trendspotting: Attending these events keeps you informed about emerging trends and offers educational sessions that can enhance your knowledge and collecting strategies.

- 11.3 Online Forums and Social Media

- Expanding Knowledge Base: Online platforms provide access to a global community of collectors, offering diverse perspectives, real-time updates on trends, and a wealth of educational resources.

- Community Engagement: Participating in online discussions and sharing your collection can help you build a reputation, gain feedback, and form valuable connections with other collectors.

- Buying and Selling: Social media and forums offer dedicated marketplace groups and networking opportunities that facilitate private sales and trades, often with greater trust and transparency.

- 11.4 Networking with Other Collectors

- Building Valuable Connections: Networking allows you to establish trust, collaborate on acquisitions, and gain access to insider opportunities that can significantly enhance your collection.

- Continuous Learning: Engaging with other collectors fosters continuous learning, exposing you to new perspectives and experiences that can broaden your understanding of collecting.

- Mentorship and Guidance: Networking also offers opportunities to find mentors and, eventually, become a mentor yourself, contributing to the growth and enrichment of the collecting community.

- 11.5 Finding Mentors and Experts

- The Importance of Mentorship: Mentors provide personalized guidance, share valuable experiences, and connect you with broader networks, all of which are crucial for your growth as a collector.

- Consulting with Experts: Experts offer specialized knowledge that is critical for authentication, valuation, and preservation, helping you make informed decisions that protect and enhance your collection.

- Integrating Expert Advice: Regular interactions with experts contribute to your ongoing education, ensuring that your collection is well-maintained, accurately valued, and aligned with your long-term goals.

Chapter 11 emphasizes that building connections within the collecting community is not just about enhancing your collection—it's about enriching your overall experience as a collector. By actively engaging with clubs, attending events, participating in online forums, networking with peers, and seeking out mentors and experts, you position yourself to achieve greater success, knowledge, and fulfillment in your collecting journey.

Chapter 12: Resources and Further Reading

As a collector, having access to high-quality resources and reliable information is crucial for deepening your knowledge and making informed decisions. Chapter 12 explores the essential resources and avenues for further reading that can significantly enhance your collecting journey. Whether you're seeking books, online databases, museum exhibits, or educational courses, this chapter provides a comprehensive guide to the best sources of information.

12.1 Recommended Books and Guides

Books and guides are indispensable resources for any collector, providing in-depth knowledge, historical context, and practical advice that are essential for building and maintaining a valuable collection. This section explores the types of books and guides that are most beneficial for collectors, offering guidance on how to build a personal library that supports your collecting endeavors.

1. Essential Reading for Collectors

Certain books are considered must-haves for collectors, offering foundational knowledge that every serious enthusiast should possess.

A. Classic References

- Timeless Knowledge: Classic reference books are often the cornerstone of a collector's library. These works provide comprehensive overviews of specific collecting categories, such as antique furniture, rare coins, or vintage toys. They offer detailed descriptions, historical backgrounds, and often include price guides that help collectors understand the value of items.

- Authority and Expertise: Written by renowned experts in the field, these books are respected for their accuracy and depth of information. They often cover the history, production techniques, and identification markers that are crucial for verifying authenticity and assessing value.

B. Specialized Guides

- Focused Insights: Specialized guides delve deeply into specific niches within the collecting world, offering targeted advice and insights. These books are ideal for collectors who have a focused interest, such as a particular artist, era, or type of artifact.

- Practical Advice: Many specialized guides provide practical advice on aspects like restoration, care, and display of items, helping collectors maintain and enhance the value of their collections over time.

C. Comprehensive Overviews

- Broad Perspective: For those who are new to collecting or interested in exploring multiple areas, comprehensive overviews offer a wide-angle view of the collecting landscape. These books cover various categories, providing a solid foundation for understanding the different types of collectibles, market trends, and acquisition strategies.

- Guidance for Beginners: These overviews are particularly useful for beginners, offering clear explanations and step-by-step guides to help new collectors get started with confidence.

2. Keeping Up with New Publications

The world of collecting is constantly evolving, and staying up-to-date with the latest publications ensures that your knowledge remains current and relevant.

A. Latest Editions and Updates

- Revised Information: New editions of classic references and guides often include updated information, reflecting changes in market trends, newly discovered items, and advancements in restoration techniques. Keeping up with these editions is essential for staying informed.

- Incorporating New Research: As new research and discoveries are made, updated editions provide the most accurate and comprehensive information available, ensuring that collectors have access to the latest insights.

B. Book Reviews and Recommendations

- Community Insights: Joining collector forums or following industry publications that review books can help you discover valuable resources that you might otherwise overlook. Reviews often highlight the strengths and weaknesses of new publications, guiding you toward the best additions to your library.

- Expert Opinions: Look for recommendations from respected figures in your collecting niche. Their endorsements can lead you to high-quality resources that align with your specific interests and needs.

C. Building a Personal Library

- Curating Your Collection: Just as with your collectibles, building a personal library of essential books and guides is an investment in your expertise. A well-curated library allows you to quickly reference important information, deepen your understanding of your collection, and enhance your ability to make informed decisions.

- Long-Term Value: Some rare or out-of-print books can appreciate in value over time, making them valuable assets in their own right. These books not only serve as knowledge resources but also add to the prestige of your collection.

3. Utilizing Books for Research and Verification

Books are not just for casual reading; they are critical tools for research and verification in the collecting process.

A. Authenticity Verification

- Identifying Key Markers: Many reference books include detailed descriptions and images of authenticity markers, such as maker's marks, signatures, or production techniques. These details are crucial for verifying the authenticity of items in your collection.

- Cross-Referencing Information: Using multiple books to cross-reference information can help ensure that your assessments are accurate. This practice reduces the risk of acquiring counterfeit or misattributed items.

B. Historical Context

- Understanding Provenance: Books that delve into the history of specific items or collecting categories provide valuable context that can enhance your understanding of an item's provenance. This knowledge is essential for assessing the historical significance and value of your collection.

- Cultural Significance: Many books explore the cultural significance of collectibles, offering insights into how items were used, perceived, and valued in their original contexts. This understanding can add depth to your appreciation of your collection and guide your acquisition strategies.

C. Enhancing Display and Preservation

- Display Techniques: Books often include sections on the best practices for displaying items, considering factors like lighting, environmental conditions, and aesthetic presentation. These techniques help you showcase your collection in a way that maximizes its visual impact and protects it from damage.

- Preservation Guidelines: Reference guides frequently offer advice on preserving items, including recommended storage conditions, cleaning methods, and materials to avoid. Following these guidelines ensures that your collection remains in excellent condition for future generations.

Building a personal library of recommended books and guides is a fundamental step in becoming a knowledgeable and successful collector. These resources provide the foundation for informed decision-making, offering insights that are essential for verifying authenticity, understanding historical context, and maintaining the value of your collection. By carefully selecting and utilizing these books, you can significantly enhance your expertise and ensure that your collecting journey is both fulfilling and rewarding.

12.2 Online Resources and Databases

In the digital age, online resources and databases have become indispensable tools for collectors. These platforms offer real-time access to a wealth of information, from market trends and price guides to detailed records of provenance and historical data. This section explores the various online resources and databases that can enhance your collecting journey, providing you with the knowledge and tools needed to make informed decisions.

1. Specialized Databases

Specialized online databases are designed to provide collectors with in-depth information on specific types of collectibles, offering access to archives, market data, and expert analyses.

A. Access to Archives

- Provenance Records: Many specialized databases offer detailed provenance records, allowing you to trace the ownership history of an item. This information is crucial for verifying authenticity and understanding the historical significance of your collection.

- Historical Data: Access to archives that include historical records, production details, and previous auction results helps you gain a deeper understanding of the items you collect. This context is essential for assessing value and making informed purchasing decisions.

B. Price Guides and Market Data

- Real-Time Market Insights: Online price guides provide up-to-date information on the current market value of items, helping you determine fair prices for buying or selling. These guides often include data from recent auctions, private sales, and dealer listings.

- Trend Analysis: By analyzing market data, you can identify trends in the collecting world, such as which categories are gaining popularity or which items are appreciating in value. This information can guide your acquisition strategy and help you stay ahead of market shifts.

C. Authentication Tools

- Digital Verification: Some online databases offer tools for digital authentication, where you can compare your items with verified examples. This can include high-resolution images, detailed descriptions, and expert evaluations to help you verify the authenticity of your collection.

- Expert Consultations: Many platforms provide access to experts who can offer advice or authentication services directly through the site. This service can be invaluable when dealing with high-value or rare items where verification is critical.

2. Forums and Discussion Groups

Online forums and discussion groups are valuable resources for engaging with other collectors, sharing knowledge, and staying informed about the latest developments in the collecting community.

A. Interactive Learning

- Peer-to-Peer Knowledge Sharing: Forums provide a space for collectors to ask questions, share experiences, and offer advice. Engaging in these discussions helps you learn from the experiences of others, gaining insights that can improve your collecting practices.

- Expert Moderation: Many forums are moderated by experts who can provide authoritative answers and steer conversations towards productive discussions. This ensures that the information shared is accurate and reliable.

B. Staying Informed

- Real-Time Updates: Forums and social media groups allow you to stay informed about the latest news, trends, and events in the collecting world. Members often share information about upcoming auctions, new discoveries, and market fluctuations.

- Community Alerts: Active participation in these groups can also provide early alerts to potential pitfalls, such as counterfeit items circulating in the market or sudden drops in the value of certain collectibles.

C. Networking Opportunities

- Building Connections: Online forums are excellent platforms for networking with other collectors, dealers, and experts. These connections can lead to opportunities for trades, private sales, and collaborations on research or projects.

- Sharing Resources: Members often share valuable resources, such as links to useful databases, articles, or tools that can help you in your collecting journey. These shared resources can save you time and provide new avenues for exploration.

3. Online Auctions and Marketplaces

The rise of online auctions and marketplaces has transformed the way collectors buy and sell items, offering access to a global market with a wide range of collectibles.

A. Research Before You Buy

- Seller Verification: Online marketplaces often include seller ratings, reviews, and verification badges that help you assess the reliability of sellers. Checking these ratings before making a purchase can protect you from fraudulent transactions and ensure that you are dealing with reputable sellers.

- Item Descriptions and Photos: Detailed item descriptions and high-quality photos are crucial when buying online. Ensure that the listings provide all necessary information, such as condition reports, provenance, and any certificates of authenticity.

B. Access to Global Markets

- Diverse Offerings: Online marketplaces connect you with sellers from around the world, giving you access to items that may not be available in your local area. This global reach can help you find rare and unique items to add to your collection.

- Competitive Pricing: The vast selection of items on online platforms often leads to competitive pricing, allowing you to find deals that might be difficult to achieve in traditional brick-and-mortar stores or auctions.

C. Real-Time Market Insights

- Price Tracking: Many online auction sites offer tools that allow you to track the final sale prices of items similar to those in your collection. This real-time data helps you stay informed about the current market value of your collectibles.

- Auction Alerts: Setting up auction alerts for specific items or categories ensures that you are notified when items of interest become available. This feature helps you act quickly on opportunities to acquire desirable pieces.

Online resources and databases are essential tools for modern collectors, providing instant access to information, community support, and market opportunities. By leveraging these digital platforms, you can enhance your knowledge, make informed decisions, and connect with a global network of collectors and experts. These resources not only make collecting more accessible but also empower you to grow and refine your collection in ways that were previously unimaginable.

12.3 Museums and Exhibitions

Museums and exhibitions play a vital role in the world of collecting, offering collectors opportunities to view rare items, gain inspiration, and deepen their understanding of historical and cultural contexts. These institutions provide a rich source of knowledge and exposure that can significantly influence your collecting practices. This section explores the importance of museums and exhibitions for collectors and how to make the most of these resources.

1. Permanent Collections

Museums often house extensive permanent collections that serve as benchmarks for collectors, offering insights into the significance, rarity, and presentation of various items.

A. World-Class Collections

- Benchmarking Quality: Visiting world-class collections allows you to see some of the finest examples of items in your collecting category. Observing these items in person helps you understand what distinguishes top-tier pieces in terms of craftsmanship, condition, and provenance.

- Learning from the Best: Museums curate their collections with great care, often focusing on items of exceptional quality and historical importance. Studying these items can refine your eye for quality and help you set higher standards for your own collection.

B. Educational Displays

- Detailed Information: Museum displays are accompanied by detailed labels and explanations, providing historical context, descriptions of materials and techniques, and insights into the cultural significance of the items. This information can deepen your understanding and appreciation of similar items in your collection.

- Curatorial Perspectives: The way museums present their collections, including how items are grouped and interpreted, can offer new perspectives on how to approach and organize your own collection. Learning from curatorial choices can inspire you to rethink how you display or categorize your items.

C. Preservation Techniques

- Best Practices in Conservation: Museums follow stringent conservation practices to preserve their collections. Observing these methods can provide valuable lessons on how to care for your own items, including ideal storage conditions, handling procedures, and preventive conservation strategies.

- Inspiration for Preservation: Seeing how museums protect and maintain their collections can inspire you to implement similar measures in your own home, ensuring that your items remain in excellent condition for future generations.

2. Temporary Exhibitions

Temporary exhibitions offer unique opportunities to explore specific themes, periods, or artists in greater depth, providing inspiration and new avenues for collecting.

A. Thematic Focus

- Deep Dives into Specific Areas: Temporary exhibitions often focus on a particular theme, artist, or period, offering a concentrated exploration of a specific aspect of collecting. These exhibitions can introduce you to new areas of interest or deepen your knowledge in a niche you're already passionate about.

- Curated Insights: These exhibitions are curated by experts who bring together significant items, often from multiple collections, to tell a cohesive story. The insights provided by these curators can expand your understanding and inspire new collecting goals.

B. Rare and Unique Items

- Opportunities to View Rare Items: Temporary exhibitions frequently include items that are not part of the museum's permanent collection, sometimes on loan from private collections or other institutions. This offers a rare opportunity to see and study items that you might not otherwise have access to.

- Limited-Time Access: Because these exhibitions are temporary, they offer a unique, time-sensitive opportunity to engage with specific items or themes. Taking advantage of these exhibitions can enrich your collecting experience and provide unique insights that are not available in standard museum visits.

C. Interactive and Multimedia Elements

- Enhanced Learning Experiences: Modern exhibitions often include interactive elements, such as multimedia displays, virtual reality experiences, or hands-on activities. These tools can provide a more engaging and immersive learning experience, helping you connect with the material in new and meaningful ways.

- Supplementary Resources: Many temporary exhibitions are accompanied by catalogs, guidebooks, and lecture series that offer additional information and perspectives. These resources can be valuable additions to your personal library and further enhance your understanding of the exhibition's focus.

3. Networking and Learning Opportunities

Museums and exhibitions are not just about viewing items; they are also valuable venues for networking and learning from experts and fellow collectors.

A. Museum Events

- Lectures and Panels: Museums often host events such as lectures, panel discussions, and symposiums featuring curators, historians, and other experts. These events provide opportunities to learn from leading voices in the field and engage in discussions about current trends, historical research, and collecting practices.

- Exclusive Tours and Receptions: Some museums offer exclusive tours or receptions for members or donors, providing a more intimate setting to view collections and interact with curators. These events can offer deeper insights and allow you to ask specific questions about items or collecting strategies.

B. Connecting with Experts

- Direct Access to Curators and Historians: Attending museum events often provides the opportunity to meet and interact with curators, historians, and other experts. These connections can lead to valuable advice, new insights, and even potential mentorship opportunities.

- Collaborative Projects: Engaging with museum professionals can lead to collaborative projects, such as contributing to exhibitions, publications, or research initiatives. These collaborations can enhance your reputation as a serious collector and provide unique opportunities to work with rare and significant items.

C. Building Relationships with Other Collectors

- Shared Experiences: Museums and exhibitions attract other collectors who share your interests, offering a natural setting to meet and network. Sharing your experiences and discussing exhibits with fellow collectors can lead to new friendships, collaborations, and opportunities for trades or acquisitions.

- Learning from Peers: Engaging with other collectors at these events allows you to exchange knowledge and strategies, learning from their successes and challenges. This peer-to-peer learning can be invaluable in refining your own collecting approach.

Museums and exhibitions are rich resources for collectors, offering opportunities to see rare and significant items, learn from expert curators, and connect with other collectors and professionals in the field. By actively engaging with these institutions, you can gain new insights, refine your collecting strategies, and enhance the overall quality and value of your collection.

12.4 Educational Courses and Workshops

Educational courses and workshops are powerful tools for collectors seeking to deepen their knowledge, refine their skills, and stay current with the latest developments in the field. These learning opportunities offer hands-on experience, expert instruction, and the chance to engage with other passionate collectors. This section explores the benefits of enrolling in educational courses and attending workshops, as well as how to choose the right ones for your collecting goals.

1. Professional Development

Investing in your education through specialized courses and workshops can significantly enhance your expertise and the quality of your collection.

A. Specialized Courses

- In-Depth Knowledge: Specialized courses offer focused instruction on specific areas of collecting, such as art history, conservation techniques, or the appraisal process. These courses are often taught by industry experts and provide a comprehensive understanding of the subject matter, allowing you to apply this knowledge directly to your collecting activities.

- Tailored to Collectors: Many courses are designed specifically for collectors, addressing the unique challenges and considerations they face. Whether you're looking to learn about a particular artist, period, or type of collectible, there are courses available that cater to your specific interests.

B. Certification Programs

- Formal Recognition: For collectors looking to deepen their expertise and gain formal recognition, certification programs in fields such as appraisal, conservation, or curation offer a structured curriculum and certification upon completion. These credentials can enhance your credibility as a collector and may open doors to new opportunities within the collecting community.

- Professional Advancement: Certification programs not only provide valuable knowledge but also position you as a more serious and informed collector. This can lead to opportunities such as speaking engagements, consulting roles, or collaborations with museums and other institutions.

C. Continued Learning

- Staying Current: The world of collecting is dynamic, with new techniques, trends, and discoveries emerging regularly. Enrolling in courses ensures that you stay updated with the latest developments, allowing you to adapt your collecting strategies accordingly.

- Building Expertise Over Time: Continuing education through regular courses allows you to build your expertise progressively. This approach helps you develop a deep and nuanced understanding of your collecting niche, making you a more knowledgeable and confident collector.

2. Hands-On Workshops

Workshops offer practical, hands-on learning experiences that are essential for mastering specific skills related to collecting, such as restoration, preservation, and cataloging.

A. Practical Skill Development

- Hands-On Experience: Workshops provide the opportunity to practice skills in a controlled, supportive environment. Whether you're learning how to restore a painting, catalog a collection, or identify forgeries, these workshops offer direct, practical experience that is difficult to acquire through books or online courses alone.

- Expert Guidance: Workshops are typically led by seasoned professionals who provide personalized instruction and feedback. This expert guidance ensures that you learn the correct techniques and avoid common mistakes that could harm your collection.

B. Interactive Learning

- Engagement with Peers: Workshops often involve collaborative activities and group discussions, allowing you to learn not only from the instructor but also from your peers. This interaction can provide new perspectives and insights, enhancing your overall learning experience.

- Immediate Application: The skills and knowledge gained in workshops can be immediately applied to your collection. For example, after attending a workshop on conservation, you can return home with the confidence and skills needed to better care for your items.

C. Access to Specialized Tools and Materials

- Learning with the Right Tools: Many workshops provide access to specialized tools and materials that you might not have at home. Learning to use these tools under expert supervision allows you to gain a deeper understanding of their application and importance in the collecting process.

- Experimentation and Exploration: Workshops offer a safe space to experiment with new techniques and materials, helping you discover the best methods for caring for and enhancing your collection.

3. Online Learning Platforms

For collectors who prefer the flexibility of learning at their own pace, online courses and webinars offer an accessible alternative to in-person classes.

A. Flexibility and Convenience

- Learn at Your Own Pace: Online courses allow you to learn at your own pace, making them ideal for collectors with busy schedules. Whether you prefer to study late at night or on weekends, online platforms provide the flexibility to fit education into your life.

- Wide Range of Topics: The variety of online courses available means you can find instruction on virtually any topic related to collecting, from beginner to advanced levels. This allows you to tailor your learning experience to your current needs and goals.

B. Access to Global Experts

- Expert Instruction from Anywhere: Online platforms often feature courses taught by leading experts from around the world. This global access allows you to learn from the best, regardless of your location.

- Diverse Perspectives: Online learning also exposes you to diverse perspectives and approaches, enriching your understanding of collecting practices from different cultures and regions.

C. Cost-Effective Learning

- Affordable Options: Many online courses are more affordable than in-person classes, making them accessible to a broader audience. Additionally, the elimination of travel and accommodation costs makes online learning a cost-effective option for gaining valuable knowledge.

- Free Resources and Webinars: Many institutions and experts offer free webinars and resources that can provide valuable insights without any financial investment. These resources are excellent for collectors who are just starting out or who want to explore a new area of interest before committing to a paid course.

4. Choosing the Right Course or Workshop

Selecting the right educational opportunities is crucial for getting the most out of your investment in learning.

A. Assessing Your Goals

- Identify Learning Objectives: Before enrolling in a course or workshop, identify what you hope to achieve. Are you looking to develop a specific skill, gain certification, or broaden your knowledge in a particular area? Understanding your goals will help you choose the right program.

- Matching Course Content: Review the course syllabus or workshop agenda to ensure it aligns with your learning objectives. Look for programs that offer a balance of theoretical knowledge and practical application.

B. Researching Instructors and Institutions

- Check Credentials: Research the credentials of the instructors and the reputation of the institution offering the course or workshop. Ensure that they have the expertise and experience necessary to provide high-quality instruction.

- Read Reviews and Testimonials: Look for reviews and testimonials from past participants to gauge the effectiveness of the course. Positive feedback from other collectors can be a good indicator of the program's value.

C. Balancing Time and Commitment

- Consider Your Schedule: Choose courses or workshops that fit your schedule and level of commitment. Intensive programs may require a significant time investment, while shorter workshops or online courses might be more manageable if you have limited time.

- Evaluate Long-Term Benefits: Consider the long-term benefits of the course or workshop. Will it provide skills or knowledge that will significantly enhance your collecting activities? Investing in education should yield long-term returns in terms of expertise and the quality of your collection.

Educational courses and workshops are invaluable resources for collectors looking to enhance their knowledge, develop practical skills, and stay current with the latest trends and techniques. By choosing the right programs and actively engaging in these learning opportunities, you can significantly elevate your collecting practices, making your collection more valuable, well-preserved, and informed by the highest standards of the field.

12.5 Finding Reliable Information

In the world of collecting, having access to reliable information is essential for making informed decisions, verifying the authenticity of items, and ensuring the overall integrity of your collection. However, the vast amount of information available today—both online and offline—can make it challenging to discern what is trustworthy. This section explores strategies for finding and verifying reliable information that you can confidently rely on in your collecting endeavors.

1. Vetting Sources

Not all sources of information are created equal. It's crucial to evaluate the credibility of the sources you rely on to ensure the accuracy and reliability of the information they provide.

A. Authority and Expertise

- Established Experts: Information from established experts in the field, such as well-known authors, academics, and professionals with years of experience, is generally more reliable. These individuals often have a proven track record of contributions to their area of expertise, making their insights trustworthy.

- Reputable Institutions: Reputable institutions, such as museums, universities, and well-known auction houses, are valuable sources of accurate and thoroughly vetted information. Their publications, databases, and educational resources are typically held to high standards of accuracy and scholarship.

B. Peer Reviews and Recommendations

- Scholarly Publications: Peer-reviewed journals and academic publications are excellent sources of reliable information. The peer-review process ensures that the research and conclusions presented have been critically evaluated by other experts in the field.

- Community-Endorsed Resources: In the collecting community, certain resources may be widely endorsed by respected collectors and experts. Recommendations from trusted individuals within your network can guide you to reliable books, websites, and other informational resources.

C. Cross-Referencing Information

- Multiple Sources: To verify the accuracy of information, cross-reference it with multiple reliable sources. If several credible sources corroborate the same details, the information is more likely to be accurate.

- Avoiding Bias: Be mindful of potential biases in the sources you use. Cross-referencing helps mitigate the impact of any single source's bias, providing a more balanced perspective on the information.

2. Avoiding Misinformation

Inaccurate or misleading information can lead to costly mistakes in collecting. Developing strategies to identify and avoid misinformation is crucial for protecting your collection and making sound decisions.

A. Critical Analysis

- Questioning Sources: Always approach information with a critical mindset. Ask questions about the source's credibility, the evidence provided, and the potential motives behind the information. If something seems too good to be true, it's worth investigating further.

- Fact-Checking: Fact-checking is an essential practice in avoiding misinformation. Use reliable fact-checking websites, consult experts, and compare information with established references to verify its accuracy.

B. Recognizing Red Flags

- Sensational Claims: Be wary of sensational claims or information that seems exaggerated or unsupported by evidence. Such claims are often designed to attract attention rather than provide reliable insights.

- Lack of Citations: Information that lacks proper citations or references should be approached with caution. Reliable sources typically provide clear citations that allow you to trace the information back to its original context.

C. Protecting Yourself from Scams

- Verifying Sellers and Sources: When dealing with sellers or sources of information online, ensure they are reputable and have positive reviews from other collectors. Avoid dealing with unknown or poorly reviewed entities, as they may be involved in scams or providing misleading information.

- Staying Updated: Scammers often adapt their tactics, so staying informed about the latest scams in the collecting world is essential. Participating in online forums and staying connected with the collecting community can help you stay alert to new threats.

3. *Continual Verification*

Collecting is an ongoing process that requires continual verification of information as new discoveries are made and markets evolve. Staying updated and regularly revisiting your sources of information is key to maintaining a well-informed collecting strategy.

A. Regular Updates

- Staying Current: The collecting world is dynamic, with new research, market trends, and discoveries emerging regularly. Make it a habit to update your knowledge by following the latest publications, attending workshops, and consulting with experts.

- Revisiting Previous Information: As new information becomes available, it's important to revisit previous assumptions and knowledge. What was considered accurate in the past may be revised or expanded upon with new evidence.

B. Engaging with the Community

- Feedback from Peers: Engaging with the collecting community through forums, social media, and local clubs allows you to gather feedback on new information and insights. This collective wisdom can help verify the reliability of information and provide additional perspectives.

- Networking with Experts: Regularly consulting with experts in your field ensures that you stay informed about the latest developments. These professionals can provide guidance on interpreting new information and integrating it into your collecting practices.

C. Continuous Learning

- Lifelong Education: Collecting is a journey of continuous learning. Embrace opportunities to expand your knowledge through courses, workshops, and reading. The more informed you are, the better equipped you will be to navigate the complexities of collecting and avoid pitfalls.

- Adapting to Change: Be prepared to adapt your collecting strategies as new information emerges. Flexibility and a willingness to revise your approach based on reliable information will help you build a collection that is both valuable and historically significant.

Finding reliable information is the foundation of successful collecting. By vetting your sources, avoiding misinformation, and continually verifying your knowledge, you can make informed decisions that protect and enhance your collection. As you build your expertise, these practices will become second nature, guiding you toward becoming a more knowledgeable and confident collector.

Chapter 12 Review: Resources and Further Reading

Chapter 12, *Resources and Further Reading*, emphasizes the importance of accessing reliable information and educational opportunities to enhance your collecting journey. The chapter covers essential tools and strategies for building knowledge, verifying authenticity, and staying informed about the latest developments in the collecting world. Here's a summary of the key points:

- 12.1 Recommended Books and Guides

- Essential Reading: Classic references and specialized guides are crucial for deepening your knowledge in specific collecting areas. These books offer detailed insights into the history, craftsmanship, and value of collectibles.

- Building a Personal Library: Curating a library of relevant books and guides is an investment in your expertise. Keeping up with the latest editions and updates ensures your knowledge remains current and comprehensive.

- Research and Verification: Books serve as critical tools for verifying the authenticity and historical context of items in your collection. Cross-referencing multiple sources helps ensure accuracy.

- 12.2 Online Resources and Databases

- Specialized Databases: Online databases provide access to provenance records, price guides, and market data, essential for making informed decisions about buying, selling, and valuing collectibles.

- Forums and Discussion Groups: Engaging in online forums offers a platform for peer-to-peer learning, staying informed about trends, and networking with other collectors and experts.

- Online Auctions and Marketplaces: These platforms connect you with a global market, offering diverse items and real-time insights into current market trends. However, thorough research and caution are advised to avoid misinformation and scams.

- 12.3 Museums and Exhibitions

- Permanent Collections: Museums house world-class collections that provide benchmarks for quality and authenticity. Studying these items can refine your eye for collecting and offer inspiration for your own collection.

- Temporary Exhibitions: These specialized exhibits offer deep dives into specific themes or periods, providing unique insights and exposure to rare items that may influence your collecting direction.

- Networking and Learning Opportunities: Museums and exhibitions are ideal venues for connecting with experts, attending educational events, and building relationships with fellow collectors.

- 12.4 Educational Courses and Workshops

- Professional Development: Specialized courses and certification programs enhance your expertise and credibility as a collector, offering in-depth knowledge in areas like appraisal and conservation.

- Hands-On Workshops: These provide practical experience in skills such as restoration and preservation, with expert guidance that can be directly applied to your collection.

- Online Learning Platforms: For flexibility and convenience, online courses and webinars offer access to global experts and diverse topics, making education more accessible to collectors at all levels.

- 12.5 Finding Reliable Information

- Vetting Sources: It's crucial to rely on reputable sources, such as established experts and institutions, and to cross-reference information from multiple sources to ensure accuracy.

- Avoiding Misinformation: Critical analysis and fact-checking are essential for avoiding misleading information that could negatively impact your collecting decisions.

- Continual Verification: Staying updated with the latest research, engaging with the community, and adapting to new information are key to maintaining a well-informed collecting strategy.

Chapter 12 underscores the importance of equipping yourself with reliable resources and ongoing education to make informed decisions and enhance the value of your collection. By building a strong foundation of knowledge, leveraging digital tools, and actively engaging with the collecting community, you ensure that your collecting journey is both successful and fulfilling.

Chapter 13: Conclusion

The conclusion of your collecting journey serves as a reflective and forward-looking chapter, offering an opportunity to consider where you've been, where you are, and where you might go in the future. This chapter will guide you through the process of reflecting on your achievements, encouraging continued exploration, offering final practical advice, and considering the future of the antiques and collectibles market.

13.1 Reflecting on Your Collecting Journey

Reflecting on your collecting journey is an essential exercise that allows you to appreciate your growth, understand the evolution of your collection, and acknowledge the milestones you've achieved along the way. This reflection not only helps you appreciate your accomplishments but also provides insights that can guide your future endeavors.

1. Understanding Personal Growth and Development

As a collector, your journey has likely involved significant personal growth. Reflecting on this development can help you appreciate how far you've come and how your approach to collecting has matured.

A. Expanding Knowledge and Expertise

- Deepening Understanding: Over time, your understanding of your chosen collecting niche has deepened. Reflect on how your ability to identify, assess, and appreciate the items in your collection has grown. Consider the specific areas where you've developed expertise, such as recognizing authenticity markers, understanding historical context, or identifying high-quality materials.

- Broadening Interests: Consider how your interests may have broadened as you've gained more knowledge. Perhaps you've ventured into new areas of collecting or developed an appreciation for items that initially didn't capture your attention. Reflect on how this broadening of interests has enriched your collecting experience.

B. Developing Skills

- Research and Analysis: Reflect on the research skills you've developed. Whether it's through reading, attending lectures, or consulting experts, your ability to gather and analyze information has likely improved. Consider how these skills have helped you make more informed decisions about your acquisitions.

- Preservation and Care: Consider the skills you've acquired in preserving and caring for your collection. From understanding proper storage techniques to knowing how to handle delicate items, these skills are crucial for maintaining the value and integrity of your collection.

C. Emotional and Intellectual Enrichment

- Personal Fulfillment: Reflect on the emotional satisfaction and intellectual stimulation that collecting has brought into your life. Consider how the pursuit of knowledge, the thrill of discovery, and the joy of acquisition have enriched your life. Reflect on how your collection has become a source of pride and a representation of your personal interests and passions.

2. Evaluating Milestones and Achievements

Milestones and achievements are significant markers in your collecting journey. Reflecting on these moments allows you to appreciate your progress and set new goals for the future.

A. Significant Acquisitions

- Key Pieces: Reflect on the most significant acquisitions in your collection. What are the pieces that stand out as particularly valuable, rare, or meaningful? Consider the stories behind these acquisitions—whether they were long-sought-after items, serendipitous finds, or significant investments.

- Building a Cohesive Collection: Consider how these key pieces have contributed to the overall cohesion of your collection. Reflect on how each significant acquisition has helped shape the narrative and focus of your collection.

B. Completion of Collections

- Achieving Goals: If your collecting journey involved completing specific sets or themes, reflect on the sense of accomplishment that came with reaching those goals. Consider the challenges you overcame to complete these collections and the satisfaction of seeing your vision realized.

- Setting New Goals: Reflecting on past achievements can also inspire you to set new goals for the future. Consider how your accomplishments have influenced your current collecting objectives and how they might shape your future pursuits.

C. Recognition and Community Engagement

- Gaining Recognition: Reflect on any recognition you've received within the collecting community. Whether it's through publications, exhibitions, or acknowledgments from peers, consider how these moments of recognition have validated your efforts and contributed to your reputation as a knowledgeable collector.

- Contributing to the Community: Consider how your involvement in the collecting community has evolved. Reflect on the relationships you've built, the knowledge you've shared, and the ways in which you've contributed to the broader community of collectors.

3. Analyzing the Evolution of Your Collection

Your collection has likely evolved over time, reflecting changes in your interests, knowledge, and focus. Analyzing this evolution can provide valuable insights into your collecting journey and help you plan for the future.

A. Shifts in Focus

- Changing Interests: Reflect on how your focus may have shifted as your knowledge and experience have grown. Perhaps you've narrowed your focus to a more specific niche, or maybe you've expanded your collection to include new categories or periods. Consider how these shifts have influenced the direction of your collection.

- Refining Your Collection: As your interests have evolved, you may have refined your collection by curating it more selectively. Reflect on how you've made decisions about what to keep, what to sell, and what to acquire. Consider how these decisions have helped you build a more cohesive and meaningful collection.

B. Curation and Organization

- Developing a System: Reflect on the systems you've developed for curating and organizing your collection. Consider how you've cataloged your items, documented their provenance, and maintained records of their condition and value. Reflect on how these systems have contributed to the overall quality and coherence of your collection.

- Display and Presentation: Consider how you've chosen to display your collection. Reflect on the choices you've made regarding how to present your items, whether in your home, in exhibitions, or online. Consider how these choices have enhanced the visibility and appreciation of your collection.

C. Long-Term Vision

- Planning for the Future: Reflect on your long-term vision for your collection. Consider how this vision has guided your decisions about acquisitions, preservation, and display. Reflect on how your collection fits into the broader narrative of your life and what legacy you hope to leave through it.

- Legacy and Impact: Consider the impact you want your collection to have in the future. Whether you plan to pass it on to future generations, donate it to a museum, or continue to build it over time, reflect on how you want your collection to be remembered and appreciated by others.

Reflecting on your collecting journey is a powerful exercise that can deepen your appreciation for the experiences and growth you've achieved. By understanding your personal development, evaluating your milestones, and analyzing the evolution of your collection, you can gain valuable insights that will guide your future collecting endeavors.

13.2 Encouragement for Continued Exploration

The world of collecting is vast, ever-changing, and filled with endless opportunities for discovery. As you reflect on your journey so far, it's important to recognize that there is always more to explore, learn, and achieve. This section encourages you to embrace new challenges, continue your education, and stay engaged with the collecting community as you move forward in your collecting endeavors.

1. Embracing New Interests and Challenges

Continued exploration is key to keeping your collecting experience fresh, exciting, and rewarding. By embracing new interests and challenges, you can expand your horizons and deepen your connection to the world of antiques and collectibles.

A. Exploring Unfamiliar Territories

- Branching Out: Consider venturing into new areas of collecting that you haven't yet explored. Whether it's a different historical period, a new type of collectible, or a different cultural artifact, branching out can lead to exciting discoveries and broaden your understanding of the collecting world.

- Diversifying Your Collection: Expanding your collection to include diverse items can not only make your collection more interesting but also increase its overall value and significance. Reflect on areas where you might diversify, such as incorporating contemporary pieces, exploring global art, or focusing on lesser-known niches within your existing interests.

B. Challenging Yourself

- Setting New Goals: Challenge yourself by setting new, ambitious goals for your collection. This could involve acquiring a particularly rare or valuable piece, completing a difficult set, or curating an exhibition of your collection. These goals can reignite your passion and give you a renewed sense of purpose in your collecting journey.

- Pushing Your Boundaries: Take on projects that push you out of your comfort zone. Whether it's learning a new skill related to preservation, engaging in detailed research for a scholarly publication, or collaborating with other collectors on a joint venture, challenging yourself in new ways can lead to significant personal and professional growth.

C. Embracing the Unknown

- Openness to Serendipity: Sometimes, the most rewarding discoveries are those that are unexpected. Be open to serendipity in your collecting journey—whether it's stumbling upon a rare item at a flea market, discovering a new area of interest through a conversation, or finding inspiration in an unexpected place. Embrace these moments of chance as opportunities for growth and exploration.

- Adaptability: The collecting world is dynamic, and being adaptable is key to thriving within it. Stay open to changes in the market, new trends, and emerging technologies that may impact how you collect. Flexibility and a willingness to adapt will ensure that your collecting practices remain relevant and rewarding.

2. Continual Learning and Engagement

Lifelong learning and active engagement with the collecting community are essential for staying informed, inspired, and connected. By committing to ongoing education and participation, you can continuously refine your collecting practices and contribute to the broader community.

A. Pursuing Education

- Expanding Your Knowledge: Continue to pursue education through courses, workshops, and seminars that deepen your understanding of your collecting niche. Whether it's studying the history and craftsmanship of specific items, learning about market trends, or gaining new skills in preservation, education is the foundation of informed collecting.

- Staying Informed: Keep up with the latest research, publications, and news in the collecting world. Subscribe to relevant journals, follow industry blogs, and participate in online forums to stay informed about developments that could impact your collection. This ongoing education ensures that you remain knowledgeable and prepared to make informed decisions.

B. Engaging with the Community

- Building Relationships: Active participation in the collecting community is a valuable way to exchange knowledge, share experiences, and build lasting relationships. Attend conventions, fairs, and exhibitions to meet fellow collectors, dealers, and experts. These interactions can lead to new opportunities, collaborations, and friendships that enrich your collecting journey.

- Sharing Your Passion: Consider ways to share your passion with others, whether through mentoring new collectors, giving talks, writing articles, or simply participating in discussions. Sharing your expertise not only helps others but also deepens your own understanding and appreciation of your collection.

C. Contributing to the Collective Knowledge

- Publishing and Presenting: If you have developed significant expertise in a particular area, consider contributing to the collective knowledge of the collecting community by publishing articles, giving presentations, or curating exhibitions. These contributions help preserve and disseminate valuable information, ensuring that your knowledge benefits others.

- Participating in Collaborative Projects: Engage in collaborative projects with other collectors, institutions, or researchers. Whether it's co-authoring a book, contributing to a museum exhibition, or participating in a group acquisition, collaboration can lead to new insights and achievements that would be difficult to accomplish alone.

3. Innovation and Adaptation

The world of antiques and collectibles is constantly evolving, driven by changes in technology, market dynamics, and cultural trends. Embracing innovation and adaptation is crucial for keeping your collection relevant and thriving in the modern era.

A. Embracing Technology

- Digital Tools and Platforms: Leverage the power of technology to enhance your collecting practices. Use digital tools for cataloging, research, and market analysis. Engage with online auction platforms, social media, and virtual exhibitions to discover new items, connect with other collectors, and stay informed about market trends.

- Exploring Digital Collectibles: As the collecting landscape evolves, digital collectibles and NFTs (non-fungible tokens) are becoming increasingly popular. While traditional collectors may be hesitant to embrace this new medium, exploring digital art and collectibles can open up new avenues for collecting and investment.

B. Adapting to Market Trends

- Staying Ahead of Trends: The antiques and collectibles market is influenced by trends that can shift rapidly. Stay ahead of these trends by regularly analyzing market data, attending industry events, and following expert opinions. Adapting your collecting strategy to align with emerging trends can enhance the value and appeal of your collection.

- Reevaluating Your Collection: Periodically reevaluate your collection in light of current market trends and personal interests. Consider selling items that no longer align with your focus or that have reached peak value, and reinvest in areas that are gaining popularity or hold long-term potential.

C. Preparing for the Future

- Long-Term Planning: As you continue to explore new areas and adapt to changes, it's important to have a long-term plan for your collection. Consider how your collection will evolve over the coming years and what legacy you want to leave. This might involve planning for future acquisitions, documenting the history and provenance of your items, or making arrangements for your collection's future care and ownership.

- Sustainability and Ethical Collecting: Consider the sustainability and ethical implications of your collecting practices. As awareness of environmental and cultural preservation grows, adopting sustainable and ethical collecting practices can enhance the integrity of your collection and ensure that it remains relevant and respected in the future.

Encouragement for continued exploration is about embracing the ongoing journey of collecting with enthusiasm, curiosity, and an open mind. By challenging yourself to explore new interests, committing to lifelong learning, engaging with the community, and adapting to the evolving landscape, you can ensure that your collecting experience remains dynamic, fulfilling, and impactful.

13.3 Final Tips and Advice

As you bring your journey through the world of antiques and collectibles to a close, it's essential to consolidate the knowledge and experience you've gained. This section provides final tips and advice to ensure that you continue to grow, protect, and enjoy your collection for years to come.

1. Prioritize Preservation and Ethical Practices

Preservation and ethical practices are fundamental to maintaining the value and integrity of your collection. By focusing on these areas, you can safeguard your antiques and collectibles for future generations.

A. Proper Care and Maintenance

- Routine Inspections: Regularly inspect your items for signs of wear, damage, or environmental stress. Early detection of issues can prevent further deterioration and preserve the item's condition.

- Climate Control: Ensure that your collection is stored in a stable environment with controlled temperature and humidity levels. This is especially important for delicate materials such as paper, textiles, and wood, which can be easily damaged by fluctuations in climate.

B. Ethical Collecting

- Respect Provenance: Always research and verify the provenance of an item before acquiring it. Ensuring that items are legally and ethically sourced not only protects your collection but also upholds the integrity of the collecting community.

- Avoid Illicit Trade: Be vigilant in avoiding items that may be tied to illicit trade, such as looted artifacts or forgeries. Engage with reputable dealers and auction houses, and stay informed about regulations and laws regarding the acquisition and sale of antiques and collectibles.

C. Sustainable Practices

- Environmental Considerations: Be mindful of the environmental impact of your collecting practices. Where possible, opt for sustainable materials and practices, such as using archival-quality storage solutions and minimizing the carbon footprint of your collection activities.

- Conservation Efforts: Consider contributing to conservation efforts related to the items you collect. Supporting museums, historical societies, or environmental initiatives can enhance the cultural and historical significance of your collection.

2. Stay Informed and Engaged

Continuous learning and active engagement with the collecting community are key to remaining a knowledgeable and connected collector. By staying informed and involved, you can adapt to changes and continue to enjoy your collecting journey.

A. Ongoing Education

- Continual Learning: Commit to lifelong learning by attending seminars, reading relevant literature, and participating in workshops. Staying up-to-date with the latest research, techniques, and market trends ensures that you make informed decisions regarding your collection.

- Mentorship Opportunities: If you have gained significant expertise, consider mentoring newer collectors. Sharing your knowledge not only helps others but also reinforces your own understanding and keeps you engaged with the community.

B. Community Involvement

- Networking: Build and maintain relationships with other collectors, dealers, and experts. Networking can lead to new opportunities, such as collaborative projects, special acquisitions, or invitations to exclusive events.

- Participating in Events: Attend auctions, fairs, and exhibitions regularly. These events provide invaluable opportunities to see rare items, learn from experts, and stay connected with the latest developments in the collecting world.

C. Giving Back

- Sharing Knowledge: Contribute to the community by writing articles, giving talks, or participating in discussions. Your insights can help others and enrich the collective knowledge of the field.

- Philanthropic Efforts: Consider supporting initiatives that align with your collecting interests, such as funding scholarships for conservation studies or donating items to museums and educational institutions.

3. Plan for the Future

Planning for the future is crucial in ensuring the long-term preservation and enjoyment of your collection. By considering the legacy you want to leave, you can make informed decisions that reflect your values and goals.

A. Long-Term Care

- Documentation: Maintain thorough records of each item in your collection, including provenance, appraisals, and any restoration work. Proper documentation ensures that future generations understand the significance and value of your collection.

- Insurance: Protect your collection with appropriate insurance coverage. Ensure that your policy reflects the current value of your items and includes provisions for loss, damage, or theft.

B. Succession Planning

- Passing on Your Collection: Consider what will happen to your collection after you are no longer able to care for it. Whether you plan to pass it on to family members, donate it to a museum, or sell it, make these arrangements well in advance to ensure your wishes are respected.

- Legacy Projects: Think about how you can leave a lasting impact through your collection. This could involve setting up a scholarship fund, creating an educational exhibit, or establishing a trust to preserve your collection for future generations.

C. Adapting to Change

- Embracing New Trends: Stay open to new trends and technologies in the collecting world. Whether it's exploring digital collectibles or adapting to shifts in market demand, being flexible ensures that your collection remains relevant and dynamic.

- Evolving Your Focus: Periodically reevaluate your collection to ensure it aligns with your evolving interests and goals. Don't hesitate to sell or trade items that no longer fit your vision, and reinvest in areas that inspire you.

Final tips and advice are about ensuring that your journey as a collector remains fulfilling, sustainable, and impactful. By prioritizing preservation, staying informed, engaging with the community, and planning for the future, you can continue to enjoy the world of antiques and collectibles for years to come.

13.4 The Future of Antiques and Collectibles

As we look ahead, the world of antiques and collectibles is poised for exciting developments and challenges. The future will be shaped by technological advancements, changing market dynamics, and evolving cultural attitudes. This section explores the key trends and factors that will influence the future of collecting, offering insights into how collectors can adapt and thrive in this ever-evolving landscape.

1. Technological Advancements

Technology is set to play a significant role in transforming the way we collect, buy, sell, and preserve antiques and collectibles. Understanding and leveraging these advancements will be crucial for staying relevant in the future.

A. Digital Tools and Platforms

- Online Marketplaces: The rise of online marketplaces has already revolutionized how collectors buy and sell items. In the future, these platforms will become even more sophisticated, offering enhanced search capabilities, virtual showrooms, and AI-driven recommendations tailored to individual collectors' preferences.

- Augmented Reality (AR) and Virtual Reality (VR): AR and VR technologies will allow collectors to experience antiques and collectibles in new and immersive ways. Virtual exhibitions, online auctions, and digital recreations of rare items will provide collectors with unprecedented access to pieces that were previously out of reach.

B. Blockchain and Provenance Verification

- Blockchain Technology: Blockchain is expected to become a vital tool in verifying the provenance and authenticity of antiques and collectibles. By creating immutable records of ownership and transaction history, blockchain can help prevent fraud and provide collectors with confidence in the legitimacy of their acquisitions.

- Digital Certificates of Authenticity: As blockchain technology becomes more widespread, digital certificates of authenticity will become the norm. These certificates will be permanently linked to the item's digital history, making it easier to track and verify its provenance.

C. Digital Collectibles and NFTs

- Non-Fungible Tokens (NFTs): The rise of NFTs has introduced a new category of digital collectibles. While traditional collectors may be hesitant to embrace this medium, NFTs are likely to become an integral part of the collectibles market, offering new opportunities for investment and expression.

- Integration with Traditional Collectibles: The future may see a blending of digital and physical collectibles, where items are paired with corresponding NFTs, providing a dual experience that appeals to both tech-savvy collectors and traditionalists.

2. Changing Market Dynamics

The market for antiques and collectibles is constantly evolving, influenced by economic conditions, generational shifts, and cultural trends. Understanding these dynamics will help collectors navigate the market and make informed decisions.

A. Evolving Tastes and Preferences

- Generational Shifts: As younger generations begin to enter the collecting world, their tastes and preferences will shape the market. Millennials and Gen Z collectors may favor items with a strong connection to pop culture, sustainability, or social justice, leading to shifts in demand for certain types of collectibles.

- Cultural Influences: The global nature of the market will continue to introduce new cultural influences into the collecting world. Collectors will increasingly seek out items that reflect diverse cultures and histories, leading to a more inclusive and varied market.

B. Economic Factors

- Market Volatility: Economic conditions will continue to impact the collectibles market, with periods of volatility creating both risks and opportunities. Collectors who stay informed and adaptable will be better positioned to capitalize on these fluctuations.

- Investment Potential: The investment potential of antiques and collectibles will remain a significant driver for many collectors. As other investment avenues become more saturated or volatile, the appeal of tangible assets like antiques may grow, especially for those seeking to diversify their portfolios.

C. Globalization and Accessibility

- Global Marketplaces: The increasing globalization of the antiques and collectibles market will provide collectors with greater access to items from around the world. This expanded reach will also introduce more competition, making it essential for collectors to develop a deep understanding of market trends and regional variations.

- Accessibility for New Collectors: The future will likely see initiatives aimed at making collecting more accessible to a broader audience. This could include educational resources, lower barriers to entry in online marketplaces, and increased visibility of diverse collecting communities.

3. Cultural and Environmental Considerations

The future of collecting will also be shaped by cultural and environmental considerations, as awareness of these issues continues to grow. Collectors will need to adapt their practices to align with evolving societal values.

A. Sustainability in Collecting

- Environmental Impact: As environmental concerns become more prominent, collectors will need to consider the sustainability of their practices. This might involve choosing items with a lower environmental footprint, supporting artisans who use sustainable methods, or advocating for eco-friendly policies within the collecting community.

- Upcycling and Reuse: The trend of upcycling and repurposing antiques and collectibles will likely gain momentum, as collectors seek to reduce waste and breathe new life into old items. This approach not only supports sustainability but also encourages creativity and innovation in collecting.

B. Ethical Collecting Practices

- Cultural Sensitivity: Collectors will need to be increasingly aware of the cultural significance of the items they acquire. Ethical collecting will involve respecting the heritage and context of items, avoiding the purchase of culturally sensitive artifacts, and ensuring that acquisitions do not contribute to the erosion of cultural heritage.

- Transparency and Accountability: The demand for transparency in the provenance and acquisition of collectibles will continue to grow. Collectors, dealers, and institutions will be expected to adhere to higher standards of accountability, ensuring that items are ethically sourced and legally obtained.

C. Preserving Cultural Heritage

- Supporting Conservation Efforts: As the importance of preserving cultural heritage becomes more widely recognized, collectors will play a crucial role in supporting conservation initiatives. This could involve donating to museums, participating in preservation projects, or advocating for policies that protect cultural heritage.

- Educating Future Generations: The future of collecting will also depend on passing down knowledge and appreciation for antiques and collectibles to future generations. Collectors can contribute by engaging in educational outreach, mentoring young collectors, and ensuring that their collections are accessible for learning and inspiration.

4. The Role of Innovation and Tradition

The future of antiques and collectibles will be defined by the interplay between innovation and tradition. Collectors who embrace new technologies while respecting the rich history and traditions of collecting will be well-positioned to navigate this dynamic landscape.

A. Balancing Modernity and History

- Incorporating Technology: While it's essential to embrace new technologies, it's equally important to maintain a connection to the historical and cultural significance of antiques and collectibles. This balance will ensure that the collecting tradition remains vibrant and relevant in the modern era.

- Respecting Craftsmanship: As the world becomes increasingly digital, the appreciation for traditional craftsmanship and tangible artifacts will likely grow. Collectors who prioritize items that showcase exceptional craftsmanship and historical value will continue to find meaning and satisfaction in their collections.

B. Innovating Collecting Practices

- New Forms of Collecting: The future may introduce entirely new forms of collecting, driven by technological advancements and cultural shifts. Staying open to these innovations will allow collectors to expand their horizons and discover new passions within the collecting world.

- Adapting to Change: The ability to adapt to change will be crucial for collectors in the future. This includes being open to new types of collectibles, embracing different collecting methods, and staying informed about emerging trends that may influence the market.

C. Preserving the Collecting Tradition

- Passing Down Knowledge: One of the most important roles collectors can play is preserving the knowledge and traditions of collecting for future generations. This involves not only maintaining collections but also sharing expertise, mentoring younger collectors, and contributing to the broader community's understanding of antiques and collectibles.

- Ensuring Longevity: Collectors should consider how to ensure the longevity of their collections, both physically and in terms of cultural significance. This may involve planning for the future care and disposition of their collections, as well as advocating for the preservation of the collecting tradition as a whole.

The future of antiques and collectibles is filled with possibilities, challenges, and opportunities. By staying informed, embracing innovation, and respecting tradition, collectors can continue to find joy, meaning, and success in their collecting endeavors. Whether you're a seasoned collector or just beginning your journey, the future offers endless potential for discovery and growth.

Chapter 13 Review: Reflecting on Your Collecting Journey and Preparing for the Future

Chapter 13 explores the culmination of your journey as a collector and offers insights into the future of antiques and collectibles. Here's a breakdown of the key sections and takeaways:

13.1 Reflecting on Your Collecting Journey

- Appreciate Your Progress: Reflect on the growth, challenges, and successes you've experienced as a collector. Understanding your journey helps to reinforce your passion and informs your future decisions.

- Recognize Milestones: Take note of the significant milestones in your collecting journey, such as acquiring rare pieces or mastering new skills, and use them as motivation for future endeavors.

13.2 Encouragement for Continued Exploration

- Embrace New Interests: Branch out into new collecting categories or niches to keep your experience fresh and engaging. Exploring unfamiliar territories can lead to exciting discoveries.

- Challenge Yourself: Set new goals and take on challenges that push you beyond your comfort zone. Whether it's acquiring rare items or curating an exhibition, these challenges will keep your passion alive.

- Stay Open to Serendipity: Be open to unexpected opportunities and discoveries in your collecting journey. Adaptability is key to thriving in the ever-changing world of antiques and collectibles.

13.3 Final Tips and Advice

- Prioritize Preservation: Focus on proper care and maintenance to safeguard your collection for future generations. This includes climate control, regular inspections, and ethical collecting practices.

- Stay Informed and Engaged: Continuous learning through education and community involvement is essential for staying relevant and knowledgeable in the collecting world.

- Plan for the Future: Consider the long-term care and succession of your collection, including documentation, insurance, and legacy planning.

13.4 The Future of Antiques and Collectibles

- Technological Advancements: Embrace emerging technologies like blockchain for provenance verification and AR/VR for immersive collecting experiences. These innovations will shape the future of the collecting world.

- Changing Market Dynamics: Stay aware of market trends and economic factors that influence the value and demand for collectibles. Adapt your strategy to align with these shifts.

- Cultural and Environmental Considerations: Sustainability and ethical collecting will become increasingly important as society evolves. Be mindful of the environmental and cultural impact of your collecting practices.

- Balancing Innovation and Tradition: Incorporate new technologies while respecting the historical and cultural significance of antiques. This balance ensures that your collecting practices remain vibrant and relevant.

Chapter 13 emphasizes the importance of reflecting on your journey, embracing continuous exploration, and preparing for the future. By following these insights, you can ensure that your experience as a collector remains fulfilling and impactful, both now and in the years to come.

Chapter 14: Appendices

The appendices in this guide provide valuable resources and tools to enhance your collecting journey. These supplementary materials are designed to be practical, accessible, and essential for collectors at any stage. From a comprehensive glossary to checklists, contact information, sample forms, and quick reference guides, these appendices will serve as your go-to resources for navigating the world of antiques and collectibles.

14.1 Glossary of Terms from A to Z

The "Glossary of Terms from A to Z" is an essential reference that provides clear, concise definitions of key terms used in the world of antiques and collectibles. This section ensures that collectors, whether beginners or experts, have a solid understanding of the specialized vocabulary they will encounter.

A

- Aging

  - *Definition*: The natural process by which materials change over time due to wear, exposure to elements, or environmental factors.

  - *Example*: The aging of leather can result in a rich patina that enhances the character and value of antique books.

- Appraisal

  - *Definition*: The process of determining the value of an item, usually conducted by a professional appraiser.

  - *Example*: An appraisal is crucial before selling an antique to ensure you receive a fair price.

B

- Biedermeier

  - *Definition*: A style of furniture and interior design that emerged in Central Europe between 1815 and 1848, characterized by simple, elegant designs.

- *Example*: Biedermeier furniture is known for its functionality and understated beauty, making it a popular choice among collectors.

- *Brocade*

- *Definition*: A rich fabric, usually silk, woven with a raised pattern, typically with gold or silver threads.

- *Example*: Antique brocade textiles are highly valued for their intricate designs and luxurious feel.

C

- *Craquelure*

- *Definition*: A network of fine cracks on the surface of paintings, ceramics, or other materials, often caused by aging or drying.

- *Example*: The craquelure on a painting can provide insights into its age and authenticity.

- *Curio*

- *Definition*: A rare, unusual, or intriguing object, often collected for its unique characteristics.

- *Example*: Collectors of curios might seek out items like Victorian-era medical instruments or unusual tribal artifacts.

D

- *Damascening*

- *Definition*: The art of inlaying different metals into one another, often gold or silver into a dark background, to create intricate patterns.

- *Example*: Damascened weapons and jewelry are prized for their intricate designs and historical significance.

- *Depreciation*

- *Definition*: The decrease in the value of an item over time, usually due to wear and tear, market changes, or lack of demand.

- *Example*: Not all antiques appreciate in value; some may experience depreciation depending on trends and condition.

E

- Ephemera

- *Definition*: Printed or written items originally meant for short-term use, now often collected for their historical significance.
- *Example*: Vintage concert tickets and old postcards are examples of ephemera that can be valuable to collectors.

- Etching

- *Definition*: A printmaking technique where an image is incised into a surface, usually metal, using acid.
- *Example*: Etchings by famous artists like Rembrandt are highly sought after in the art market.

F

- Faience

- *Definition*: A type of tin-glazed earthenware, often brightly colored and used in decorative pottery.
- *Example*: Faience pottery from ancient Egypt is renowned for its vibrant blue-green glaze.

- Filigree

- *Definition*: Delicate ornamental work made from twisted gold or silver wire, often used in jewelry.
- *Example*: Antique filigree jewelry is valued for its intricate design and craftsmanship.

G

- *Gilding*

- *Definition*: The process of applying a thin layer of gold leaf or gold paint to a surface, often for decorative purposes.

- *Example*: Gilded frames from the Baroque period are admired for their opulence and craftsmanship.

- *Grisaille*

- *Definition*: A painting technique using shades of gray to create a monochromatic effect, often used to mimic sculpture.

- *Example*: Grisaille paintings were popular during the Renaissance for their ability to simulate stone reliefs.

H

- *Hallmark*

- *Definition*: An official mark or series of marks stamped on items made of precious metals, certifying their content and purity.

- *Example*: A hallmark on a piece of silverware can reveal its place of origin, maker, and year of production.

- *Hydration*

- *Definition*: The process of adding moisture to an item, often used in the conservation of organic materials like wood and leather.

- *Example*: Proper hydration can prevent cracking and warping in antique wooden furniture.

I

- *Intaglio*

- *Definition*: A technique in which an image is carved into a surface, and the resulting impression holds ink for printing.

- *Example*: Intaglio prints are valued for their fine detail and are often used in currency and official documents.

- *Iridescence*

- *Definition*: A rainbow-like play of colors caused by the refraction of light, often seen in glass and certain minerals.

- *Example*: Iridescent glass, such as that produced by Tiffany Studios, is highly prized by collectors.

J

- *Japanning*

- *Definition*: A type of lacquerwork that originated in Europe, designed to imitate Asian lacquerware.

- *Example*: Japanned furniture and decorative items were popular in the 18th century and are now sought after by collectors.

- *Jugendstil*

- *Definition*: A style of art, architecture, and design that emerged in Germany and Austria in the late 19th century, known as Art Nouveau in other regions.

- *Example*: Jugendstil jewelry is characterized by flowing lines and natural forms, similar to the Art Nouveau movement.

K

- *Kilim*

- *Definition*: A flat-woven carpet or rug made in regions such as Turkey, Iran, and the Caucasus, known for its geometric patterns.

- *Example*: Antique Kilim rugs are valued for their intricate designs and cultural significance.

- *Knotting*

- *Definition*: A technique used in textiles, especially rugs, where yarns are knotted to create patterns or add texture.

- *Example*: The knotting technique used in Persian carpets is a key factor in their durability and intricate designs.

L

- *Lacquer*

- *Definition*: A liquid applied to objects that dries to form a hard, protective, and often shiny surface, commonly used in Asian art.

- *Example*: Lacquered boxes from Japan are highly collectible for their craftsmanship and decorative appeal.

- *Lithograph*

- *Definition*: A print made by drawing on limestone with a greasy substance and then treating the stone so that ink adheres only to the drawing.

- *Example*: Lithographs by artists like Toulouse-Lautrec are highly valued in the art market.

M

- *Marquetry*

- *Definition*: The art of applying pieces of veneer to a structure to form decorative patterns, often seen in furniture.

- *Example*: Antique marquetry furniture from the 18th century is prized for its intricate and elaborate designs.

- *Millefiori*

- *Definition*: A glasswork technique that produces distinctive patterns resembling flowers, often used in paperweights and jewelry.

- *Example*: Millefiori paperweights are popular collectibles due to their vibrant colors and intricate designs.

N

- *Nacre*

- *Definition*: Also known as mother-of-pearl, a smooth, iridescent substance forming the inner layer of some shells, often used in jewelry and decorative items.

- *Example*: Nacre is commonly used in inlays for antique furniture and musical instruments.

- *Neoclassical*

- *Definition*: An artistic and architectural style that emerged in the mid-18th century, drawing inspiration from classical antiquity.

- *Example*: Neoclassical furniture is known for its elegant lines and references to ancient Greek and Roman design.

O

- *Ormolu*

- *Definition*: Gilded bronze or brass used for decorating furniture and other objects.

- *Example*: Ormolu mounts on 18th-century French furniture are a sign of luxury and high craftsmanship.

- *Overglaze*

- *Definition*: A method of decorating ceramics where the decoration is applied over the initial glaze and fired again.

- *Example*: Overglaze porcelain from China, known as "famille rose," is highly collectible for its delicate colors and intricate designs.

P

- *Patina*

- *Definition*: The surface layer that develops on metals and other materials due to aging, often valued for its aesthetic qualities.

- *Example*: The green patina on bronze sculptures is often seen as a desirable feature that adds character and authenticity.

- *Provenance*

- *Definition*: The documented history of an item, detailing its origin, ownership, and authenticity.

- *Example*: A strong provenance can significantly increase the value of an antique, as it provides assurance of the item's history and legitimacy.

Q

- *Quadrant*

- *Definition*: A quarter-circle panel or a quarter of a circular object, often used in furniture design.

- *Example*: Antique quadrant tables are collectible for their unique folding design, which allows them to be compact yet functional.

- *Quatrefoil*

- *Definition*: A decorative element that consists of four partially overlapping circles, often used in Gothic and Renaissance architecture and design.

- *Example*: Quatrefoil designs are commonly seen in antique jewelry, particularly in brooches and pendants.

R

- *Repoussé*

- *Definition*: A metalworking technique where a malleable metal is ornamented or shaped by hammering from the reverse side to create a raised design.

- *Example*: Repoussé silverware from the Victorian era is highly valued for its detailed and elaborate patterns.

- *Rococo*

- *Definition*: An 18th-century artistic movement and style, characterized by ornate decoration, asymmetry, and playful themes.

- *Example*: Rococo furniture is known for its intricate carvings, elaborate decorations, and graceful curves.

S

- *Silhouette*

- *Definition*: An image, often of a person's profile, in which the subject is represented as a solid shape of a single color, typically black.

- *Example*: Silhouette portraits were popular in the 18th and 19th centuries and are now collectible for their simplicity and charm.

- *Sgraffito*

- *Definition*: A technique in pottery and painting where layers of color are scratched to reveal a pattern or the underlying layer.

- *Example*: Sgraffito pottery is admired for its intricate designs and historical significance, particularly in Italian Renaissance ceramics.

T

- *Tessera*

- *Definition*: A small block of stone, tile, glass, or other material used in the construction of a mosaic.

- *Example*: Tesserae were used to create intricate mosaic floors and wall decorations in ancient Roman villas.

- *Tortoiseshell*

- *Definition*: A material produced from the shell of the hawksbill turtle, used historically in jewelry, inlays, and other decorative arts.

- *Example*: Antique tortoiseshell combs and boxes are highly prized, though modern conservation efforts restrict the trade of tortoiseshell.

U

- *Ukiyo-e*

- *Definition*: A genre of Japanese woodblock prints and paintings, depicting subjects from everyday life, including landscapes, theater, and pleasure quarters.

- *Example*: Ukiyo-e prints, particularly those by artists like Hokusai and Hiroshige, are sought after by collectors for their beauty and cultural significance.

- *Urushi*

- *Definition*: A type of lacquer used in traditional Japanese art, derived from the sap of the urushi tree and known for its durability and glossy finish.

- *Example*: Urushi lacquerware, such as boxes and trays, is prized for its deep, rich color and smooth, polished surface.

V

- *Verdigris*

- *Definition*: A green or bluish patina formed on copper, brass, or bronze surfaces due to oxidation over time.

- *Example*: The Statue of Liberty is a famous example of verdigris, which gives the statue its distinctive green color.

- *Vinaigrette*

- *Definition*: A small container used to hold aromatic substances, such as vinegar, to mask unpleasant odors, often worn as jewelry in the 18th and 19th centuries.

- *Example*: Antique vinaigrettes are collectible for their intricate designs and historical charm.

W

- *Wabi-sabi*

- *Definition*: A Japanese aesthetic that finds beauty in imperfection, transience, and simplicity, often applied to ceramics and other art forms.

- *Example*: Wabi-sabi ceramics are valued for their natural, unpretentious appearance and the unique marks of the artist's hand.

- *Wainscoting*

- *Definition*: Wooden paneling that lines the lower part of the walls of a room, often used in period interiors.

- *Example*: Antique wainscoting, particularly from the Georgian and Victorian eras, adds architectural interest and value to historic homes.

X

- *Xylography*

- *Definition*: The art of engraving on wood, particularly for printing purposes; also known as woodcut.

- *Example*: Xylography was a popular method of printing in Europe during the 15th century, with works like Albrecht Dürer's woodcuts being highly collectible.

Y

- *Yard of Ale*

- *Definition*: A long, narrow drinking glass, typically holding about a yard of ale (approximately three pints), often used in pub challenges.

- *Example*: Antique yard of ale glasses are collectible, particularly those from the 19th century, often engraved with intricate designs.

- *Yūgao*

- *Definition*: A term from Japanese art, referring to the "moonflower," a common motif in ukiyo-e prints symbolizing fleeting beauty and transience.

- *Example*: Yūgao imagery in ukiyo-e prints is often sought after for its delicate beauty and symbolic meaning.

Z

- Zellige

- *Definition*: A form of Islamic art and architecture, consisting of mosaic tilework made from individually hand-cut tiles set in plaster to create intricate geometric patterns.

- *Example*: Zellige tiles from Morocco are highly prized for their vibrant colors and intricate patterns, often used in fountains, floors, and walls.

- Zither

- *Definition*: A musical instrument consisting of a flat wooden soundbox with numerous strings stretched across it, played by strumming or plucking.

- *Example*: Antique zithers are collectible, particularly those from the late 19th and early 20th centuries, known for their craftsmanship and historical significance.

This glossary serves as a vital reference tool, helping collectors at all levels understand the terminology that is essential to navigating the world of antiques and collectibles. By familiarizing themselves with these terms, collectors can enhance their appreciation for the items they collect and make more informed decisions in their collecting journey.

14.2 Checklists for Collectors

The "Checklists for Collectors" section provides practical and structured tools to guide collectors through various aspects of collecting. Each checklist is organized to ensure that collectors can easily follow the steps needed to make informed decisions, whether buying, appraising, preserving, or selling items.

1. Buying Checklist

This checklist helps collectors make informed decisions when purchasing new items for their collection.

A. Research the Item

- Authenticity: Verify the item's authenticity through provenance, marks, or expert opinions.

- Historical Context: Understand the historical significance and background of the item.

- Market Value: Compare prices from multiple sources to ensure you're paying a fair market value.

B. Inspect the Condition

- Physical Condition: Check for any damage, repairs, or alterations that could affect value.

- Restoration Work: Determine if any restoration has been done and how it impacts the item's value.

- Original Parts: Ensure all parts and components are original and not replacements.

C. Verify the Seller

- Reputation: Research the seller's reputation through reviews, testimonials, and past sales.

- Guarantees: Ask about return policies, warranties, or guarantees offered by the seller.

- Legal Compliance: Ensure the seller is compliant with all legal requirements, including permits and licenses.

D. Consider Future Value

- Investment Potential: Assess whether the item has the potential to appreciate in value over time.

- Market Trends: Be aware of current market trends that might affect future demand for the item.

2. Appraisal Checklist

This checklist ensures that collectors accurately assess the value of their items, whether for insurance, resale, or personal knowledge.

A. Select a Qualified Appraiser

- Credentials: Choose an appraiser with recognized credentials, such as membership in a professional appraisal organization.

- Specialization: Ensure the appraiser specializes in the type of item being evaluated.

- References: Ask for references or check reviews from previous clients.

B. Prepare the Item

- Documentation: Gather any documentation, including provenance, previous appraisals, and certificates of authenticity.

- Condition Report: Prepare a detailed report on the item's condition, including any known repairs or restorations.

C. Understand the Appraisal Process

- Appraisal Methods: Familiarize yourself with the appraisal methods the appraiser will use, such as comparative market analysis or cost approach.

- Fees and Costs: Understand the fees associated with the appraisal and ensure they are clearly outlined before proceeding.

- Final Report: Ensure the appraisal report includes a detailed description of the item, its condition, and the appraiser's valuation, along with any relevant photographs.

3. Preservation Checklist

This checklist helps collectors maintain and preserve the condition of their items over time.

A. Environmental Controls

- Temperature: Maintain a consistent temperature suitable for the specific materials in your collection (e.g., cooler temperatures for textiles and paper).

- Humidity: Control humidity levels to prevent mold, warping, or cracking.

- Light Exposure: Minimize exposure to direct sunlight and strong artificial light to prevent fading and deterioration.

B. Handling and Storage

- Protective Gear: Use gloves or other protective gear when handling delicate items to prevent oils and dirt from causing damage.

- Proper Storage: Store items in appropriate containers, such as acid-free boxes for paper items or padded cases for fragile objects.

- Display Considerations: When displaying items, ensure they are properly supported and protected from environmental risks.

C. Regular Maintenance

- Cleaning: Clean items using appropriate methods and materials, taking care not to damage delicate surfaces.

- Inspections: Regularly inspect items for signs of wear, damage, or environmental effects, and address any issues promptly.

- Documentation: Keep detailed records of any maintenance or restoration work performed on the items.

4. Selling Checklist

This checklist guides collectors through the process of selling items, ensuring they achieve the best possible outcome.

A. Preparing the Item for Sale

- Cleaning and Restoration: Ensure the item is clean and, if necessary, restored to enhance its appeal without compromising its integrity.

- Documentation: Gather all relevant documentation, including provenance, appraisals, and certificates of authenticity.

B. Setting the Right Price

- Market Research: Research current market trends and comparable sales to set a competitive and realistic price.

- Appraisal: Consider getting a professional appraisal to establish a baseline value for the item.

- Negotiation Strategy: Develop a negotiation strategy, including your minimum acceptable price.

C. Choosing the Selling Platform

- Auction Houses: Consider selling through reputable auction houses for high-value items.

- Online Platforms: Use online marketplaces for wider reach, but ensure you understand the platform's fees and policies.

- Private Sales: For rare or unique items, consider private sales to known collectors or dealers.

These checklists are designed to help collectors at every stage of their journey, ensuring that they can make informed, strategic decisions while managing and growing their collections.

14.3 Contact Information for Appraisers and Experts

The "Contact Information for Appraisers and Experts" section provides a curated list of reputable professionals who specialize in appraisals, authentication, and expert advice on various types of antiques and collectibles. This section connects collectors with trusted resources to ensure the accuracy, authenticity, and proper valuation of their items.

1. Selecting the Right Expert

This checklist helps collectors choose the most suitable appraiser or expert for their needs.

A. Identify the Type of Expertise Needed

- Specialization: Determine the specific type of appraisal or expertise required (e.g., fine art, furniture, jewelry, coins).

- Experience Level: Look for professionals with extensive experience in the specific category of your collectible.

B. Verify Credentials

- Professional Affiliations: Ensure the expert is affiliated with recognized professional organizations (e.g., American Society of Appraisers (ASA), International Society of Appraisers (ISA)).

- Certification: Check if the expert holds any certifications or qualifications relevant to their field.

C. Consider Location

- Local Experts: For large or fragile items, consider working with a local expert to avoid shipping risks.

- International Experts: If you have a unique or high-value item, consider consulting with an international expert who specializes in that specific niche.

2. Recommended Appraisers and Experts

This list provides contact details, including websites, for highly regarded appraisers and experts across various categories of antiques and collectibles.

A. Fine Art

- Sotheby's Fine Art Appraisals (New York, USA)

- Specialization: European paintings, modern art, and sculptures.
- Contact: info@sothebys.com | +1-212-606-7000
- Website: www.sothebys.com

- Christie's Art Appraisals (London, UK)

- Specialization: Asian art, Old Masters, and contemporary art.
- Contact: appraisals@christies.com | +44-20-7839-9060
- Website: www.christies.com

B. Furniture

- Cottone Auctions (Geneseo, USA)

- Specialization: American and European antique furniture from the 17th to 19th centuries.

- Contact: info@cottoneauctions.com | +1-585-243-1000

- Website: www.cottoneauctions.com

- Osenat Auction House (Paris, France)

- Specialization: French and Italian furniture, particularly from the Louis XV and XVI periods.

- Contact: contact@osenat.com | +33-1-8010-9870

- Website: www.osenat.com

C. Jewelry

- American Gem Society (AGS) (Las Vegas, USA)

- Specialization: Antique and vintage jewelry, gemstones, and watches.

- Contact: info@ags.org | +1-702-255-6500

- Website: www.americangemsociety.org

- Jewellery Valuers Association (JVA) (London, UK)

- Specialization: Antique jewelry, diamonds, and rare gemstones.

- Contact: admin@thejva.org | +44-20-7613-4445

- Website: www.thejva.org

D. Coins and Currency

- Stack's Bowers Galleries (New York, USA)

- Specialization: Rare coins, paper currency, and historical medals.

- Contact: info@stacksbowers.com | +1-800-458-4646

- Website: www.stacksbowers.com

- *Künker Numismatics (Osnabrück, Germany)*

- Specialization: European coins from ancient to modern times.

- Contact: contact@kuenker.de | +49-541-96202-0

- Website: www.kuenker.de

E. Textiles

- *The Textile Conservation Studio (Norfolk, UK)*

- Specialization: Antique textiles, quilts, and tapestries.

- Contact: info@textileconservation.co.uk | +44-1603-895746

- Website: www.textileconservation.co.uk

- *Ratti Textile Center at the Metropolitan Museum of Art (New York, USA)*

- Specialization: European tapestries and handwoven fabrics from the Renaissance period.

- Contact: textilecenter@metmuseum.org | +1-212-650-2400

- Website: www.metmuseum.org

3. Tips for Working with Appraisers and Experts

This checklist offers advice on how to effectively collaborate with appraisers and experts.

A. Preparing for the Consultation

- Documentation: Provide any relevant documentation, including previous appraisals, provenance, and purchase receipts.

- Condition Report: Prepare a detailed report on the item's condition to help the appraiser understand its current state.

B. Questions to Ask

- Valuation Method: Ask about the methods they use for valuation and how they apply to your specific item.

- Turnaround Time: Inquire about how long the appraisal or consultation will take.

- Fees: Clarify the fees involved and whether they are based on an hourly rate or a percentage of the item's value.

C. Follow-Up

- Final Report: Ensure you receive a comprehensive written report that includes the item's description, condition, market value, and any other relevant details.

- Future Consultations: Establish a relationship for future appraisals or advice as your collection evolves.

This section is designed to connect collectors with trusted professionals who can provide accurate and reliable appraisals, ensuring that they can make informed decisions about the valuation and care of their antiques and collectibles.

14.4 Sample Valuation Forms

The "Sample Valuation Forms" section provides collectors with practical templates that they can use to document the value of their antiques and collectibles. These forms are essential for appraisals, insurance purposes, record-keeping, and when selling or donating items. Each form is structured to capture all the necessary details about the item, ensuring thorough and accurate documentation.

1. Purpose of Valuation Forms

Valuation forms serve several important purposes in the management of a collection:

A. Insurance

- Coverage Documentation: Ensures that each item in the collection is adequately insured based on its appraised value.

- Claim Support: Provides essential information in the event of a loss or damage claim, helping to facilitate the claims process.

B. Appraisal

- Record Keeping: Maintains a detailed record of each item's appraised value, condition, and other relevant details.

- Value Tracking: Helps collectors monitor changes in value over time, which is crucial for understanding market trends and making informed decisions.

C. Sale and Donation

- Sales Preparation: Provides potential buyers with a clear and professional valuation of the item.

- Donation Documentation: Offers necessary information for tax deductions when donating items to museums or charitable organizations.

2. Components of a Valuation Form

Each sample valuation form is designed to include key components that capture the most important details about an item. Below is a breakdown of these components:

A. Item Description

- Title/Name: The official name or title of the item.

- Category: The type of item (e.g., furniture, jewelry, painting).

- Dimensions: Measurements of the item (e.g., height, width, depth for furniture; diameter for coins).

- Materials: The primary materials used (e.g., oak, silver, canvas).

- Maker/Artist: The name of the creator, if known.

B. Provenance

- Ownership History: A detailed history of the item's previous ownership.

- Acquisition Date: The date the collector acquired the item.

- Purchase Price: The original purchase price of the item.

- Source: The origin of the item (e.g., auction house, private sale).

C. Condition Report

- Overall Condition: A general assessment of the item's condition (e.g., excellent, good, fair, poor).

- Detailed Notes: Specific details about any damage, wear, or restoration.

- Photographs: Attached images showing the item from multiple angles, highlighting key features and any imperfections.

D. Appraised Value

- Current Market Value: The appraised value of the item based on current market conditions.

- Appraisal Date: The date the appraisal was conducted.

- Appraiser's Name and Credentials: Information about the appraiser who provided the valuation.

E. Additional Notes

- Special Considerations: Any unique factors that may affect the item's value, such as historical significance or rarity.

- Comparative Sales: Notes on recent sales of similar items that support the appraised value.

3. Sample Valuation Form Templates

Here are examples of how these forms might be structured for different types of collectibles:

A. Furniture Valuation Form

- Item Description: Victorian Mahogany Sideboard

- Provenance: Purchased from Sotheby's, New York, 2015

- Condition Report: Minor scratches on the surface, original brass handles intact

- Appraised Value: $12,000

- Appraiser's Name and Credentials: Jane Doe, Certified Appraiser, ASA

B. Jewelry Valuation Form

- Item Description: Art Deco Diamond Brooch

- Provenance: Inherited from grandmother, family heirloom

- Condition Report: Excellent condition, all stones securely set

- Appraised Value: $8,500

- Appraiser's Name and Credentials: John Smith, Graduate Gemologist, GIA

C. Art Valuation Form

- Item Description: "Sunset Over the Hills" by Claude Monet

- Provenance: Purchased from a private collection in Paris, 1998

- Condition Report: Slight fading of colors, original frame

- Appraised Value: $150,000

- Appraiser's Name and Credentials: Emily Brown, Certified Art Appraiser, ISA

4. Tips for Using Valuation Forms

To make the most of these valuation forms, collectors should:

A. Keep Forms Updated

- Regular Reappraisals: Schedule reappraisals every few years or when there are significant changes in market conditions.

- New Acquisitions: Immediately document new items using the valuation forms to maintain an up-to-date record.

B. Store Forms Securely

- Physical Copies: Keep hard copies of all forms in a secure, fireproof location.

- Digital Copies: Store digital copies in a secure cloud storage service to ensure easy access and backup.

C. Review for Accuracy

- Double-Check Details: Regularly review the forms to ensure all information is accurate and reflects the current state of the collection.

These sample valuation forms are designed to help collectors thoroughly document their items, providing a clear and organized way to manage their collection's value, condition, and provenance. Proper use of these forms can significantly enhance the collector's ability to protect, insure, and potentially sell their antiques and collectibles.

14.5 Quick Reference Guides

The "Quick Reference Guides" section provides collectors with concise, easily accessible information on essential topics related to antiques and collectibles. These guides are designed to be practical tools that collectors can refer to frequently, helping them make informed decisions and manage their collections effectively.

1. Identification Guide

This guide helps collectors quickly identify and verify the authenticity of items based on key characteristics.

A. Common Marks and Signatures

- Pottery and Porcelain: Includes visual examples of marks from major manufacturers like Meissen, Wedgwood, and Limoges.

- Silverware: Lists hallmarks and maker's marks from well-known silversmiths, such as Tiffany & Co. and Georg Jensen.

- Art: Features signatures and monograms used by famous artists, along with tips on spotting forgeries.

B. Material Identification

- Wood Types: A quick guide to identifying different types of wood, such as oak, mahogany, and walnut, based on grain patterns and color.

- Gemstones: Basic identification features for common gemstones, including diamond, emerald, sapphire, and ruby.

- Textiles: How to distinguish between different fabrics like silk, wool, linen, and cotton based on texture and weave.

C. Style and Period Recognition

- Furniture Styles: Overview of distinguishing features of major furniture styles, such as Victorian, Georgian, and Art Deco.

- Art Movements: Quick identification of key art movements like Impressionism, Cubism, and Baroque, based on stylistic elements.

2. Valuation Factors Guide

This guide outlines the primary factors that influence the value of antiques and collectibles, helping collectors make informed assessments.

A. Age and Rarity

- Age: The impact of an item's age on its value, with tips on how to estimate the age of various types of antiques.

- Rarity: Understanding how rarity affects value, including examples of rare collectibles and how to assess rarity.

B. Condition and Restoration

- Condition Grades: Explanation of grading systems (e.g., mint, excellent, good, fair) and how condition impacts value.

- Restoration Impact: How restoration work can either enhance or diminish an item's value, depending on the quality and extent of the restoration.

C. Market Trends

- Current Demand: How to evaluate market demand for specific items, with examples of trends that have affected the value of certain collectibles.

- Economic Factors: Overview of how broader economic conditions can influence the antiques market, including tips on when to buy or sell.

3. Restoration vs. Preservation Guide

This guide helps collectors decide whether to restore or preserve an item, outlining the pros and cons of each approach.

A. Restoration Considerations

- When to Restore: Situations where restoration is advisable, such as repairing functional items or restoring items with significant damage.

- Types of Restoration: Overview of common restoration techniques, such as reupholstering, re-gluing, and repainting.

B. Preservation Techniques

- When to Preserve: Cases where preservation is preferable, such as with items of historical significance or those with original finishes.

- Preservation Methods: Techniques for preserving items in their current condition, including climate control, protective coatings, and careful handling.

C. Impact on Value

- Value Enhancement: How high-quality restoration can increase value, especially for functional items like furniture.

- Value Preservation: The importance of maintaining original materials and finishes to preserve the historical and monetary value of antiques.

4. Legal and Ethical Considerations Guide

This guide provides an overview of the legal and ethical issues that collectors need to be aware of, helping them navigate the complexities of collecting responsibly.

A. Provenance Verification

- Importance of Provenance: Why provenance is crucial in determining the legality and value of an item.

- How to Verify: Steps to take in verifying the provenance of an item, including consulting experts and checking historical records.

B. Cultural Sensitivity

- Culturally Sensitive Items: Identifying items that may be of cultural significance and the ethical considerations involved in collecting them.

- Repatriation Issues: Understanding when and how to approach the repatriation of cultural artifacts to their countries of origin.

C. Import/Export Regulations

- Customs and Duties: Overview of the regulations governing the import and export of antiques and collectibles, including tips on complying with international laws.

- Restricted Items: List of items that may be restricted or prohibited from import/export, such as ivory and endangered species products.

5. *Maintenance and Care Guide*

This guide offers practical advice on the ongoing care and maintenance of antiques and collectibles to ensure their longevity.

A. Cleaning Tips

- Safe Cleaning Methods: Guidelines for cleaning different types of materials, such as metals, wood, ceramics, and textiles, without causing damage.

- Products to Avoid: List of cleaning products and chemicals that should be avoided when caring for antiques.

B. Storage Solutions

- Climate Control: Tips on maintaining optimal temperature and humidity levels for different types of items.

- Storage Containers: Recommendations for storage containers and materials, such as acid-free boxes for documents and padded cases for fragile items.

C. Handling Practices

- Proper Handling: Techniques for safely handling antiques to avoid damage, such as using gloves and supporting items from the base.

- Display Considerations: Advice on how to display items safely, including securing heavy objects and avoiding direct sunlight.

These Quick Reference Guides are designed to be used frequently by collectors, offering straightforward, actionable advice that can be applied to a wide range of situations. Whether you need to identify an item, assess its value, decide on restoration, or ensure its long-term care, these guides provide the essential information needed to make informed decisions.

Chapter 14 Review: Essential Tools and Resources for Collectors

Chapter 14 provides a comprehensive set of tools and resources designed to support collectors in their journey. Here's a breakdown of the key sections and takeaways:

14.1 Glossary of Terms from A to Z

- Comprehensive Definitions: The glossary offers clear and concise definitions of key terms, helping collectors understand the specialized language of antiques and collectibles.

- Alphabetical Organization: The terms are organized alphabetically, making it easy to find and reference specific terms.

- Contextual Examples: Many terms include examples to illustrate their meaning and relevance in the collecting world.

14.2 Checklists for Collectors

- Structured Guidance: The checklists provide step-by-step guidance for various aspects of collecting, including buying, appraising, preserving, and selling.

- Key Considerations: Each checklist emphasizes important factors to consider, such as authenticity, condition, market value, and legal compliance.

- Practical Use: These checklists are designed to be practical tools that collectors can easily follow to ensure thoroughness and organization.

14.3 Contact Information for Appraisers and Experts

- Curated List of Professionals: This section offers a curated list of reputable appraisers and experts across various categories of antiques and collectibles.

- Selection Tips: Guidance on how to choose the right expert based on specialization, credentials, and location.

- Effective Collaboration: Tips on how to work effectively with appraisers and experts, including preparing for consultations and understanding valuation methods.

14.4 Sample Valuation Forms

- Comprehensive Templates: The sample valuation forms include all necessary details, such as item description, provenance, condition report, and appraised value.

- Versatile Use: These forms can be used for various purposes, including insurance, appraisals, sales, and donations.

- Detailed Documentation: The forms ensure that collectors maintain thorough and accurate records of their items, which is crucial for managing a collection.

14.5 Quick Reference Guides

- Essential Information: The quick reference guides provide concise, easily accessible information on identification, valuation factors, restoration vs. preservation, legal considerations, and maintenance.

- Frequent Use: These guides are designed to be practical tools that collectors can refer to frequently for quick and reliable advice.

- Comprehensive Coverage: The guides cover a wide range of topics, ensuring that collectors have the information they need to make informed decisions.

Chapter 14 equips collectors with the essential tools and resources needed to manage their collections effectively. From understanding specialized terminology to accessing expert advice, documenting valuations, and maintaining items, this chapter provides practical and actionable guidance. By utilizing these resources, collectors can enhance their ability to protect, preserve, and enjoy their collections for years to come.

About the Author

HowExpert publishes how to guides on all topics from A to Z. Visit HowExpert.com to learn more.

About the Publisher

Byungjoon "BJ" Min is an author, publisher, entrepreneur, and the founder of HowExpert. He started off as a once broke convenience store clerk to eventually becoming a fulltime internet marketer and finding his niche in publishing. He is the founder and publisher of HowExpert where the mission is to discover, empower, and maximize everyday people's talents to ultimately make a positive impact in the world for all topics from A to Z. Visit BJMin.com and HowExpert.com to learn more. John 14:6

Recommended Resources

- HowExpert.com – How To Guides on All Topics from A to Z by Everyday Experts.
- HowExpert.com/free – Free HowExpert Email Newsletter.
- HowExpert.com/books – HowExpert Books
- HowExpert.com/courses – HowExpert Courses
- HowExpert.com/clothing – HowExpert Clothing
- HowExpert.com/membership – HowExpert Membership Site
- HowExpert.com/affiliates – HowExpert Affiliate Program
- HowExpert.com/jobs – HowExpert Jobs
- HowExpert.com/writers – Write About Your #1 Passion/Knowledge/Expertise & Become a HowExpert Author.
- HowExpert.com/resources – Additional HowExpert Recommended Resources
- YouTube.com/HowExpert – Subscribe to HowExpert YouTube.
- Instagram.com/HowExpert – Follow HowExpert on Instagram.
- Facebook.com/HowExpert – Follow HowExpert on Facebook.
- TikTok.com/@HowExpert – Follow HowExpert on TikTok.

Printed in Great Britain
by Amazon

54913890R00162